JUST AND RIGHTEOUS CAUSES

Arkansas History

JEANNIE WHAYNE, GENERAL EDITOR

JUST
—AND—
RIGHTEOUS
CAUSES

Rabbi Ira Sanders and the
Fight for Racial and Social Justice
in Arkansas, 1926–1963

James L. Moses

For Muriel —
enjoy !

[signature]

THE UNIVERSITY OF ARKANSAS PRESS
FAYETTEVILLE | 2018

Copyright © 2018 by The University of Arkansas Press
All rights reserved
Manufactured in the United States of America

ISBN: 978–1–68226–075–3
e-ISBN: 978–1–61075–651–8

22 21 20 19 18 5 4 3 2 1

Designer: April Leidig

∞ The paper used in this publication meets the minimum
requirements of the American National Standard for
Permanence of Paper for Printed Library Materials z39.48–1984.

Library of Congress Control Cataloging-in-Publication Data
Names: Moses, James L., 1960- author.
Title: Just and righteous causes : Rabbi Ira Sanders and the fight for
    racial and social justice in Arkansas, 1926-1963 / James L. Moses.
Description: Fayetteville : University of Arkansas Press, 2018. |
Identifiers: LCCN 2018034904 (print) | LCCN 2018037470 (ebook) |
    ISBN 9781610756518 (electronic) | ISBN 9781682260753 (hardback)
Subjects: LCSH: Sanders, Ira E. | Rabbis—Arkansas—Biography. | African
    Americans—Relations with Jews—History. | African Americans—Civil
    rights—Arkansas—History—20th century. | Arkansas—Biography. | BISAC:
    BIOGRAPHY & AUTOBIOGRAPHY / Religious. | HISTORY / United
    States / State & Local / South (AL, AR, FL, GA, KY, LA, MS, NC, SC, TN,
    VA, WV). | SOCIAL SCIENCE / Discrimination & Race Relations.
Classification: LCC BM755.S244 (ebook) | LCC BM755.S244 M67 2018 (print) |
    DDC 296.8/341092 [B] —dc23
LC record available at https://urldefense.proofpoint.com/v2/url?u=https-3A__lccn
    .loc.gov_2018034904&d=DwIFAg&c=7ypwAowFJ8v-mw8AB-SdSueVQgSDL
    4HiiSaLKo1W8HA&r=4fo1OqKuv_3krqlYYqNQWNKNaWxXN20G1PCOL
    -2ERgE&m=U397ap21k9hC2l-D_cd9NYTwc_cnUmR5pP3te_dkT8Q&s
    =aYROyc3oYath6ok1pXCArJalZj8roYw8u1QYCxn5ve8&e=

There is in my heart as it were
a burning fire shut up in my bones, and
I weary myself to hold it in, but cannot.
—JEREMIAH 20:9

The effective rabbi sees his reward only
in the changed attitudes and social activism
in behalf of just and righteous causes.
—IRA SANDERS

CONTENTS

Acknowledgments ix

Abbreviations xi

Introduction
[3]

1
Before Little Rock
1894–1926
[13]

2
Rabbi Sanders Goes to Arkansas
1926–1934
[27]

3
Race and Poverty in the Great Depression
1929–1937
[51]

4
Birth Control, Eugenics,
and "Human Betterment"
1931–1958
[69]

5
World War II, Zionism, Cold War
1933–1954
[87]

6

The Southern Rabbi Meets the
Civil Rights Movement
1950–1957
[111]

7

The Central High Crisis and Beyond
1957–1963
[127]

8

Honors, Laurels, and Plaudits
1963–1985
[157]

Appendixes 167

Notes 173

Bibliography 203

Index 213

ACKNOWLEDGMENTS

LIKE EVERY WRITER OF HISTORY, I have many people to thank for their role in the production of this book. Arkansas Tech University provided support at every stage of this project with a research grant, travel monies, and particularly a sabbatical leave that allowed me time to complete the manuscript. Thanks to Jeff Woods and David Blanks, my dean and department head, for their enthusiastic support in the completion of this project, and for occasionally acting as very effective sounding boards for me. My good friend and colleague Peter Dykema has listened to too many stories about Ira Sanders, and through his friendship, his moral support, and our many conversations, he has helped me work out aspects of this history, probably more than he realizes. His insightful suggestions upon reading the manuscript greatly improved it.

Thanks to editors D. S. Cunningham, Molly B. Rector, and the staff at the University of Arkansas Press for all their efforts in seeing this project through to publication. The anonymous readers' suggestions made in the peer review process improved the quality of my work. This book's infancy was as a presentation to a meeting of the Southern Jewish Historical Society, and then as an article, "The Law of Life is the Law of Service: Rabbi Ira Sanders and the Quest for Racial and Social Justice in Arkansas, 1926–1963" in *Southern Jewish History*, where many parts of this book first appeared. They reappear here by kind permission of the journal and its editor Mark K. Bauman, whose skillful efforts to edit and ask questions of that article very much helped guide me as it grew into a full-length book.

Many members of Little Rock's Congregation B'nai Israel cheerfully answered my questions, sat down with me for discussions or interviews, and shared memories of Rabbi Sanders with me over the years. Of course, all of you are a part of this book. Liz Downs, the temple's former administrative assistant, provided cheerful assistance, and Rabbis Barry Block and Gene Levy answered many questions for me. Thanks to temple president Dr. Carmen Arick and to Jim Pfeifer, Phillip Spivey, and the volunteers who maintain the temple's excellent archives for allowing me unfettered access.

I am indebted to the late Carolyn LeMaster, who very early in the process of researching this work generously allowed me complete access to her voluminous personal collection of research materials and newspaper clippings regarding Arkansas Jewry. She later donated this body of documents to the Butler Center for Arkansas Studies at the Arkansas Studies Institute in Little Rock, where it now resides as the Carolyn LeMaster Arkansas Jewish History Collection, an invaluable resource on the topic.

The friendly and efficient staff of archival professionals at the Butler Center for Arkansas Studies and the Arkansas Studies Institute in downtown Little Rock always stood ready to assist with any questions or requests I had for them. A special thanks to my former Tulane classmate David Stricklin, historian par excellence and director of the Butler Center who kindly invited me to speak there on the contributions of Ira Sanders, and to the Clinton School of Public Service, who cosponsored that event. It was a blast. Thank you, David, for your assistance and your friendship over the years. You have been a role model for me as well as a good friend.

I appreciate the kind and timely assistance of Jack Eckert, public services librarian at the Center for the History of Medicine, Francis A. Countway Library of Medicine, Harvard Medical School, for his long-distance help in procuring vital materials from the Clarence Gamble Papers.

I am very fortunate to have studied under and worked with many outstanding historians over the years, but by far my largest academic debt, one I can never fully repay, is to Patrick J. Maney, my mentor when I was at Tulane University, my role model, and my friend, who has been the greatest influence in my career as a historian. If we are fortunate, we have some person to whom we can point and say "that person changed my life." For me, that person is Pat Maney. Whatever missteps, poorly constructed paragraphs, errors of fact, and misinterpretations may be contained in this book are mine and mine alone. The good stuff is because of Pat.

For Flora Louise Sanders, daughter of the late rabbi, a very special and heartfelt thank you. Kind, gracious, frank, generous of spirit, with razor sharp insight, and always willing to share memories of her father with me, Flora is a very important part of this book. Our talks over a period of many years, whether in person, via telephone, or by email, were always enjoyable and enlightening, gave me great insight into Rabbi Sanders, and have blossomed into a friendship I dearly cherish. Flora also put me in touch with Paula Sanders, grandniece of the late rabbi and professor of history at Rice University, whom I thank for her input. Her genealogical information and photos of the Sanders family contributed much to this work.

The final and most important acknowledgment is to Anna Spann Moses, my wife, my partner, my friend, and the love of my life. With her, everything is possible, including this work. I dedicate it to her.

ABBREVIATIONS

AME	African Methodist Episcopal
ACJ	American Council for Judaism
ACSW	Arkansas Conference on Social Welfare
ADL	Anti-Defamation League
AEA	Arkansas Eugenics Association
AHBL	Arkansas Human Betterment League
ASWPL	Association of Southern Women for the Prevention of Lynching
CCCLR	Capital Citizens' Council of Little Rock
CCAR	Central Conference of American Rabbis
CCSA	Central Council of Social Agencies
CWA	Civil Works Administration
FERA	Federal Emergency Relief Administration
HBF	Human Betterment Foundation
HBL	Human Betterment League
IMA	Interracial Ministerial Alliance
JCC	Jewish Community Center
NCCJ	National Conference of Christians and Jews
NRA	National Recovery Administration
PPA	Planned Parenthood of Arkansas
PWA	Public Works Administration
PWC	Public Welfare Commission (Pulaski County)
SCLC	Southern Christian Leadership Conference
UAHC	Union of American Hebrew Congregations
UALR	University of Arkansas at Little Rock
UAMS	University of Arkansas for Medical Sciences
WEC	Women's Emergency Committee to Open Our School
WPA	Works Progress Administration

JUST AND RIGHTEOUS CAUSES

Introduction

ON THE COOL EVENING of February 18, 1957, Ira Sanders, rabbi of Little Rock's Congregation B'nai Israel, arrived at the Arkansas legislative chambers inside the state capitol. He had come to speak at a public hearing then underway that would help decide the fate of four anti-integration measures before the Arkansas Senate. A vocal crowd packed the chambers to witness the various speakers who would put forth arguments about the measures, either in enthusiastic support or in outraged opposition. Numbering more than nine hundred, the spectators occupied all of the available seating on the floor and jammed the gallery overlooking the chamber. Segregation laws then in place mandated that African Americans sit in the gallery, while whites occupied the seats on the chamber floor. An overflow crowd, who could still hear, but not see, the speakers, poured out through the lobby and onto the steps of the capitol. Rarely constrained by any sense of decorum, the spectators inside the legislative chamber variously applauded, cheered, and lustily booed and jeered the speakers—including ministers, union leaders, and politicians—who took the rostrum in succession to speak out on the four measures the Arkansas House of Representatives already had adopted.[1]

A number of speakers had been slated for the evening, so Dr. Sanders patiently waited his turn. The speaker currently at the microphone was attempting to talk over the crowd's reactions. Friends had tried to dissuade Sanders from speaking at this hearing, imagining the worst for him and the Little Rock Jewish community if he spoke out publicly and passionately against segregation and for African American rights. The rabbi, though, having taken public stands for racial equality and racial justice many times before, set those concerns aside. He had carefully prepared a set of remarks he hoped would move the senators to defeat the measures. Sanders had no doubt rehearsed these remarks more than once, as he had a habit of talking privately to himself in order to practice conversations before they happened so as to clarify his intent through the precision of language. That clarity of language was now vital. It would be the speech of his life.[2]

Another speaker addressed the audience to much applause. Sanders waited. Two months shy of his sixty-third birthday, he stood a stocky six feet tall and wore a dark suit. He looked out from round spectacles that accentuated his round face and balding crown. This was Sanders' thirty-first year in Arkansas; in September 1926, he had moved to Little Rock from New York City, where he had served as the associate rabbi of Manhattan's prestigious Temple Israel, one of the nation's largest and most influential Reform synagogues. He had served Temple B'nai Israel in Little Rock since that time, becoming by far the longest-serving and most beloved rabbi in that congregation's long history, which dated back to 1866.

Sanders stood ready to address the crowd inside the legislative chamber, mentally preparing himself to take center stage while another speaker stood before the microphone. Speaking out on controversial issues was not a new endeavor for Dr. Sanders, and his thirty-one year history of good works in Little Rock and surrounding areas had made him a recognized and public figure. His tenure in Arkansas thus far had been quite eventful. A social worker as well as a Reform rabbi, Sanders had acted as a major force in the state, moving minds on a number of issues both from the pulpit and as a community leader and organizer. He had founded and led several Depression-era public service, social service, and welfare agencies as varied as the Urban League of Greater Little Rock and the Little Rock School of Social Work, and he had taken both personal and public stands for racial justice in a number of circumstances since the 1920s. He had helped found civil rights groups and fought for African American access to jobs during World War II, antilynching legislation, the desegregation of public facilities, and the general cause of equal justice before the law. He had championed the right of access to birth control and contraception for the poor by helping found Little Rock's first birth control clinic and later by assuming the leadership of Arkansas Planned Parenthood. He had dabbled for a time in the ethically murky waters of eugenics. In the years beyond 1957, he would continue to fight for an end to Jim Crow and for fair housing, and he would continue his work on behalf of numerous public agencies ranging from the Little Rock Public Library, which he helped desegregate, to the Arkansas Lighthouse for the Blind and the Arkansas Tuberculosis Association. He would do so without fanfare and with seemingly inexhaustible energy even well beyond his retirement from the pulpit in 1963.[3]

Dr. Sanders' turn to speak had come. He had long studied the prophets, especially Isaiah, from whom he took inspiration: "Learn to do well. Seek justice; relieve the oppressed" (Isa. 1:17). A lifetime spent in pursuit of these very goals put him here at this moment. The rabbi confidently approached the rostrum. The senators and the nine hundred spectators looked at him, some in anticipation, others in defiance, their eyes meeting his as he stepped up to the microphone. Hands at his sides, Rabbi Sanders stared intently out into the crowd. His face, stern and set, reflected a level of intensity palpable to the gathering. Over the years, Sanders had earned a reputation as an erudite and dynamic public speaker with precise diction and a mellow yet powerful voice. He had used his widely admired speaking abilities in a number of venues over the decades to further the causes of racial and social justice, whether before his congregation or in a wide variety of public settings. This evening, standing before the legislature, he would not disappoint.[4]

I NEVER MET RABBI IRA SANDERS; however, I have done my best to recreate his contributions in the pages of this history. His was a life well lived, a life of true consequence that I came upon in conversations with fellow congregants at Little Rock's Temple B'nai Israel, and with associates who remembered, with fondness and some with a sense of awe, his thirty-seven years in the pulpit, his remarkable works in the community, and his stands for justice and told me about them. And now, in the pages of this history, I will tell you.

For me, the career of Rabbi Ira Sanders began as simply an interesting topic for a short-term research project, but it quickly grew into something from which I could never fully get away. I initially researched Sanders for a presentation before the 2006 Little Rock meeting of the Southern Jewish Historical Society. That conference paper became the basis for articles in the journals *Southern Jewish History* and the *Pulaski County Historical Review*.[5]

After that, I set aside my work on Rabbi Sanders. Although I considered expanding the article into a fuller history and worked toward that goal for a time, life intervened, other projects and responsibilities arose, and I did not pursue it. The articles and conference presentations were enough. But even as I migrated to other research interests, this fascinating man's life remained with me, and I found myself spending time in the archives revisiting it again and again. I also grew frustrated that his historic contributions remained under-represented in the histories of Arkansas and of southern rabbis and civil rights; in essence, this book demanded that I write it. His story intersected in many ways with my life and interests as a member of Congregation B'nai Israel of Little Rock, where Sanders had served as rabbi for thirty-seven years, and as a historian with research interests in modern social and cultural history, in African American history, and in particular in the history of civil rights and

movements for reform and social justice. Finally, I dove in, encouraged by
members of the congregation who knew and admired Rabbi Sanders. I subsequently presented aspects of this research at various conferences and in a number of public and community forums ranging from synagogues to civic groups
to retirement communities. The enthusiastic receptions told me, as much as I
would like to think they were about me, that people were interested in hearing
more about the beloved rabbi and city father and his many contributions to the
community.

A prime factor that motivated me to pursue Rabbi Sanders' story was his
curious absence in the extant literature on southern Jewry, southern rabbis, and
their involvement (or lack thereof) in the fight for racial equality in America
and in the modern civil rights movement. The more I studied Sanders, who
had devoted so much of his life and energy in these areas, the more frustrated
I became at this absence. The topic of southern Jews and civil rights is a bur-
geoning field of historical inquiry, and the study of southern rabbis in particular
has produced several thoughtful and insightful works.[6] Yet detailed analyses
of Rabbi Sanders are conspicuously absent. He is often mentioned, but rarely
studied. This work seeks to remedy that oversight. It is my contention that
Sanders was a major contributor to reform and progress in Arkansas during
the mid-twentieth century and that his many important contributions make
him one of the most significant figures among southern rabbis in the twentieth
century. Sanders' life work provides a context in which one may examine the
evolution of social and racial justice in Arkansas through the thirty-seven years
of his rabbinate, from the mid-1920s through the mid-1960s. His activism and
the causes for which he fought illustrate the dynamic change of these years, and
it sheds particular light upon two critical periods in Arkansas history: the state's
battle against the Great Depression and the local civil rights struggle over the
long term. His response to the deep-seated need for social and racial reform in
the Depression era through the tumultuous 1960s provides a window through
which the reader can view the overall sweep of change during these decades
in Little Rock specifically and Arkansas and the American South in general.

Sanders' career in Arkansas also reveals the precarious position of the
Southern rabbi and the Jewish community during the civil rights struggle.
His successes illustrate very real differences between Arkansas — Little Rock,
especially — and other contentious centers of the civil rights struggle such
as Birmingham, Montgomery, Nashville, or Jackson: those cities presented
harsher, sometimes crueler environments through which to push social change,
while much of Sanders' success is due to Arkansas's evolving, more moderate
racial climate, especially after World War II, and to the much greater ecu-

menical cooperation he enjoyed, all of which allowed Sanders to pursue more openly the goals of racial and social justice and gave him advantages many of his brother rabbis of the South did not enjoy.

Essential histories connecting the actions of southern rabbis to civil rights begin with *The Quiet Voices: Southern Rabbis and Black Civil Rights, 1880s to 1990s*, edited by Mark K. Bauman and Berkley Kalin, an excellent collection of fifteen essays by leading historians on the significant rabbis of the South and their civil rights activities, devoting separate, entire chapters to ten different rabbis. Little Rock's Ira Sanders, though, is notably absent; or rather, he is badly slighted, mentioned mostly in passing on a total of only ten pages in this near-comprehensive study numbering more than four hundred pages. He is most prominently mentioned in Carolyn LeMaster's chapter, entitled "The Arkansas Story," and there in fewer than seven pages. LeMaster's massive *A Corner of the Tapestry: A History of the Jewish Experience in Arkansas, 1820s–1990s* devotes but two pages to a summary of the rabbi's life and discusses Sanders and the Jewish community's role in the Little Rock Central High School crisis on two others. LeMaster also wrote the brief profile of Rabbi Sanders for the *Encyclopedia of Arkansas History and Culture*.[7]

Clive Webb's important *Fight against Fear: Southern Jews and Black Civil Rights* touches upon aspects of Sanders' work in chapter 8, "The Rabbis." Webb credits Sanders thus: "In the twenty years that preceded the Supreme Court decision [in *Brown v. Board of Education* in 1954], no southern rabbi had campaigned more rigorously against segregation than Ira Sanders of Little Rock." Yet despite that recognition and high praise, Webb devotes but three pages to Sanders' "lifetime commitment to community action," concentrating on the rabbi's historic 1957 speech before the legislature against four pending anti-integration measures and the events surrounding the Central High crisis.[8] Webb also discusses Sanders' young successor at Congregation B'nai Israel, Rabbi Elijah Ezekiel "Zeke" Palnick, an important civil rights figure in 1960s–1970s Little Rock whose career also cries out for deeper analysis.

It is in these above works that Ira Sanders' life and activities have been thus far most fully explored. Other important works on southern rabbis and civil rights give little or no mention of Ira Sanders. Rabbi P. Allen Krause's famed interviews with twelve southern rabbis, completed in 1966 as part of his rabbinic thesis, "The Southern Rabbi and Civil Rights," and published along with new material in 2016 as *To Stand Aside or Stand Alone: Southern Reform Rabbis and the Civil Rights Movement*, under the editorship of Mark K. Bauman with Stephen Krause, is an invaluable and long-awaited addition to the literature. The core of this work is the Krause interviews from the 1960s with rabbis from

Virginia, Mississippi, Louisiana, Tennessee, Alabama, and Georgia. As he conducted no interviews with any Arkansas rabbis, Ira Sanders' important work for social and racial justice is absent in this history as well. Neither is he mentioned in the new material; indeed, his name does not even appear in the index. I consider this a stunning oversight, particularly in light of an article Krause published in the journal *American Jewish Archives* in 1969, largely based on the interviews, "Rabbis and Negro Rights in the South, 1954–1967," in which Sanders does merit a mention. In this work, Rabbi Krause discusses "some men whose pulpit preachments have been forcibly and directly to the issue," who have "advanced one further step and have joined word to deed. In the Deep South, Perry E. Nussbaum, Charles Mantinband, Alfred L. Goodman, and Ira E. Sanders might be cited as examples of such rabbis." As do most studies that include Ira Sanders, Krause very briefly notes Sanders' 1957 appearance before the Arkansas General Assembly: "Rabbi Sanders' voice was one of the few moderate utterances to be heard in Arkansas during the black year of 1957, and it took no little courage to stand up and be counted in so open a manner."[9] That, however, is the full extent of Krause's discussion of Sanders in this article. Despite the omissions, Krause's works remain vital supplements in understanding other southern rabbis facing challenges similar to those faced by Rabbi Sanders.

Many works, then, that connect southern Jewry and African American history mention Sanders, but none examine, none contextualize, and none give much detail beyond his heroic speech before the Arkansas legislature in 1957. This study is intended to fill the gap and be a useful complement to the works of Krause, Bauman, LeMaster, and Webb, as well as the growing number of biographies and histories of individual southern rabbis.

MARK COWETT, in his biography of Rabbi Morris Newfield of Birmingham, Alabama, wrote that Newfield, in order to be understood, "must be seen not only as a leader of Jews but also as a Jewish leader."[10] The same is true of Rabbi Sanders of Little Rock. Though clearly a "leader of Jews" in Arkansas, Dr. Sanders was much more than that. A trained social worker as well as a rabbi, Ira Sanders led a career as a dynamic religious and community leader in Little Rock that spanned the traumas of the Great Depression, World War II and the Holocaust, and the wrenching social and racial struggles of the 1950s and 1960s. On the occasion of his 1963 retirement, the *Arkansas Gazette* stated what Arkansans familiar with Dr. Sanders already knew: "long before most of us understood even the full meaning of terms such as social justice and human dignity, Rabbi Sanders had begun to translate these ideas into action."[11] He had a lifelong commitment to social justice in its broadest construction and was particularly committed to African American equality. An agent of change in an era of tremendous change, Sanders brought to Arkansas a desire to make a difference in his community. From the mid-1920s through the 1960s, Sanders emerged as a key figure in the evolution of attitudes and institutions related to social and racial justice in the South, providing leadership in times of crisis and calm. Sometimes controversial, often successful, and sometimes unsuccessful, Sanders sought to address the inequities he saw around him. The study of his efforts to effect progressive change and ensure the mandates of equal justice under law provide an invaluable window into mid-century Arkansas, southern Jewry, and the history of the American South in general.

The focus of this work is on the years 1926 through 1963, the span of Ira Sanders' rabbinate at Congregation B'nai Israel in Little Rock, and accordingly it is a history of Sanders' work in Arkansas, and not a full biography. Essentially, this is a public life of Ira Sanders, the study of which can offer insight into the many changes underway in Arkansas and Little Rock during these years. Nevertheless, Sanders' early life, those years before he came to Arkansas, hold important keys to understanding his passion for social justice as an adult. Chapter 1 examines these formative years and sets the stage for understanding Sanders' later contributions. By looking at aspects of his upbringing and early life, we discover where and when Sanders' ideas about equality and social justice formed and coalesced. His upbringing and youth, his years at Hebrew Union College, and his tenures as a rabbi in Allentown, Pennsylvania, and New York City reveal a young man who in many ways was shaped from youth both for the rabbinate and the pursuit of social justice by his family, his peers, his study of Isaiah and the prophets, and his own inner desire to fulfill the goals of what would later be termed "Prophetic Judaism," the tenets of which he so hungrily studied and in which he so deeply believed.[12]

Sanders arrived in Little Rock from New York only after resolving his internal struggles over whether or not to commit to a life and career in Arkansas and the South. Congregation B'nai Israel worked hard to secure Ira Sanders' services as rabbi, and once they got him, the temple leadership worked just as hard to keep him. Chapter 2 details Sanders' first years in Arkansas and his confrontations with the rigid and often brutal Jim Crow of the 1920s, a harsh system as yet untouched by the reforms and ameliorations to come in the era after World War II, changes that would make Arkansas a racially moderate state compared to its more extreme regional cohorts. Sanders openly challenged the

Jim Crow system and emerged as a high-profile community leader and advocate
for social and racial justice. He brought change both to his congregation and the
community at large. As a founder and leader of several social service agencies of
the era, Sanders made a real difference in the lives of poor Arkansans. Finding a
dearth of trained social workers in Arkansas to aid him in his mission, Sanders
almost single-handedly created the Little Rock School of Social Work to train
a new generation of professionals to assist those in need.

The twin calamities of extreme drought and the Great Depression spelled
disaster for many Arkansans, creating challenges for Sanders beyond any he
had ever experienced. Chapter 3 examines Sanders' expanding role in the community, beginning with his high-profile and reputation-making public debate
with Clarence Darrow over immortality and the existence of the human soul.
His tireless work in attempting to ameliorate the worst aspects of the Great
Depression can be seen in the relief and welfare agencies he founded and
worked in during the depression decade, perhaps most significantly the Pulaski
County Public Welfare Commission, a vital and hugely successful relief agency.
In his quest for racial justice, Sanders helped create and lead the Urban League
of Greater Little Rock and insisted that relief funds provided through groups
such as the Family Welfare Agency be made available to the needy regardless of
color. As his congregation suffered under the strains of the Great Depression,
Sanders willingly made numerous personal sacrifices such as draconian self-
imposed cuts to his own salary—cuts he never fully recouped—in order to
assist his temple with the financial emergency.

Ira Sanders' interests and training as a social worker included laboring to
ensure that women had access to safe and effective means of contraception,
especially poor women for whom such assistance was prohibitively expensive.
Accordingly, very early in his years in Little Rock, Sanders helped found
Little Rock's first birth control clinic as well as its sponsor organization, the
Arkansas Eugenics Association. Chapter 4 details the rabbi's work in the field
of reproductive rights, so critical for many poor Arkansas women during the
Depression, for whom an additional child often meant only additional hunger,
stress, and suffering. He worked side-by-side with community activist Hilda
Cornish, an associate of birth control maven Margaret Sanger and herself a
force for social progress in the Little Rock community, who collaborated with
the rabbi for decades in the area of women's access to contraception. Later,
Sanders headed the Planned Parenthood Association of Arkansas, but the rabbi
proved to be less successful as an administrator than as an inspirational leader.
The organization went broke under his tutelage. Contemporaneous with the
collapse of Planned Parenthood, Sanders organized and chaired the Arkansas

Human Betterment League, a dalliance in the dubious field of eugenics whose goal was to offer surgical sterilization to those who desired, but could not afford, the procedure. The ethical waters were muddied considerably when Sanders and the organization took up the cause of sterilizing the mentally incompetent; however, Arkansas never followed the path many other states took in passing compulsory sterilization laws or in targeting minorities for forced sterilization.

The era of World War II saw Sanders facing new challenges, handling new crises, and developing new points of view. For the rabbi, it was a time of great successes and crushing failures. Chapter 5 examines these events, including his attempts to influence the course of world events on a number of levels, from exploiting inroads to powerful figures of the era to working to get Jewish refugees resettled and out of harm's way. The Holocaust and the wartime conflicts in the United States within Reform Judaism over the creation of a Jewish political state profoundly changed his attitudes regarding Zionism. His work in the 1940s through the Urban League of Greater Little Rock helped make possible good paying jobs for African Americans in Arkansas. After the war, the rabbi took up the mantle against the emerging threat of international communism, using these opportunities to stress the virtues of American democracy and equality — including racial equality — under the law.

In the mid-century civil rights movement in the United States, the most significant social movement of the postwar era, southern rabbis played a small but important role. The black struggle for equality, though, created special concerns for southern Jews, who feared segregationist reprisals and the erosion of their status in the segregated South should their rabbis take public stands for integration. Nevertheless, Sanders and some of his southern Jewish contemporaries took such stands. Chapter 6 looks at the problems of the southern rabbi and southern Jewry in general during the struggle for equality in the south and analyzes Sanders alongside several of his like-minded contemporaries. Sanders and the Jews of Little Rock faced a different, less severe set of problems and circumstances than Jews of other prominent Southern cities thanks to a successful gradualist approach to desegregation that had been underway since the end of World War II.

The Central High crisis, the focus of Chapter 7, was the momentous exception to the more moderate policies and practices in Arkansas regarding the struggle for civil rights. The crisis moved Sanders to participate in a variety of high-profile activities, from speaking before the state legislature to participating in the so-called Ministry of Reconciliation, which garnered national attention, to facilitating controversial plans to resolve the school crisis. His public posture in favor of school desegregation led to threats upon his life, bomb threats to his synagogue, and threats against the entire Jewish community of Little Rock. Sanders then took up the cause of equal housing as a founder of the Greater Little Rock Conference on Religion and Human Relations, later called the Greater Little Rock Conference on Religion and Race.

The rabbi's 1963 retirement did not end his activities or temper his zeal for racial and social justice. Chapter 8 looks at Sanders' slowing but continued quest for social justice after his retirement. By this time, Rabbi Sanders, a well-regarded and often-honored city father, had decades of good works behind him. His final years saw him showered with plaudits and honors for a lifetime of committed service even as he continued fighting for the cause of racial justice. In these years, Sanders mentored his successor at Temple B'nai Israel, Rabbi E. E. Palnick, a dynamic civil rights activist who looked to Sanders' example for inspiration. But these years also saw Sanders fall prey to failing health, losing first his eyesight and then in 1985 his fight against a number of health problems. He died only days before what would have been his ninety-first birthday. His was a life both of deep significance and of profound consequence from whose study themes and patterns of history may be more clearly understood.

— 1 —

Before Little Rock

1894–1926

A BRIEF LOOK AT Sanders' early life provides insight into his motivations and later activities. He was born on May 6, 1894, to immigrant parents Daniel Sanders and Paulina Ackerman Sanders in Rich Hill, Missouri, seventy-five miles south of Kansas City, near the Kansas border. Founded in 1880, Rich Hill was a small farming and coal mining town of fewer than two thousand that Daniel Sanders jokingly referred to as "Poor Prairie," as there were no rich hills to be found.[1] Daniel had been born in Soetern in the Kingdom of Prussia. Daniel's father—Ira's grandfather, whom Ira called "Grandpa Sender"—was a deeply religious man, known by the villagers in Soetern as "Fromsher Sender," the most devout man in the village, from the Yiddish word *frum*, meaning pious. The family name, "Alexander," was over time shortened to "Xander," then changed by Ira's grandfather to "Sender," and finally anglicized by Daniel to "Sanders" following his immigration to the United States.

After he and his family immigrated, Daniel Sanders became a naturalized US citizen in January 1871 in Linn County, Kansas, just west of Rich Hill. He worked in Fort Scott, Kansas, as a butcher and wholesale meat packer, barely making ends meet. Daniel met Paulina Ackerman sometime after the death in 1880 of his first wife, Hannah Lederman Sanders, with whom he had a daughter, Jessie.[2] He and Paulina—whom everyone called "Lina"—married on August 13, 1883, in St. Louis, and the couple would have four children together: sons Morris, Ralph, Ira, and Gus. In 1900 the family relocated from Rich Hill to the growing frontier city of Kansas City, Missouri, where six-year-old Ira began public school. Ira's mother worried about the worldly influences upon her children in this diverse and growing metropolitan environment. In particular, she warned Ira and the other children to "never go near" two "wicked women" who lived at the end of their block because "they use rouge!"[3] Paulina instilled in young Ira a strong sense of morality, religiosity, and propriety that he would carry with him throughout his life.

Daniel and Paulina Sanders, date unknown.
Photo courtesy of Paula Sanders.

Born to the Rabbinate

Even in childhood I expected to become a rabbi.
—IRA SANDERS, 1954

Young Ira Sanders knew by the age of nine that he would become a rabbi, a feeling influenced both by a desire to help others and by his deeply religious mother Paulina, who took her two youngest sons Gus and Ira to Sabbath services every Saturday morning, and whose "one aim in life was to have one of her four sons enter the rabbinate."[4] As a child, Ira often pretended to be a rabbi, going so far as to lock himself and his younger brother Gus in their bedroom together in order to force his brother to listen to his sermons.[5] In Kansas City, Paulina tried to facilitate her son's desire to be a rabbi by arranging Hebrew lessons for him with a local Orthodox rabbi. This rabbi, though, apparently dissatisfied with his career and increasingly an object of criticism in the local Jewish community, scoffed at Ira's ambitions, pointedly asking his mother, "Why do you encourage him to become a rabbi? Rather let him be a shoemaker." An outraged Paulina then related this story to their rabbi, Dr. Harry Mayer, who said, "You go back and tell that rabbi that *he* should be a shoemaker. Ira will be a rabbi."[6]

Rabbi Harry Mayer had come to Kansas City and Congregation B'nai Jehudah from Arkansas following a two-year stint (1897–99) as rabbi of Little Rock's Congregation B'nai Israel. This Little Rock–Kansas City connection would prove very important in Sanders' later life. Mayer arranged for Ira to have Hebrew lessons, and he told young Ira that once he had "progressed sufficiently in Hebrew," he would personally mentor him in preparation for eventual admission to Hebrew Union College in Cincinnati.[7] In Dr. Mayer, young Ira had found a mentor and role model to guide him on his path to the rabbinate.

Sanders pursued his dream of the rabbinate throughout his years in the Kansas City public schools and later in Cincinnati, where the seventeen-year-old Sanders arrived on September 1, 1911, to begin his studies at Hebrew Union College (HUC), the primary training ground for Reform rabbis in the United States. He recalled that, like himself, "most students entered the Primary Department of the seminary while yet high school undergraduates and [later] attended the Collegiate Department" through the University of Cincinnati, undertaking a broad range of courses in the liberal arts that culminated in a final period of intensive rabbinical studies. While in Cincinnati, Sanders lived in a boarding house on a budget of thirty dollars per month, most of which had been borrowed from the HUC student loan fund. Of this, twenty-five dollars went to room and board (including a daily boxed lunch prepared by "Mrs. B," the stern wife of the boarding house proprietor), leaving him a five-dollar-per-month spending allowance.[8]

Sanders would relate the story of the time Mrs. B, whom he recalled as being possessed of "a rather ungovernable temper," unilaterally and unexpectedly raised the rent. In the spring, as Passover drew near, she announced an increase in the room and board to thirty dollars per month to cover, she said, the increased cost of special Passover food. Such an increase would consume Sanders' entire monthly budget. He considered the surprise increase unfair and said he would refuse to pay it; as a result, on the morning of the first day of Passover, an angry Mrs. B forcibly threw him out of the house, threating to shoot him if he returned—a very real threat considering the active rumor among the boarding house boys that Mrs. B had once, as a result of a family quarrel, threatened to shoot her own sister. Sanders communicated his ouster to his friend and classmate Julius Liebert, a young seminarian of considerable stature and strength, who accompanied Sanders back to the boarding house where Mrs. B's husband, small of stature, awaited with his hand raised to strike young Ira should he approach the door. The beefy Liebert interposed himself and said "if you as much touch a hair on that boy's head, I'll give you a whipping the like of which you have never had." Sufficiently intimidated, the landlord thought better of his planned course of action, and all parties agreed that Sanders would remain at the boarding house at the agreed-to rate of twenty-five dollars a month. Mrs. B never again broached the topic of rent increases.[9]

Sanders and his four housemates occasionally played practical jokes on the disagreeable Mrs. B. The boarding house was notorious for its skimpy mealtime portions, leading fellow resident Harvey Franklin to compose a ditty the boys sometimes would mockingly sing at meals, to Mrs. B's great consternation: "Glorious! Glorious! One cup of milk for the four of us!" The boys once concocted a scheme to increase their meager meal portions. They passed off a fellow student as the visiting learned scholar "Dr. Goop" of Berlin, and Sanders and the other boarding house boys told Mrs. B they would like to have this important guest over for Sunday dinner. She fell for the ruse, saying she felt honored to have such a visitor, and prepared a sumptuous spread for that evening's dinner; "for once," Sanders later wrote, each person "was fully sated," with Mrs. B never the wiser.[10]

Sanders received rabbinic ordination from Hebrew Union College in April 1919, as the city and the campus bustled with the return of GIs from the First World War. Sanders cited HUC president Kaufmann Kohler, "foremost theologian of his day," among other instructors, as great influences on his later life, recalling their emphasis on the traditions of prophetic Judaism.[11] Sanders later wrote that the primary realization he took from his years at Hebrew Union College was "Judaism's role in the moral drama of mankind." The Jew, wrote Sanders, has always "been under a burden of responsibility." This burden "gladly becomes a joy for him once he understands the place he fulfills in the economy of life on earth." The Jew must pursue the ideal "not of mastery, but of service" to mankind. If he does not understand this, "that he is the vehicle of a sublime purpose, if he weakly and foolishly expects that he can enjoy the privilege of being himself *without* service, better he quit than to be faithless to his divine election." Judaism has "given to the world the concept of service," a calling to a higher purpose. This call to service would be the governing concept of Ira Sanders' life in the rabbinate.[12]

Ira Sanders received his undergraduate degree from the University
of Cincinnati in June 1918. Courtesy Temple B'nai Israel,
Little Rock, Arkansas.

Allentown

Those years in Allentown were most rewarding.
—IRA SANDERS, 1978

After ordination, the twenty-five-year-old Sanders fielded a number of pulpit offers for his first rabbinate from congregations across the country. Temple Beth Israel of Tacoma, Washington, and Temple Israel of Tulsa, Oklahoma, both actively recruited Sanders in 1919, as did Congregation Keneseth Israel of Allentown, sixty-one miles northwest of Philadelphia in eastern Pennsylvania.[13] The young rabbi accepted the Allentown offer and gave his first sermon on Friday, September 12, 1919. Fluent in German, the language of his father and grandfather, Sanders was at home in *Pennsilfaanisch Deitsch*, the Pennsylvania Dutch of the area. This language and culture thrived in the region as a result of substantial German immigration to the area from the seventeenth to the late eighteenth century. Sanders realized his knowledge of conversational German would serve him well in his new pulpit when, on his first day in Allentown, the rabbi went to a cafeteria for lunch and, making his way down the line, asked the server for potatoes. "Ach die grundbeere sind all," came her high-pitched reply in Low German (*Plattdeutsch*) slang, which Sanders understood: "The potatoes are all gone." His facility with Low German gave him greater access to his congregation and community, as it allowed him to minister to congregants with very limited or no English skills. On one such occasion, Sanders visited a sick congregant who lived "on the third floor of an old dilapidated flat" and spoke almost no English. Sanders paused as he reached for the doorbell, knowing he had arrived at the right place when he saw a sign on the door scrawled in broken English: "Bell don't button. Bump."[14] His language skills helped make him a very popular rabbi in Allentown.

While in Allentown, Rabbi Sanders founded the Jewish Community Center after working hard within the community to organize and to solicit donations to build it. "The necessity of immediate funds is the only obstacle in our path at present," he wrote in 1920.[15] He and the local Jewish community dedicated the new community center later that year, and within it Sanders founded a Talmud Torah, a religious school "that gave instruction in Bible, liturgy, and simple Talmudic passages" with a faculty of five and himself as principal. "In those days," Sanders said, "the Center seemed to be the focal point around which all activities dealing with the Jew and Judaism revolved, so that I early learned a great deal about the so-called Center movement." He directed the religious school and the community center for four years. In addition to his duties as rabbi and community center director, Sanders taught primarily Orthodox children in an Allentown Jewish day school. He asked one of his Orthodox rabbinic colleagues "why they had chosen me, a Reformed rabbi, a rabbi with a liberal tendency towards everything," to teach in their day school. He was gratified at the response: "that I had a great deal of empathy for all people, in particular those in my own faith who differed from me philosophically, theologically, and otherwise." Rabbi Sanders did not neglect his own education while in Allentown. It was his habit to rise early each morning to study before breakfast, and while in Allentown he travelled weekly by train to New York City and Columbia University, leaving at two o'clock in the morning to attend classes part-time "and meet with my early morning professors." Sanders would earn his Master of Arts degree in sociology in 1926, and he began, but never completed, work towards a doctorate in sociology. He studied with and was influenced deeply by such luminaries as philosopher John Dewey, anthropologist Franz Boas, and sociologist Frank Giddings. Boas was a particular influence upon Sanders' notions of race and racism. "Boas and his students," writes historian Lynn Dumenil, "led the way in challenging hierarchical assumptions about race," finding no scientific basis for them, and refuting as deeply flawed such devices as IQ tests then used to assert African American biological inferiority.[16]

Sanders participated in and supported a variety of Jewish philanthropic causes while in Allentown, and in the process he rubbed shoulders with a few powerful figures of the era. The groups in which Sanders played an active role included the Eastern Pennsylvania Joint Distribution Committee, an arm of the American Jewish Joint Distribution Committee, established in 1914 to "facilitate and centralize the collection and distribution of funds by American Jews for Jews abroad."[17] Sanders became involved in this charitable endeavor at the invitation of two prominent businessman: Max Hess, cofounder of the Hess Brothers chain of department stores and a member of his Allentown congregation (Hess "attended regularly each Sabbath evening service" and "always sat on the last row," Sanders recalled, so as not to call too much attention to himself), and Jacob Schiff, a New York financier and one of the most prominent and generous philanthropists of his era. Schiff's firm—Kuhn, Loeb, and Company—played a key role in the financing and development of such iconic American industries as Westinghouse and AT&T, and Schiff himself generously gave to dozens of charitable causes such as New York's Montefiore Hospital and the American Red Cross. Schiff also supported through substantial contributions such institutions as the Henry Street Settlement House, Barnard College (to whom he donated $1 million), and the Tuskegee Institute.[18] Shortly before his death, Schiff invited Hess and Sanders to a meeting in his New York City office to discuss plans for their 1919–20 campaign in Eastern Pennsylvania. Sanders deemed the work of the American Jewish Joint Distribution Committee particularly important at that time, given "the chaotic period which followed World War I" in Europe.[19] He played an important role as organizer, fund raiser, and promoter of the Joint Distribution Committee's activities in Pennsylvania throughout his Allentown tenure.

Always dedicated to the furtherance of Jewish education, Sanders travelled extensively while based in Allentown as president of the Pennsylvania Federation of Religious School Teachers, which "brought together in annual sessions the educators of most of the Reform Jewish religious schools of Eastern Pennsylvania." Throughout his tenure at Congregation Keneseth Israel, he spoke often throughout the region before different groups regarding Jewish education and maintained an enthusiastic association with the Jewish Chautauqua Society of Philadelphia, whose executive secretary Jeanette Goldberg often assisted him with his work both as a rabbi and an educator.[20]

While in Allentown, Sanders played a prominent role in Keren haYesod, the Palestine Foundation Fund, established in 1920 to assist Jews in relocating to Palestine. He "travelled extensively throughout Pennsylvania conducting campaigns, giving lectures and in general," he later wrote, "encouraging and promoting Jewish life in Palestine." At this point in his life, however, Sanders was neither a Zionist nor an advocate of the creation of a Jewish state. He was not a Jewish nationalist. In Sanders' words, "the express purpose" of Keren haYesod was "to solicit money to be utilized in promoting the religious, cultural, and economic welfare of the Jewish settlers and inhabitants of Palestine." Absent from Sanders' description is any mention of the creation of a Jewish state. Zionism was not a tenet of Reform Judaism. Sanders advocated and supported Jewish life in Palestine insofar as it was the right of Jews to live unfettered alongside those of other faiths in the Holy Land. Following World War II and the horrors of the Holocaust, recalls a close colleague, Sanders' point of view shifted and he "understood the need for a sanctuary for the European Jews and he fought for it," but in the 1920s that belief did not as yet involve the establishment of a Jewish state.[21]

In 1920, Sanders met Selma Loeb, a graduate of Wellesley College who also hailed from Rich Hill, Missouri, and who in that year had moved with her family to Philadelphia. With match-making on her mind, Ira's mother Paulina had told him of "a nice family" from Rich Hill named Loeb with lovely twin daughters who lived in Philadelphia, and that Ira "should look them up."[22] So in 1920, while in Philadelphia to buy books from the Jewish Publication Society, Ira telephoned the Loebs, introduced himself, and asked, "May I come out

Rabbi Ira Sanders of Congregation Keneseth Israel, Allentown.
Courtesy Temple B'nai Israel, Little Rock, Arkansas

and see you?" When he arrived and knocked on the door, Selma answered. Ira was captivated, and it was love at first sight—he fell hard for Selma. Sanders later struggled to explain just how this happened: "Maybe because I knew her background, this was already an introduction to me—that she was—she could be—that I fell desperately in love with her." Recalls Sanders: "I always felt that that was just so much foolishness, that nobody could fall in love at first sight, that you have to learn to know a person before you can actually learn to love them." His experience in meeting Miss Loeb proved him wrong. Instantly smitten with Selma, Ira spent a sleepless night tossing and turning following their first evening together, convinced that Selma would never return his feelings, that she "was just too good for [him]." But he pursued her just the same during a ten-month, very proper courtship in which each date ended not with a kiss but with a firm handshake. On the several occasions when Ira asked for a kiss, Selma, ever conscious of propriety, would not consent. He finally summoned up enough courage to ask her to marry him on the unseasonably cold evening of June 14, 1921, in Philadelphia's Fairmount Park. As they sat on a bench together, he found himself bingeing on hot coffee out of a combination of nerves and the cold, to the point that Selma suspected that something was afoot. "Why are you drinking so much coffee?" she asked with suspicion. He then proposed. She accepted his proposal with (finally) a kiss, Sanders recalls, and by saying, "I've loved you all the time, but I couldn't let you know too much because I could not be jilted." Shortly after their engagement, Selma left on a trip to Casco Bay, Maine, and during their separation—indeed, throughout their engagement—they exchanged intimate and often passionate letters. They were married in Philadelphia on March 21, 1922, with two rabbis co-officiating—his Kansas City rabbi and mentor Harry Mayer and Albert Minda, Sanders' closest friend. Ira's younger brother Gus served as best man. It marked the beginning of a long and very happy fifty-six year marriage and partnership, as Selma also acted at times as a skillful editor of Ira's sermons. Their only child, daughter Flora Louise, was born in 1925.[23] One close friend summed up their relationship by saying, "It was a love story, Ira and Selma, plain and simple, from the first to the last, fifty-six years of love."[24]

Sanders exhibited very early in his career as rabbi his propensity for imposing religious discipline both upon himself and also upon his community, a trait he would display throughout his years as a rabbi. He saw that as part of his rabbinical duties. Accordingly, shortly after accepting the pulpit in Allentown, when Sanders became aware that the local branch of the Jewish National Workers' Alliance had scheduled a dance for a Friday night, "openly and willfully desecrating" the Sabbath, he wrote them a stern letter strongly objecting to this example of what he termed "moral degradation."[25] Friday night was a time for synagogue, not dancing.

Despite this strictness, or perhaps because of it, Sanders proved to be a very popular rabbi in Allentown. Temple Keneseth Israel's congregation doubled in size during his tenure. His facility with the local dialect and language and, reported a local newspaper, the fact that "various activities have been inaugurated with great success which have heightened the interest in the congregation," combined to make him a popular rabbi in Allentown. In addition to the establishment of the community center, "a source of great pride with him," in which Sanders played the central role, the rabbi also oversaw the opening of two Young Men's Hebrew Association branches, in Pottstown and in Pottsville, "both of which are flourishing." In appreciation, the Temple board voted for a substantial increase in Sanders' salary.[26] And, as throughout his career, Sanders did not hesitate to use his Allentown pulpit to further the ends of social justice. As related in the *Allentown Morning Call*, Sanders "estimated social justice to be the great contribution to the world from Israel, and his plea was that this dream and vision of social justice be worked out here and now." On November 26, 1922, he translated those ideas into action as he spoke out from the pulpit against Henry Ford and his anti-Semitic *Dearborn Independent* newspaper, "attacking the malicious insults that have been printed" therein. Sanders, in previewing the sermon in the temple's newsletter, wrote that "every Ford owner and Jew should be present."[27] Similarly, at a memorial service held in February 1924 following the death of former president Woodrow Wilson, Sanders took the opportunity to preach a message of equality and "the common brotherhood of man."[28] Allentown marked the beginning of Ira Sanders' socially conscious rabbinate and his devotion to improving his local community, traits evident to the larger Jewish community as he considered his career options after four years in Pennsylvania.

Misfire: New York City

I was just a little cog in a great big wheel.
—IRA SANDERS, 1978

Prominent Jewish leaders around the country took notice of Ira Sanders' good works in Allentown. Dr. Maurice Harris, since 1882 the senior rabbi of New York City's prestigious Temple Israel and "one of the nation's most prominent spokesmen for progressive Judaism," was aware of Sanders' estimable pulpit skills and his prodigious work in the Allentown community, particularly his role in creating and directing the Jewish Community Center.[29] Temple Israel had recently built such a center for study and recreation in Manhattan. Harris hoped to lure Sanders away from Allentown and so sent him a brief telegram on Tuesday, May 27, 1924: "I am seeking an Associate Rabbi for Temple Israel New York. Would you consider it? Will you preach Saturday, May thirty-first?" The date was only *four days* hence. This offer presented Sanders almost no time to ponder what could be the opportunity of a lifetime: the chance to serve as a rabbi in one of the largest, most influential, and most prestigious Reform congregations in the nation and perhaps succeed to the role of senior rabbi, given the fact that Dr. Harris had already served Temple Israel as rabbi for more than forty-two years. Sanders scribbled a response in pencil on the back of the telegram and sent it immediately via return telegram: "Glad to consider associateship. Will preach Saturday May 31. Sincerest thanks for consideration. Letter follows."[30]

Sanders got the job. Barely thirty years old, he had been hand-picked to serve in one of the most high-profile Reform temples in the nation. The *Kansas City Jewish Chronicle* approvingly noted, "he will be one of the youngest rabbis in a metropolitan pulpit," and under his leadership, Temple Israel "will in all probability branch out in new directions that will enlarge its membership and increase its prestige."[31] Nearly one thousand people attended Sanders' installation service on September 19, 1924. His initial sermon was a clear sign of things to come: "The Law of Life is the Law of Service," in which he exhorted "high-minded men to don the armor of Elijah and wear that mantle of service," a sentiment that became his life's credo.[32]

Sanders had very quickly earned a reputation as a dynamic and powerful pulpit presence. In New York, as in Allentown, Sanders developed a "persuasively mellow" style of speaking that he used for the rest of his life, his words coming in "assured, authoritative tones," and a style greatly enjoyed and admired by most listeners, but found by some to be "a bit off-putting."[33] He spoke like the intellectual that he was, clearly and precisely, with a florid formality, each sermon a stage performance equally at home in the pulpit or under the Chautauqua tent. In later years, Sanders wistfully recalled, "I've always been a sucker for anything that had to do with the stage, and might even have tried to be an actor if I had thought it acceptable to my family."[34] His flair for the dramatic was evident in the way he punctuated his smooth, resonant, yet academic delivery with the dense vocabulary of a highly educated man, each sermon structured with the highs and lows of drama. These erudite, well-crafted performances for the most part found very receptive audiences.

For some, though, he spoke almost too formally, and there were those who found his delivery overdone. Early in his career, his was the oratory of the nineteenth-century speaker on the Chautauqua circuit, and sometimes his sermons suffered for it: "The Jewish problem in America," he said in a 1925 sermon, "can be solved by the corralling of our educational forces. No people is so ignorant of its life-forces as are we Jews; we must reestablish ourselves upon our ancient patrimony-religious education."[35] This style of sermonizing presented a picture of erudition and educational accomplishment that Sanders seemed almost to need to project.

Sanders did possess a measure of insecurity. "He was brave in many ways," recalls his daughter Flora, "and fearful in many ways. He was one of the most sensitive people I've ever met." He had a habit in private of talking to himself as a means to work out problems or to practice conversations before they took place. Precision of language was very important to him. He enjoyed being in the center of things, but personally he could be distant, and his formal, often stentorian speaking skills aided in creating or projecting a strong image of confidence that hid or masked some of those inner insecurities.[36] Sanders thought of himself as learned and scholarly, and he wanted others to see those qualities in him as well. To some degree, perhaps to a large degree, he sought to impress. The academic delivery of his sermons, punctuated as they were with dense vocabulary and formal structure, helped to mold and create that impression among his audiences.

As in Allentown, at New York's Temple Israel, Sanders often preached conservative messages of religious discipline, urging his congregation to remain devout, avoid temptations of the flesh, and engage themselves in meaningful social service. The changing, freer moral standards and the liberal evolution of women's roles in the 1920s found qualified support from Ira Sanders, who wanted to see that new vitality channeled in productive ways. In a November 1924 sermon, Sanders gave his unflattering and somewhat alarmist characterization of the Roaring Twenties: unless there "is a slackening in the maddening pace America is setting," he said, "our country is doomed to destruction." The America of this century "is an impetuous, restless, neurotic America" where "play has become an obsession to many of us, an all absorbing interest in life." As for the New Woman feminism popular at the time, Sanders offered a critical assessment: "Our women are becoming ignorant of the homely virtues of domesticity, spending their hours in dressing, parading, gadding, 'mah jongging', and cigarette smoking, refusing to translate their leisure moments into worthwhile social service." Sanders concluded, "One panacea, one salvation, one hope is left alone. Power, religious power—not creedal, not doctrinal, but ethical in content, in fervor, in meaning—a religion of righteousness." Only following such an establishment "will America rise to its true dignity and worth."[37] Sanders, as most spiritual shepherds of religious flocks, was not above reprimanding his congregation and steering them down the straight and narrow way.

The bustling New York City of the 1920s, six million people strong, was not a good fit for Rabbi Sanders. He admitted, "I felt that I was just a very, very unimportant individual in a very large, surging amalgam of individuals and institutions," a situation unbefitting a man such as Sanders, who enjoyed being in the center of things. "I was just a little cog in a great big wheel. [The city] offered me no community life whatsoever, and so I was very anxious to leave New York."[38] Ira and Selma would stay in New York only two years, an active but otherwise unsatisfying time for both of them. Sanders found "his greatest source of satisfaction" in New York working in the community with social work pioneer Lillian Wald, who had championed public health nursing and housing reform and in 1895 had founded New York's famed Henry Street Settlement House.[39] Like Sanders, Wald abhorred racial prejudice and insisted that all classes offered at Henry Street be integrated. She had been a cofounder of the National Association for the Advancement of Colored People (NAACP), whose inaugural meeting took place on May 30, 1909, at the Henry Street Settlement House.[40] But aside from the social work Rabbi Sanders did in the community, he disliked life in New York City. As a sensitive man who enjoyed attention, Sanders craved a smaller setting where he could make a more significant impact. Rabbi Sanders, recalls his daughter Flora, also "felt constrained" in New York "because of his rabbinical duties that left too little time for his family," a sentiment Selma shared. Though an accomplished Wellesley graduate, Selma remained at heart a "small-town person" who decried the city's "lack of community warmth," preferred staying at home, and in any event was not much of an "organization woman." Selma also felt "very dependent" upon Ira, in part because of a hearing impairment from which she suffered that got worse later in life.[41] These reasons contributed to his serious consideration in 1925, and even more in 1926, of offers for the pulpit of the largest Reform congregation in Arkansas, Congregation B'nai Israel of Little Rock.

Such a dramatic relocation, from the nation's largest Reform temple in the nation's largest city to the relatively bucolic atmosphere of a small southern city with a single Reform congregation, intrigued Sanders. The Little Rock move offered him the possibility of a much smaller congregation in a much smaller city more to his liking, where his abilities and interests as a social worker could be exercised to their fullest. There his level of educational attainment, his academic style, and his erudite presence would set him apart much more than in New York City. In addition, he would be the *only* Reform rabbi in the entire city of Little Rock, and with his education and training in sociology and social work, he could be a difference-maker in Arkansas, putting him very much in the center of things and thus ameliorating his insecurities. Sanders seriously considered a move to Arkansas.

— 2 —

Rabbi Sanders Goes to Arkansas

1926–1934

WHEN IRA SANDERS ARRIVED in Little Rock in 1926, he faced challenges he had not yet seen in his young career as a rabbi and social worker. After conquering his initial doubts about relocating to the South, Sanders got to work both within his congregation and in the community at large, a community rigidly segregated by the entrenched culture of white supremacy, pervasive Jim Crow laws, casual and overt racial prejudice, and racially restrictive customs he had always found repugnant. It was the nadir of American race relations, an era of violence and racism lasting from the end of Reconstruction in 1877 through the 1930s; and in Sanders' first months in Arkansas, the inequities of race and the cruelties of racism seemingly met him at every turn. In addition, the young rabbi had entered a culture of want well beyond his experience. An overwhelmingly rural and poor state, Arkansas suffered from generalized poverty, a dearth of social service institutions, and a dramatic shortage of trained social work professionals. The disastrous combination of the Great Depression and the extreme drought of 1930–31, twin calamities that struck Arkansas only three years after his arrival, served to exacerbate these problems.

This new and challenging milieu represented to Sanders a set of interrelated social problems to be worked out. Eager to put his training and education as both a spiritual leader and a social worker to the test, he went to work almost immediately. Within days of his arrival, he rushed into the vacuum, providing community leadership and playing a key role in the creation of various assistance programs and social service institutions for those in need, whose work ranged from providing general welfare assistance to training a new generation of social workers to increasing access to birth control among the poor. When he encountered the entrenched institutional racial preferences and Jim Crow discrimination then characteristic of the South, including Arkansas and Little Rock, he pushed against them, often alone, and sometimes to great effect. Sanders quickly became a potent and driving force in the community.

In *The Provincials*, Eli Evans' bestselling look at Southern Jewry, he wrote, "The southern atmosphere is pleasant for a rabbi; they are respected, are called 'doctor,' and many of them stay for long periods of time." For religiously conservative Christian southerners, the rabbi seems "the very embodiment of the prophets themselves." These "deep-voiced, dramatic men"—certainly an apt description of Ira Sanders—"deeply impressed the fundamentalist community with their appearance and bearing." As one southern rabbi added, "You can't help yourself." If the local community "treats you like some Old Testament prophet, you start acting that way."[1] Even as a young man, Sanders fit the bill perfectly.

Recruiting Dr. Sanders

What have I done?

—IRA SANDERS, 1926

Although the Jewish presence in Arkansas dates to 1838, members of the Little Rock Jewish community did not formally establish Congregation B'nai Israel until November 1866, in the aftermath of the American Civil War. Morris Navra, a successful dry goods proprietor and Prussian immigrant who had settled in Little Rock in 1855, served as the first president of the temple, and in 1867 the sixty-six member congregation retained Samuel Peck as its first rabbi. Lay leaders like Navra, Phillip Pfeifer, and Phillip Ottenheimer, along with Jewish families including the Lasker, Menkus, Kempner, Cohn, Ehrenberg, Levy, and Samuels families—many of whose descendants remain a part of Congregation B'nai Israel more than 150 years later—were critical in its founding.

Peck served as rabbi for only one year, and a succession of many rabbis followed over the next thirty years, none of whom served more than eight years. Near the turn of the twentieth century, Rabbi Harry Mayer left Little Rock for Kansas City, Missouri, where he would serve as young Ira Sanders' rabbi and mentor. Rabbi Louis Wolsey assumed the pulpit in 1899 and remained eight years, followed by Louis Witt, whose twelve-year tenure from 1907 to 1919 was at the time the longest of any in the congregation's history. Following Witt came the brief rabbinate of James Heller (1920) and that of Emanuel J. Jack (1921–1925). The pulpit stood vacant as the congregation entered its sixtieth year in 1926.[2]

In the mid-1920s, the congregation and its leadership for the most part consisted of business owners, professionals, and retailers, solidly middle class or

upper middle class, and respected members of the Little Rock business and
retail community. Temple president Maurice L. Altheimer served as the president of Twin City Bank in North Little Rock, while Temple board member
Leo Pfeifer owned Pfeifer's Department Store, one of the largest and most
prestigious in the city. The other large department and specialty stores of Little
Rock — M. M. Cohn, Kempner's, and Blass — all were also Jewish-owned, and
their proprietors were all members of Congregation B'nai Israel.[3]

With the upcoming departure of Emanuel Jack in 1925, the Temple board
set out to hire a new rabbi. Rabbi Jack, a World War I veteran, had been an
activist rabbi in Little Rock, playing a leadership role in both the local Veterans
of Foreign Wars chapter and the American Legion, and he had taken great
interest in furthering interfaith and cultural dialogue in the community. Jack
had a keen interest in the contemporary "Better Understanding" interfaith ini-
tiatives that accompanied the aftermath of the large-scale Jewish immigration
that marked the era. In 1925, Rabbi Jack initiated Better Understanding Week
in Arkansas, an effort both to engender better racial and ethnic understanding and to respond to the racist and anti-Semitic rhetoric of proliferating nativist
and white supremacist organizations such as the Knights of the White Camellia
and the Ku Klux Klan. The Klan had chartered a group in Little Rock in the
early 1920s that quickly grew to more than 7,500 members at its peak; nation-
ally, the Klan would grow to more than five million strong by mid-decade.[4] Like
Emanuel Jack, Ira Sanders of Temple Israel in New York City had a background
as a community activist, and Sanders and the leaders of Congregation B'nai
Israel were aware of each other when the need to find Jack's replacement arose.

Little Rock knew of Ira Sanders through their former rabbi Harry Mayer,
Sanders' mentor in Kansas City. A committee of Congregation B'nai Israel
representatives approached Ira Sanders of New York's Temple Israel in 1925
about the possibility of accepting the Little Rock pulpit soon to be abandoned
by Rabbi Jack, but Sanders refused. Though not particularly happy in New
York City, he had been Temple Israel's associate rabbi for only one year, so he
declined any interest in Little Rock, deciding to give Manhattan another year.

Little Rock's Reform temple soldiered on through the remainder of 1925 and
into 1926 without a permanent rabbi. Lay leaders like Maurice Altheimer often
led services during this period. Late in May 1926, the temple board tried again
to secure Sanders' service. They had been very impressed with him and were
reluctant to consider anyone else for their pulpit. Acquiring a rabbi of Sanders'
reputation and experience from the prestigious Temple Israel of the City of
New York would be a coup for the Little Rock congregation, so the board dispatched temple president Altheimer and board member Leo Pfeifer as delegates

to New York to again see and hear Rabbi Sanders in action, hoping this second attempt to secure Sanders' services would be more fruitful. Perhaps another year in New York City had altered Sanders' position.

On a cool late May evening, unbeknownst to Sanders, Arkansans Altheimer and Pfeifer sat attentively among the congregation in the voluminous sanctuary of Temple Israel as Sanders rose to take the pulpit. With his usual learned formality, and in mellifluous voice and typically precise diction, he delivered a sermon whose theme of sectional reconciliation seemed tailor-made for the Arkansans: "Why the North and the South Should Meet." Altheimer and Pfeifer and the rest of Little Rock's temple board badly wanted Sanders, both for his prodigious pulpit abilities and likely because they had tired of being without a rabbi to replace Emanuel Jack, now gone for a year.[5] In Sanders, the board saw a man who hailed from the general region, who radiated a palpable aura of erudition, and who possessed a style and scholarly bearing they admired. His sermon and its delivery illustrated just these qualities for Altheimer and Pfeifer. They were deeply impressed. After talking with Sanders, who indeed now expressed a much greater interest in their offer, the men arranged for him to make a brief visit to Little Rock in early June 1926 to interview formally with the search committee and to deliver a Friday night sermon to the congregation — the same sermon on sectional unity that Altheimer and Pfeifer had heard and enjoyed in New York.

Sanders' June 4 meeting with the committee and his Friday evening sermon both went very well. Like the search committee, the congregation as a whole also seemed deeply impressed with Sanders; accordingly, the Congregation B'nai Israel board of trustees moved very quickly, immediately pressing forward with the business of securing his services as rabbi. The board took the unusual step of calling a meeting on the Sabbath, the next day, Saturday, June 5, 1926, during which trustee Lasker Ehrman made a motion "that the Board approve the actions of Messrs. Altheimer and Pfeifer in bringing Rabbi Sanders to Little Rock, and unanimously recommend to the congregation that Rabbi Sanders be elected at a salary of $10,000 a year for three years." The motion passed, and the group then called a special meeting of the entire congregation for 7:30 p.m. on Tuesday evening, June 8, "for the purpose of electing a rabbi." Board president Maurice Altheimer presided over the meeting attended by two hundred or so congregants, where Myron Lasker moved that the congregation as a whole accept Sanders at the salary and time agreed to by the board. The motion carried unanimously and enthusiastically.[6] Actually, at this meeting the temple board members presented the question to the Congregation B'nai Israel membership as a fait accompli, since they had in fact already offered Sanders the position by way of a telegram sent immediately after their Saturday decision to hire him, armed with the foreknowledge that the congregation ardently backed him. The Little Rock Reform Jewish community was moving very quickly to get Sanders on board. The entire hiring process had been a whirlwind— Altheimer and Pfeifer's visit to New York, Sanders' trip to Little Rock, his interview and sermon, the board meeting, the board's offer to Sanders, the rabbi's acceptance, and the congregational meeting and vote of support—all had taken place in little more than one week. This congregation clearly wanted Sanders, and the young rabbi reciprocated, seemingly swept up in the tidal wave of affection as he accepted their offer via return telegram from New York almost at the same time as the congregation met Tuesday evening.

Following Rabbi Sanders' acceptance of the job offer, a delighted Maurice Altheimer wrote him on June 9, 1926, in order to impress upon the young rabbi just how much Congregation B'nai Israel wanted him as their spiritual leader: "You have made us very happy over your coming. You would surely have been overjoyed at your enthusiastic election." He described the scene to Sanders: "As soon as you were nominated and seconded, there were calls that the motion be put; it was carried by a large shout of 'ayes,' and when I called for 'nos,' there was complete silence—then, handclapping." Altheimer added, "We are going to make you and Mrs. Sanders very happy here. We know you will be a wonderful inspiration to us all."[7] It was important that Sanders know the deep regard Little Rock's Reform Jewish community held for him, and just how intensely they desired his services. Leo Pfeifer also wrote to the rabbi, adding that Sanders' telegram accepting the position made "Mr. Altheimer and I feel as if we had accomplished something wonderful; in fact, I do not remember a time in the history of Little Rock where our congregation was so unanimously in favor of any one as they were in your election."[8] The *Arkansas Democrat* added its voice to the chorus of admiration and anticipation, noting that Sanders "has displayed a keen interest in the cooperative functioning of Jewish ideals with civic ideals."[9]

Back in New York, though, Sanders had begun to second-guess himself, as growing doubts about the significant move gnawed at him. The entire process had occurred so quickly, and though pleased with Congregation B'nai Israel and its offer, he now seemed uncertain of his desire to leave New York. This would be, after all, a dramatic move for him, Selma, and infant Flora. What is more, he had been in New York only two years and, upon reflection, had not been particularly impressed with his brief look at the city of Little Rock. Is this

Downtown Little Rock circa 1920. Library of Congress.

where he wanted to raise a family? Had he given Temple Israel enough time as its associate rabbi? Would a move to Little Rock really give him what he was seeking?

Sanders may have inadvertently revealed this hesitation while in Little Rock, or perhaps his acceptance was less enthusiastic than the temple board had hoped. In any event, the Little Rock committee seemed to have sensed or at least anticipated Sanders' indecision, and in an attempt to make plain their sincere desire to secure his services, they took several further steps to convince Sanders to come to Little Rock. In what may have been a coordinated effort on the part of the board to ensure they landed their catch, search committee member Preston Pfeifer sent Sanders a reassuring telegram: "You will be received with much gratification as Little Rock is certainly anxiously awaiting spiritual leadership."[10] Two days later, yet another board member, Myron Lasker, wrote to Sanders, "It was my honor, as well as pleasure, to place your name in nomination and if you could have been listening on the outside, am sure it would have pleased you very much to witness the happiness and joy which our congregation manifested when you were elected as our rabbi."[11] As added insurance, after Sanders left Little Rock, the board asked former Congregation B'nai Israel rabbi Louis Wolsey, then serving as the rabbi of Philadelphia's Congregation Rodeph Shalom, to take Sanders in hand and convince him to come to Arkansas. Wolsey "cornered" Sanders at a small Philadelphia restaurant and enthusiastically went about the business of selling Ira Sanders on Little Rock. Sanders still was not sure he wanted to commit to relocating to the South. He still had time to back out and tell the Little Rock congregation to keep searching for a rabbi. Wolsey painted an intriguing picture for Sanders, telling him of the particular challenges and opportunities "for a man with foresight" that a southern rabbinate and a smaller congregation presented. The opportunity to be an agent of real change in the challenging environment of the American South in general and of Arkansas and Little Rock specifically did have undeniable appeal to the social worker in Sanders, who finally relented, agreeing with Wolsey's assessment that Little Rock "offered a challenge older communities did not have."[12] Sanders attempted to put away his doubts as he, Selma, and baby Flora prepared to leave New York for a new life in Arkansas.

Arrival in Little Rock

I've been sold a bill of goods. I'm going home.
—IRA SANDERS, 1926

Ira Sanders arrived in Little Rock with more than a measure of trepidation. He stepped off the Hot Springs Special at the downtown railroad depot on a hot and humid Wednesday morning, September 1, 1926, during the midst of a late summer heat wave. Sanders recalled it as "the hottest day I've ever experienced."[13] With the morning temperature already above ninety degrees, a committee of temple members met Rabbi and Mrs. Sanders at the train station; the women among the group took Mrs. Sanders in hand while the men "took Dr. Sanders around," as per instructions from Temple president Maurice Altheimer, then away on business in New York, who stressed in his instructions to the welcoming committee the importance of getting the new arrivals settled in quickly "so he gets ready OK for the [upcoming High] Holidays."[14] For his part, however, Sanders immediately felt a strong, almost overwhelming sense of buyer's remorse. While standing there in the train station under a broiling Arkansas sun, doubts raced through his mind as the reality of the move became suddenly apparent. This was more than a world away from New

York City, it seemed. "What have I done?" Sanders thought.[15] Later that day, feeling he had been "sold a bill of goods," he stared out the window of his Hotel Lafayette room at "this wilderness" below. Feeling singularly unimpressed, Sanders dejectedly thought, "It looks like a prairie. I don't think I can stay here. I'm going home." The late summer heat wave, with temperatures hovering in the mid-nineties for three full weeks after his arrival, did not help matters. He seriously considered packing up the family and returning to New York, but several persuasive conversations with members of his new congregation, coupled with pangs from his own conscience, convinced him to stay.[16] If at the end of his three year contract, he still felt unease over the move, he could simply opt to move on. The thirty-two-year-old Sanders preached his inaugural sermon two days later. As in New York, this first sermon signaled to the Little Rock congregation their new rabbi's priorities: "The Law of Life is the Law of Service."[17]

Determined to give his new congregation his best, despite his initial misgivings about staying, Ira Sanders hit the ground running in Little Rock, and a receptive congregational board, very eager to make their new rabbi happy, welcomed his activism. In only his second meeting with the Congregation B'nai Israel board of trustees, on October 12, 1926, he presented an ambitious agenda for change for the upcoming year. Included were the organization of a parent-teacher association "so the mothers of religious school students would meet once a month with teachers" and the establishment of a "normal school" for religious school teachers to begin in November. He told the board he would begin conducting a regular "study circle under the auspices of the Council of Jewish Women," and he then called for the complete refurbishment of the vestry room into a library for pupils and congregants which, he told the board, would "mean the purchase of shelving, tables, chairs, [and] lighting." He also wanted to see the congregational newsletter, the *Temple Chronicle*, published weekly rather than monthly. The board unanimously agreed to everything.[18] Sanders clearly signaled to his board and his congregation that education would be a priority for him, and the board backed him. The various reforms Sanders and the board implemented were well received, and during the temple's well-attended annual meeting of January 1927, congregants overwhelmingly voiced their support for their new rabbi with a gushing resolution: "It is the sense of this congregation that we are conscious of the splendid spiritual leader we have been so fortunate as to secure; that we appreciate his high ideals, his earnestness and zeal for our spiritual welfare, and his scholarly attainments, as well as his thorough Jewishness; that we will endeavor to evidence these feelings by cooperating with him insofar as may be within our power by our attendance at

Rabbi Ira Sanders in his first year at Temple B'nai Israel, 1927.
Courtesy Temple B'nai Israel, Little Rock, Arkansas.

Divine services and in every other way in which we may be called upon to do so." In this resolution, the congregation, still wooing him, demonstrated their sincere desire that he remain in Little Rock for the long term. Altheimer, speaking as board president, added that "by his civic work, he has endeared himself to our entire community."[19] Sanders had been in Little Rock only four months, but in that time, he had clearly and deeply impacted his congregation and was fast becoming a felt presence in the local community.

Congregation B'nai Israel would continue to heap praise upon their rabbi on a regular basis. It seemed that this Little Rock congregation had gotten exactly what it wanted when they hired Sanders in 1926, and they wanted him to know it, especially during the time of that initial three-year contract. Since its founding in 1866, Congregation B'nai Israel had not retained the services of any one rabbi for a term longer than twelve years. The average term of service had been much less than that, about four years, with most of the temple's previous rabbis serving for terms of three or fewer years.[20] Eager for greater stability and to retain Dr. Sanders' services for the long term, they remained mindful both of his initial misgivings about Little Rock and the looming approach of 1929, the expiration date of that initial contract. Accordingly, through 1927 and 1928, the congregation and the board praised their rabbi for the record again and again. During the January 1928 annual congregational meeting, board member Lasker Ehrman lauded Sanders for his work in the community, "having heard words of praise on all sides of Dr. Sanders' good work," while Altheimer reported that "on the many public appearances which Dr. Sanders has been called upon to make, he has requited himself in a highly satisfactory manner, bringing credit and praise to us." In these first three years, the board simply did not refuse Sanders during board meetings, unanimously approving his requests for, among other things, additional monies for books for the new library and paid advertisements "announcing the subject of his sermons" to be placed in the *Arkansas Gazette* on a weekly basis.[21] The board went so far as to throw Rabbi Sanders a surprise party on May 7, 1928, his thirty-fourth birthday. Touched by the sentiment, Sanders told the board that "one of the greatest joys I have had in your midst is the spirit of friendliness and closeness that I have felt for you," which in turn "renews in me an eagerness to give all that I have in me."[22] Having recruited him from Manhattan's prestigious Temple Israel and eminently satisfied with his performance thus far, Congregation B'nai Israel wanted very much to keep the erudite Dr. Sanders in Little Rock.

All of the wooing paid off. In 1929, the board offered—and with his initial reluctance to remain in Little Rock now a thing of the past, Sanders accepted—a renewed contract as rabbi of Congregation B'nai Israel. The board voted unanimously in January of that year to reelect Sanders and award him a new five-year contract to begin in August 1929. They agreed to extend both Sanders' term of service and his salary. Given the seemingly flush economy of the time, the board increased his salary from an annual remuneration of $10,000 to one of $12,000, an impressive sum for that time.[23] With this new contract in place and the decision to remain in Arkansas made, Sanders settled into an ever-enlarging role in the Little Rock community and the continuing work of making his adopted home a better place—and there was much to do. It had been only a matter of days after Rabbi Sanders' 1926 arrival in Little Rock that he personally confronted many of the stark practical and cultural differences presented by his newly adopted community.

Confronting Jim Crow

Why do you object to my sitting in the back?
—IRA SANDERS, 1926

When Ira Sanders arrived in Little Rock in 1926, the city, like the state of Arkansas and the South in general, had in place a rigid set of laws and customs regarding racial segregation. This period in African American history has been called the nadir of race relations, corresponding roughly to the period from the end of Reconstruction to the 1930s, and marking the lowest point of racial comity in American history, in some regards worse than slavery in its disregard for black lives. During the period of Reconstruction (1865–1877) following the Civil War, the US Congress sought to establish legal equality regardless of race throughout the South by means of three constitutional amendments and numerous federal laws. Every state of the former Confederacy, each now firmly back in the hands of Democrats known as Redeemers, responded with what came to be known as Jim Crow laws, a slew of legislative restrictions designed to keep in place the system of racial hierarchy and white privilege that was the legacy of the newly defunct antebellum slave system. In 1868 the Arkansas legislature contributed Act 52, mandating racially segregated education; later, the state's Separate Coach Law of 1891 required separate rail facilities based on race. Those laws as well as similar actions, notes historian Cherisse Jones-Branch, "set the stage for legislation to ensure that black citizens were marginalized in mainstream life in Arkansas, a process that occurred most rapidly in urban areas" such as Little Rock.[24]

The US Supreme Court abetted such efforts. The 1883 decisions known as the Civil Rights Cases stated that the Fourteenth Amendment's Equal Protection Clause applied only to governmental discrimination and not to the discriminatory practices of private businesses, therefore opening the door for widespread racial segregation and denial of services at restaurants, theaters, and any other public facilities. The court's 1896 decision *Plessy v. Ferguson* upheld the validity of "separate, but equal" segregation laws. In the wake of these court decisions, the Arkansas legislature passed the 1903 Streetcar Segregation Act, which did not require separate cars but did mandate "separate, but equal" areas on every car. In practice, this meant African Americans had to take the back and whites the front, and black patrons had to give up their seats in the "colored" seating areas to whites if the designated white area filled. Passengers who refused to sit in the appropriate racially assigned areas were subject to a $25 fine. In addition to these restrictions, black men (and after the passage of the

Nineteenth Amendment in 1920, black women) lost access to the ballot through devices such as the poll tax, literacy tests, and the 1906 institution of the "white primary." Intimidation and violence also kept the African American population in check. Every state of the former Confederacy (as well as most states outside the South) enacted such "Jim Crow" laws, covering nearly every aspect of life.[25] Institutionalized racial preferences that upheld white supremacy both in custom and before the law were an established and harsh fact when Ira Sanders arrived in Arkansas in 1926. It would take the progressive reforms and gradual plans for desegregation of the years after World War II to ameliorate the harshness of the segregation Arkansas experienced during the nadir.

Nothing Ira Sanders had seen in Allentown or Manhattan prepared him for Little Rock's world of rigid racial preferences, discriminatory regulations and customs, and overt and casual public racism. Arkansas represented a dramatically different environment for Sanders, an environment replete with the unique challenges of a southern rabbinate of which Rabbi Louis Wolsey had spoken when recruiting him for Little Rock, a conversation that helped convince Sanders to come to Arkansas.

Very shortly after his arrival in Little Rock, Ira Sanders ran headlong into the reality of racial segregation in Arkansas in two dramatic incidents that both outraged and inspired the young rabbi and in the process moved his entire career along its eventual path. Sanders did not own an automobile when he came to Little Rock, so he rode the electric streetcar to his office in the Temple. On one of the first such occasions, he boarded the sparsely occupied trolley and moved toward the back, taking a seat near the rear of the car. He found the signs designating "colored" and "white" seating areas "appalling," but he was more naïve than bold in his choice of seating that day.[26] The conductor watched with a disapproving eye as Sanders took his seat in the rear section beside an African American man, an act in stark violation of both the Streetcar Segregation Act and local custom. The alarmed conductor rushed immediately to the rear of the car and confronted Sanders, telling him first, he must be new in town, and second, "You know, here in the South the niggers and the whites do not sit together. Will you kindly come up to the front?" Taken aback by the request as well as the casual use of a harsh racial epithet, the rabbi stared up at the conductor. Sanders had not intended to commit an act of civil disobedience, but instead had simply wandered down the aisle and taken a seat as he had done dozens of times in Allentown and New York City. Now, however, the conductor's visceral reaction had transformed Sanders' action from the mundane act of commuting to work into the dramatic act of challenging the racial status quo. Sanders became defensive, feeling his notions of fairness, equality, and decency under assault. He had always found the notion of racial segregation repugnant, and in the moment, in these circumstances, he almost reflexively decided he would challenge it. Without relinquishing his seat, Sanders looked up at the streetcar conductor. "Why do you object to my sitting in the back?" he said. "This is a free country—can't a person ride where he pleases?"[27] Unmoved, the conductor pressed the issue, making it very clear that he would not allow Sanders to keep his chosen seat in the "colored section." The situation quickly escalated as each man raised his voice in a heated and confrontational dialogue. Sanders, balding and bespectacled, but a substantial six feet tall, was prepared to fight the man; instead—livid, red-faced, and seething with righteous indignation—he exercised restraint and complied, moving to the front of the car. The indignity, though, both to him and his unknown bench-mate, had been done. Once he arrived at the temple, he scrapped his planned sermon for the upcoming Friday evening service and instead prepared a new sermon: "The Jim Crow Law." That Sabbath evening, before his new southern congregation, Sanders scathingly denounced racial discrimination, preached the equality of all before God, and predicted the absolute demise of Jim Crow within twenty-five years. Such laws, Sanders said, "are obsolete" and would be "almost forgotten" by that time. Any law that robs the individual of dignity and freedom could not stand.[28]

The streetcar incident moved Rabbi Sanders to take immediate action in the form of a sharply worded sermon, but the stark racial inequalities he saw around him also led him to take other, more concrete actions. A ghastly lynching Sanders witnessed mere months after his confrontation on the streetcar only compounded his desire to take decisive action against racism and Jim Crow. In May 1927 a marauding white mob murdered John Carter, an African American man accused of assaulting a white woman in her car. The mob captured and hanged Carter from a utility pole, after which more than two hundred bullets were fired into his lifeless body; the mob then chained his corpse to an automobile and dragged it through the streets of downtown Little Rock, finally stopping at the intersection of Ninth and Broadway Streets, the commercial center of Little Rock's African American community, where on two corners stood the Mosaic Templars building, the national headquarters of that historically black fraternal organization, and the Bethel African Methodist Episcopal Church.[29] Only four blocks north, at Fifth and Broadway, stood Temple B'nai Israel.

As Ira Sanders looked on in horror, the lynch mob, which would eventually reach five thousand strong, filled the streets and built a large bonfire on the streetcar tracks in the intersection of Ninth and Broadway, stoking it with furniture, doors, and pews they ransacked from the church and nearby black businesses. Carter's body burned while members of the white mob claimed parts of the charred corpse as "souvenirs" and rampaged through the abutting black residential area in what the *Arkansas Gazette* angrily characterized as a

"Saturnalia of savagery." One member of the mob brazenly directed traffic with Mr. Carter's severed, charred forearm.

The police, meanwhile, did nothing. Gov. John Martineau, out of town but mortified upon hearing of the lynching and the accompanying white rioting mere blocks from the state capitol, immediately called in the National Guard to restore order. The lynching both horrified Sanders and moved him to action. "When I saw that dreadful lynching," Sanders said understatedly, "I was convinced that I had come into a community that needed a lot of education." The young rabbi attended a "magnificent" mass meeting to protest the lynching and was gratified to see Little Rock's progressive *Arkansas Gazette* come out "in very, very vehement terms of denunciation." The lynching "forcibly brought home the whole problem of a better understanding between the different groups in the community" and helped inspire Sanders' ongoing and active role in promoting racial and social justice and in bettering relations between black and white Arkansans.[30]

As the lynching of John Carter graphically illustrated for the young rabbi, "the cleavage between blacks and whites in the community was wide; rapport between them was almost nil." In response, he became a member of the Little Rock chapter of the National Association for the Advancement of Colored People (NAACP) and also accepted a seat on the advisory committee of the Arkansas council of the Association of Southern Women for the Prevention of Lynching (ASWPL), the local arm of a rapidly-growing national organization founded in 1930. By 1936 the ASWPL had nearly forty thousand southern signatories to a pledge "to create a new public opinion in the South which will not condone for any reason the acts of mobs or lynchers." The group focused on education rather than political action, disbursing by that same year more than seventy-six thousand copies of anti-lynching pamphlets and materials.[31]

The Rabbi as Rabbi

This pulpit was offered me as a free one,
and it will continue to remain such.
—IRA SANDERS, 1928

Rabbi Sanders' sermons on racial and social injustice, of which "The Jim Crow Law" was the first of many, met with general approval.[32] While the congregation was anxious to keep Sanders in Little Rock and happy, the rabbi and his new congregation had struck genuine chords of affinity very early on. Like many within the Little Rock community as a whole, the congregation over the years of Sanders' tenure as rabbi generally held moderate to progressive views on issues of race, and within the walls of the temple, many congregants could feel free to nod approvingly at the rabbi's words and voice progressive opinions. Nonetheless, like Jews in other southern communities, publicly most Little Rock Jews remained much more cautious because of their standing in the larger community as prominent businessmen and retail merchants. In short, they tended to keep their views to themselves. Southern Jews were aware that their standing in the region might grow more precarious should they be perceived as "agitators" or threats to the social, and especially the racial, status quo. The 1920s and 1930s in America, after all, saw not only institutionalized Jim Crow but generalized and overt anti-Semitism on display as well, and the 1915 Leo Frank lynching in Atlanta remained fresh in Southern Jewish minds.[33]

Yet even during these years of casual public anti-Semitism and racial prejudice, that sense of caution almost never hampered Rabbi Sanders. He was not one to lead marches, to be sure, but he did lead through education, by example, and by virtue of his rapidly growing stature and influence in the larger community. He often used his pulpit as a place to persuade and educate, and in his sermons he tended to integrate themes near and dear to him: service to God and community; the basic and essential equality of all people; and engaging the community through civic involvement.

His sermons gained additional gravity and authority by virtue of his use of language and his style of speaking, the primary qualities of which congregants in Little Rock still speak when they reminisce about Rabbi Sanders, and perhaps the prime characteristic that had endeared Sanders to the congregational search committee in the first place. His sermonizing style reflected a depth of intellect respected over the years by the congregation, and the sermons themselves were made sharper by the keen editing skills of his wife Selma.[34] As to the delivery of those sermons, the vast majority of congregants through the years agreed about both their delivery and their tone. "He had an outstanding speaking voice," recalls Jerry Jacobson, a congregant at whose 1960 wedding Rabbi Sanders officiated. He "spoke in a precise manner," and his services "were all seriousness." Maxwell Lyons II recalls Sanders as "an imposing person" with a "stentorian voice, demanding," and James Pfeifer, who grew up with Sanders as his rabbi and as part of a confirmation class tutored by Sanders, called the rabbi "a great orator," going on to say, "His sermons were serious—no puns, no forgotten candlesticks, no jokes, and you were expected to sit and listen with no bathroom breaks or kids talking. He expected his confirmands to speak accordingly and," recalls Pfeifer, "practice we would, in front of him, from the pulpit." Sanders' voice was "crystal clear with every syllable enunciated perfectly." Congregant Eugene P. Levy said, perhaps only half-jokingly, "When I was a little boy I did not know the difference between Rabbi Sanders and God." Detractors might describe Sanders' delivery as "pompous," but says Pfeifer, "He really wasn't. I think he was driven by perfection, especially in the temple, and he expected that from others." Jacobson has a similar recollection, calling Sanders "a stern taskmaster" who in later years "developed a certain sweet quality. He was one of a kind."[35]

The *Arkansas Gazette* agreed, characterizing Sanders' oratory and voice some years later as "persuasively mellow and resonant," coming in "assured, authoritative tones which also manage to remain friendly to the point of geniality." There is "the look of a scholar, yes," noted the *Gazette* in describing Sanders, "but not of the idle dreamer. His is the look of a practical man, a business man, which is exactly what he is. Humanity—or God, if you will—is Rabbi Sanders' business." With Sanders, there seems to be "a purposefulness that eliminates waste of energy, an impression of great strength—not of muscular force, perhaps, but certainty of purpose. You get the impression that in moving from one objective to another he travels by the most economical route, a straight line."[36]

In addition to his qualities of gifted oratory and religious discipline, Ira Sanders was very much a classical Reform rabbi, which was exactly what this classically Reform congregation wanted. "We were so Reform," joked long-time congregant Alan Thalheimer, "that we closed on the High Holidays!"[37] Little Rock's Congregation B'nai Israel had been among the first congregations in the United States to join the national Reform Jewish organization created in 1873, the Union of American Hebrew Congregations (UAHC), and to adopt the Union Prayer Book for its services.[38] The strong Reform tradition would continue under Ira Sanders. There would be little to no Hebrew during services; confirmation rather than bar mitzvahs; traditional organ and choirs provided music in services that closely resembled church services in their overall feel. Indeed, many Reform congregations, though not Little Rock's, even held services on Sundays to more closely conform to their Christian neighbors. Reform Judaism does not recognize *kashrut*, the kosher laws, and neither did Sanders, as evinced by his personal love for bacon and BLTs. Rabbi and Mrs. Sanders (like many Reform Jews) consented to their young daughter Flora's desire to have a Christmas tree during the holiday season; but, in the Sanders' case and at Selma's insistence, only for one day, and with the blinds closed. Afterward, as Flora Sanders recalls, "Mother made us . . . throw it in the incinerator!"[39]

Like the kosher laws, Zionism was not a tenet of Reform Judaism, and in these early years before the establishment of the State of Israel, the congregation and the rabbi agreed that discussions of Zionism should not emanate from the pulpit, as both he and many of his congregants, who held disparate views on the topic, believed it was a controversial topic best left for discussion outside the sanctity of the synagogue.

A potential point of contention between the rabbi and his congregation came with the 1928 presidential election and Sanders' endorsement of Catholic Democratic candidate Al Smith of New York and his running mate, Arkansas senator Joseph T. Robinson. Sanders had always been a vociferous advocate of unfettered freedom for his pulpit, and this incident further tested his ability to address controversial matters from the bema. In October 1928, Sanders announced in the *Temple Chronicle* his upcoming sermon "Shall We Elect a Roman Catholic President?" This controversial topic elicited an immediate response from some temple members who preferred that Sanders "not discuss such a highly volatile subject" from the pulpit. A committee of two approached the rabbi and in essence tried to bribe him into silence, offering Sanders a check for one hundred dollars to purchase books for the new library in exchange for his opting to deliver a sermon on a more benign topic. Outraged, Sanders told the men, "Do you think I should sell myself for a mess of pottage? This pulpit was offered me as a free one, and it will continue to remain such." He delivered the sermon to a crowded sanctuary audience, and an impressed Arkansas Democratic Party subsequently asked to have the sermon reprinted in order to distribute it to Democrats throughout the state. After that, Sanders proudly recorded in his journal, "My stock rose heavily." His congregation knew, he wrote, "[I] had not come into their midst to play second fiddle. Like the prophet of old, justice and fair play flamed in [my] heart as though it were 'burning fire shut up in my bones.'"[40] Sanders had stood firm for the freedom of his pulpit and had triumphed, earning him the recognition and validation from his congregation and the community that he seemed both to want and need. It would not be the last time he stood firm for control of his pulpit.

Sanders' conception of the ideal rabbi was centered in the classical Reform tradition as reflected in the so-called Pittsburgh Platform, drawn up in 1885 in a conference called by a man who in later years would be one of his Hebrew Union College mentors, college president Kaufmann Kohler. The planks of the Pittsburgh Platform became the tenets of modern Reform Judaism in their rejection of many traditional rituals and practices as "outdated," and the platform's concurrent embrace of "the struggle for truth, justice, and righteousness in modern society."[41] These tenets of modern Reform Judaism conveniently aligned with the concepts of the social worker in Sanders, making the profession of Reform rabbi an ideal vehicle for him. Rabbi Sanders' deep and abiding interest in racial and social justice had other sources as well. He grew up in the public schools of Kansas City and Cincinnati and attended integrated classes at Columbia University, going "to school with all peoples, and I felt that they were all one."[42] One of the factors that motivated him to pursue a career as a rabbi in the first place was his interest, even as a child, "in the promotion of good will between peoples."[43] His study of sociology and social work at Columbia also had been motivated by his desire to make a difference in the world. He embraced the Jewish concept of *tikkun olam* (repairing the world), a call to social action and social justice which teaches that people bear the ultimate responsibility for working together in the here and now towards a just and equitable society. Finally, Sanders' study of the biblical prophets, particularly Isaiah, "who railed against the injustices of his day," also factored into his life of social activism.[44] He was not alone. Many reform rabbis of his generation, North and South, also had an abiding interest in social and community activism.[45] But for Sanders, social work was equal parts profession and avocation, and one of the first things he noticed upon arriving in Arkansas was a lack of trained social workers. For a poor state very much in need of trained professionals to assist its citizens in need, this for Sanders represented a crisis. To answer this crisis, in addition to his other community involvements, Sanders took it upon himself to establish a school for social workers.

The Little Rock School of Social Work

The first lesson we must learn in life is the lesson of understanding.
—IRA SANDERS, 1927

Within days of his arrival in Little Rock, Sanders established himself as an active force in the community. By the time he founded the Little Rock School of Social Work in 1927, he had already become involved in a number of other community organizations. "My first two institutions that dealt with the health and well-being of the community," Sanders later recalled, "were the public library and the Arkansas Tuberculosis Association." Vera Snook, who had just become the librarian at the main branch of the Little Rock Public Library, asked Sanders shortly after his arrival to serve on the library's board of directors, a position he gladly accepted and retained for more than fifty years. Also in Sanders' first few months in Arkansas, Erle Chambers, who had been the first woman to serve in the Arkansas General Assembly (1923–26) and in 1926 served as the executive secretary of the Arkansas Tuberculosis Association, asked Sanders to sit on the board of that organization. Again, he remained a force in that organization for over four decades.[46]

IRA E. SANDERS

newly elected

President

of the

Central Council of

Social Agencies

BOARD OF DIRECTORS OF THE COMMUNITY FUND

Board of Directors is composed of one representative of each member agency and eleven citizens representing the giving public.

DIRECTORS REPRESENTING THE PUBLIC

John F. Boyle	Herbert Wolfe	J. B. Webster	J. J. Harrison	Emmet Morris
Sidney Florsheim	C. J. Griffith	E. L. Bruce, Jr.	Dr. F. Vinsonhaler	Mrs. Julian Blass

DIRECTORS REPRESENTING THE AGENCIES

Mrs. F. V. M. Haley	H. G. Pugh	Mrs. J. F. Lenon	Mrs. Elbert Brack
Mrs. J. E. Fry	D. L. Menkus	Mrs. C. C. Rose	Mrs. J. E. Watson
Mrs. W. S. Rawlings	J. K. Poch	Mrs. D. D. Terry	Ben D. Brickhouse
A. J. Reap	G. Dennison Cherry	W. A. McDonnell	
Horace Chamberlain	Florance Donahue	Dr. Ira E. Sanders	

Flyer announcing the election of Ira Sanders as president
of the Little Rock Central Council of Social Agencies, 1927.
Courtesy Temple B'nai Israel, Little Rock, Arkansas.

Several months after his September 1926 arrival in Little Rock, Sanders also became the president of the Central Council of Social Agencies (CCSA). First organized in 1924 as part of Little Rock's Community Fund, the CCSA was intended "to raise, collect, and disburse funds for the agencies caring for the social needs of Little Rock." Composed of representatives "of all social agencies," the CCSA served as a sort of clearinghouse for social service agencies in Little Rock and, like all other such agencies in the city, received its funding through local taxation and the Community Fund. Charles Wickard, the CCSA's secretary-treasurer, asserted that "Sanders is not only well educated in sociology, but he has that practical experience which makes him of utmost value in the handling of our community problems." As president of the CCSA, Sanders led the organization in undertaking a comprehensive study of "community conditions and problems" through the use of "the spot map system," which would highlight the areas in the city of greatest "poverty, bad health, and juvenile delinquency." Sanders explained, "With the use of this map, our social agencies and those interested in social work will be able to visualize and know at a glance just which parts of the city are problem centers. We know," concluded the rabbi, "that approximately 75 per cent of poverty is caused by illness, as is about 50 per cent of delinquency. It stands to reason, therefore, that if we can prevent sickness we should have less poverty and less crime."[47] This system allowed Sanders to locate problem areas and allocate funds and resources accordingly. From his arrival in September 1926, Sanders worked to meet the many social challenges presented by his new home, but his social work took place in a state with few social workers in it and no educational institution to train them. He resolved to address that serious shortage by the most direct route possible: through creating a school of social work himself.

This school was perhaps Sanders' most significant contribution in his first years in Arkansas. By October 7, 1927, just over a year after his arrival, he had completed all of the necessary groundwork to open the doors of a fully operational and accredited college-level institution. This organizational feat becomes even more remarkable when one considers that he accomplished it in addition to his rabbinic responsibilities and his other community commitments. He noted that, upon his arrival in Arkansas, the state had fewer than a dozen trained social workers and no facility or school to train new ones. Realizing "how important it was for the community of Little Rock — Arkansas also — to have trained social workers," he set forth to create such as school.[48] Already the president of Little Rock's Central Council of Social Agencies, Sanders asked the board of the Little Rock Community Fund, "the fiscal policy maker of the Council," to tender the start-up funds, and the board "unanimously made an appropriation to start the school."[49] Sanders then went about the formidable task of organizing and designing the curriculum, locating and hiring instructors, finding an appropriate meeting space, recruiting administrators, and promoting the school in the community. He did it all in less than a year. The Little Rock School of Social Work, operating under the auspices of the University of Arkansas, opened its doors on October 7, 1927, in the Young Women's Christian Association building downtown at Fourth and Scott Streets. Sanders served as the program director, taught classes, and corralled key city leaders including Little Rock school superintendent R. C. Hall and Southern Methodist bishop H. A. Boaz to serve on the board. Dr. Frank Vinsonhaler, dean of the Arkansas

Little Rock School of Social Work

Announcing the opening of the Little Rock School of Social Work, Monday, October 7, 7:30 o'clock, Y. W. C. A. Building, Fourth and Scott Streets.

Courses offered in Social Psychology; Family Case Work; Principles and Techniques of Social Work; Social Research. All work done in the School of Social Work is accredited by the University of Arkansas—two credits per two hours of year's work. Instruction given bi-weekly, until June, in all courses. Hours of instruction to be arranged at the opening night of school.

School open to all those interested in the field of sociology.

Tuition for students wishing credit from School of Social Work —$10.00 per year, payable $5.00 per semester, in advance: University credit—$10.00 additional per course for two hours work bi-weekly, payable in advance.

ALL STUDENTS MUST REGISTER MONDAY EVENING, OCTOBER 7th, 7:30 O'CLOCK
Y. W. C. A. Building, Fourth and Scott

IRA E. SANDERS, Dean,
Little Rock School of Social Work.

P. S.—Inasmuch as some prospective students may be in attendance at the Little Rock Junior College on Monday, the opening night, the Registrar will be in attendance also on Tuesday evening, October 8th, for the placing of students in their classes

Announcement for the opening of the Little Rock School of Social Work, 1927. Courtesy Temple B'nai Israel, Little Rock, Arkansas.

School of Medicine, served as president. The school offered accredited junior and senior level courses such as social psychology, family casework, and social research. Sanders himself taught many of the courses, including Principles and Techniques of Social Work and Modern Social Problems. The board set tuition at ten dollars per two hours of coursework, with a five dollar registration fee.[50]

The Little Rock School of Social Work opened with an initial enrollment of sixty students, including two African American women. Following the inaugural orientation meeting between Sanders and the students, a contingent of three white students approached the rabbi: "You know, Dr. Sanders, in the South the Negroes and the whites do not go to school together, and we very much object to having any of these women who are with us to be in our school."[51] As with his confrontation over segregated seating with the streetcar conductor the previous year, Sanders again found himself face-to-face with questions of race, segregation, and equal treatment. He turned the confrontation into what could be called a teachable moment tinged with an air of ultimatum. In a quiet but stern manner, he told the students "Of course the first lesson we must learn in life is the lesson of understanding, to know how the other person feels before we can do any kind of work in life." Sanders stated that the women in question had qualifications equal to their own or to any of the others, and certainly as great a need. "If fifty-eight students do not care to attend the school, they certainly are at liberty to leave, but these two women — those two will remain."[52] He offered to refund the fees of any student who chose to withdraw.

Having taken a stand for equality and racial integration in the Jim Crow-dominated Little Rock of 1927, his concern shifted to the real possibility that an accompanying exodus of white students might jeopardize his dream of a school for social work. To his pleasant surprise, attendance did not decline, and for a time, Sanders had removed a racial barrier in Little Rock higher education: his school of social work successfully held racially integrated classes. But it was not to last. Once Little Rock school superintendent R. C. Hall became aware that the African American women attended the school on an equal basis with the white students, he notified the University of Arkansas, under whose name and supervision the school operated. The university leadership intervened by refusing to allow the integrated classes as per the university's practices, despite the rabbi's wishes and the evident acquiescence of the white students. They ordered Sanders to dismiss the black women from the school in order to maintain the university's policy of strict racial exclusion. Sanders did all he could to allow the women to remain, but the administrators were unmoved — they insisted the rabbi remove the women from the rolls. The rabbi reluctantly acquiesced to the demand, unwilling to sacrifice the entire endeavor for the sake of challenging the racial exclusionism of the system. The Little Rock School of Social Work thereafter operated as a whites-only institution until the economic stresses of the Great Depression forced its closure in 1932.[53] In May 1930 the school graduated an initial class of forty social workers, all white.

One of the African American women Sanders had been forced to dismiss was Sadye Allen Thompson. She had read in the newspaper of the opening of the school for social work, applied, been accepted for the initial fall semester, and enrolled in a class taught by Sanders. In the aftermath of the three students approaching Sanders with their objections to her attending, she recalled that Sanders "polled the class and found that the other students would not object to her staying." The question seemed settled, and a few months passed during which Thompson continued to attend classes without incident. The rabbi then summoned her late in the following semester to say that university administrators had become aware of the integrated classes. "Against the rabbi's wishes," Thompson recalled, school segregation policies forced her to leave the class. The other African American woman had already left, having moved from the Little Rock area. "I guess I was in the class maybe from fall until spring," and then Sanders called her in to see him. "He told me in a nice way," she remembered. "What I'm about to tell you," Sanders said, "I don't know *how* to tell you." He said he'd rather "take a whipping" than have to give her this news. He told her how the school had overridden his desire that she be allowed to stay, and that in fact she would have to leave. "I don't want you to think it is the members of the class, because I have polled all the members," he reassured her. Thompson also said that her classmates were sorry and missed her. "You know, they had all said that they wanted me to attend. But it was just that policy—I could understand that; Rabbi Sanders had nothing to do with that."[54] Sanders and Ms. Thompson would keep in touch throughout their lives.

Little Rock provided fertile ground for Sanders' mission of social justice and racial equality, and he had much to do given the city's relative dearth of social service institutions as the 1920s drew to a close. Almost immediately upon arriving in Arkansas, Sanders had been a whirlwind of activity, joining, founding, and participating in a variety of civic and community organizations such as the School of Social Work. The onset of the Great Depression, however, brought challenges of a scale Sanders had never before seen.

3

Race and Poverty in the Great Depression

1929–1937

ARKANSAS AND LITTLE ROCK faced a multitude of problems during the Great Depression, and Ira Sanders offered many different solutions to address the suffering of both his congregation and the community at large. The antipoverty and social justice measures Sanders helped institute and through which he actively worked following his arrival, including the Little Rock School of Social Work, would all either strain or buckle under the weight of the Great Depression. As early as 1930, the relatively few other social service agencies that existed across Arkansas likewise were reeling, stretched to the breaking point and beyond by the triple disasters of Depression, severe drought, and the catastrophic aftermath of the Mississippi River flood of 1927, which caused many to overcome their apprehension about being "on the dole" and look to private and governmental agencies for help.[1] Sanders' efforts during the years of the Great Depression border on the heroic. He waged a one-man campaign to shore up and in many cases create from scratch effective institutions and individual measures to combat the poverty and welfare crises in Little Rock and Pulaski County. Particularly mindful of the special problems faced by African Americans already suffering under the restrictions of Jim Crow, Sanders knew the strains brought on by the drought and the Depression would weigh disproportionately upon segregated and marginalized black Arkansans. With a dearth of federal assistance coming to Arkansas from the Hoover administration and the hit-or-miss nature of later New Deal relief programs, Sanders' social welfare efforts in Arkansas during the Great Depression took on even greater significance.

The Great Debate

Man is soul, even as soul is man.
—IRA SANDERS, 1930

One of Rabbi Sanders' proudest achievements took place almost contemporaneously with the onset of the Great Depression in Arkansas: the founding of the Congregation B'nai Israel Temple Men's Club, for many years the only organization in Little Rock to sponsor public lectures in the arts and sciences. After an initial meeting on January 16, 1930, and an organizational luncheon on February 14, 1930, the group held its first official meeting on April 1, 1930. The Temple Men's Club's first great event, though, was a debate on November 3, 1930, between Ira Sanders and famed attorney and avowed atheist Clarence Darrow on the topic "Is Man Immortal?"

In many ways, the Sanders-Darrow debate represents the moment of Ira Sanders' broad acceptance within the larger Little Rock Christian and secular community. Sanders conceived of the idea of a debate with Darrow as a means to raise funds for the new Temple Men's Club. The rabbi wrote to Darrow inviting him to participate and was somewhat surprised when he accepted: Darrow would debate for his standard speaking fee of $500. Sanders then had tickets printed to offer for sale, and he arranged for the rental of the newly constructed Little Rock High School auditorium for $250. The Temple Men's Club needed robust ticket sales in order to cover the expenses of setting up the event, but ticket sales were slow, and the event was in danger of losing money until a local Christian fundamentalist minister, who had twice written to Sanders unsuccessfully requesting and then demanding to be added to the program to give "a Christian's opinion," angrily took to the radio with a bitter anti-Semitic tirade consisting, Sanders later said, of "some of the most vituperative language I have ever heard." The radio minister concluded his rant by exclaiming, "The rabbi will burn in hell for a thousand years!" Ticket sales then skyrocketed, and a crowd of nearly three thousand people attended the standing-room-only event.[2]

A committee of three, including Rabbi Sanders, met Darrow's train, which arrived from Chicago several hours late. Internationally famous from having defended Tennessee schoolteacher John T. Scopes only five years earlier in the infamous "Monkey Trial" of July 1925, the controversial Darrow was, as Sanders described him, "a rather old looking, stoop shouldered man" possessed of "an unusually keen sense of humor." Despite Darrow's late arrival, the committee offered to drive him down to the tourism and resort city of Hot Springs to see the fabled and supposedly curative waters. Darrow curtly replied, "Why

Ira Sanders and Clarence Darrow, 1930, Little Rock, Arkansas.
Courtesy Temple B'nai Israel, Little Rock, Arkansas.

should I go to Hot Springs? I don't have syphilis!"[3] Despite their wide age disparity — Darrow was 73, Sanders, 36 — and differing philosophies, Sanders and Darrow got on well; the rabbi, particularly, had great respect for the famed attorney.

The debaters took the stage on the evening of November 3, 1930. Over the span of more than two and one-half hours, the rabbi and the attorney argued the question of immortality before a rapt audience. The crowd that filled the Little Rock High School auditorium "applauded generously" for each man as they made their respective points. Sanders surprised Darrow by not referencing God or religion at all in his remarks; instead, he argued the question of immortality as a scientific one, a question of the "conversion of mass and energy." He said, "Man has qualities over and above what are necessary to cope with his environment." Why should this be, he asked, unless this superiority of man enables him to survive death in some form? Yet he said he did not pretend to know anything about the specifics of such survival. Sanders argued for the scientific validity of man as "a unity within himself — one unitary whole with no independent parts." People did not *possess* souls, he said: "Man *is* soul, even as soul is man." Darrow countered by reiterating that the immortality of the soul represented not a scientific but a religious concept, "a myth built upon wishful religious thinking" with "not a shred of evidence to support such a belief." Darrow said, "no one has ever touched a soul or has seen one in a test tube. Empirically, therefore, the soul is unreal." The lively exchange resulted in much positive press coverage for the rabbi, which noted that Sanders' eloquent defense of an afterlife "made a deep impression" with the audience, who "applauded him vigorously."[4] In the process, Sanders earned the respect and a measure of admiration from Arkansas's Christian community in the face of the celebrated agnostic's arguments. This goodwill represented capital that the rabbi could tap into in the years to come when he championed sometimes controversial causes.

The local consensus was that the rabbi had "beaten" Darrow in the debate, though many in the crowd noted that the men approached the topic from such differing viewpoints, with "Rabbi Sanders presenting his thoughts in a broad, philosophical way, and Mr. Darrow contending from a personal and emotional angle," that the two debaters "never quite met."[5] One witness to the debate later recalled, "I remember Darrow being surprised that Rabbi Sanders did such a good job. I don't think he expected much of a debate from a small-town rabbi."[6] Rev. Paul Quillian, pastor of Winfield Methodist Church, wrote Sanders the day after the debate: "Not only did you entirely discomfit your opponent, you thrilled and inspired me along with the major portion of your audience." He congratulated the rabbi on his "masterful" presentation and his "unique but valid" approach to the topic. "Mr. Darrow in fact was driven to resort to trivial humor to hide his complete rout." Sanders and the debate became the topic for Quillian's next Sunday sermon. Little Rock's "only organization with a distinguished lecture course," the Temple Men's Club later brought to Little Rock such luminaries as historian Will Durant and radio journalist H. V. Kaltenborn.[7]

Sanders became involved in many different aspects of Little Rock civic life from the beginning, establishing himself in the community as a force for good. His positive relationship with the Little Rock secular and Christian communities would pay important dividends in later years; in the shorter term, however, the social, political, and economic stability of Arkansas and of Little Rock began to slide dangerously toward disaster as the Great Depression and historic drought hammered the state.

Catastrophe

The stomachs of the black people are just as
important as the stomachs of the white.
— IRA SANDERS, 1931

The twin disasters of drought and Depression struck Arkansas almost simulta-neously. The Great Depression hit first. Coming in the wake of the catastrophic stock market collapse of October and November 1929, it owed much to several preexisting problems in the American economy. A speculative implosion led to panicked selling and to stock prices spiraling downward at a dizzying pace as investors faced financial ruin. The crash of the stock market helped bring on the Depression as it triggered a series of equally disastrous events. Since much of the market speculation had been funded through borrowed money, in an environment with few regulations to prevent banks themselves from risking depositors' funds in the market, the crash dragged an already weak banking system down along with it. Banks failed at an epidemic rate, and depositors, seeing the banking system quickly collapse around them, lined up to withdraw funds from their banks, fearing such a failure would hit them. In a self-fulfilling prophecy, these mass withdrawals—runs on the bank—in fact helped trigger a cascade of further bank failures that lasted throughout the Hoover years. In these days before federal deposit insurance, millions of bank patrons lost every-thing and in many cases were plunged into poverty. A severe maldistribution of wealth exacerbated the problem, as the top 5 percent of the population received over one-third of the national income. Such piling of wealth on one end of the economic scale mandated that, in a consumption-production economy, the top 5 percent do one-third of all the spending, which did not—and could not—occur. Investments stalled as caution replaced confidence, and due to the lack of purchasing power amongst the bottom 95 percent, consumer spending declined as consumption could not keep pace with production, forcing lay-offs, busi-ness closures, shift eliminations, and rising unemployment. As unemployment rose, purchasing power further declined, creating a vicious downward spiral of declines in spending leading to increasing unemployment leading to further declines in spending. Business failures in an already unstable business structure accelerated, as investment firms and holding companies, many of which more closely resembled pyramid schemes with interconnected tentacles everywhere in the economy, went bankrupt and took down other firms that had invested in them. Retrenchment followed, creating deflationary pressures that squeezed whatever earnings there were and brought new investment to a virtual halt.[8]

The Depression hit Arkansas doubly hard because the man-made catastrophe of economic collapse coincided with two natural disasters: the aftermath of catastrophic flooding in 1927 and a bout of severe drought in 1930–31 that turned saturated farmland into dust. About 80 percent of Arkansans in 1930 lived in rural areas in varying degrees of poverty; for these Arkansans, flood damage and the drought constituted much greater calamities than the Depression. During the height of the drought, temperatures routinely topped 100 degrees and rose as high as 113 in August, and there was no precipitation for a ten-week summertime stretch, leading to famine. Commodities prices, in the basement since the early 1920s, remained very low. Cotton sold for a mere 5 ½ cents per pound, less than the cost to plant and harvest it. Rural families, sharecroppers, tenant farmers and their families, and the urban poor faced starvation as gardens withered and died under the intense heat, and no federal assistance came. The Hoover administration relied upon the Red Cross, state and local governments, and private charity to handle the emergency, clinging tightly to the president's philosophy of self-help and volunteerism as a solution to the Depression. But the Red Cross and many other charitable agencies buckled or faced bankruptcy under the tremendous demand for assistance. Having dealt with historic flooding, and now with crippling drought and widespread economic disaster created by the Depression, many exhausted Arkansans starved. Yet under no circumstances did President Hoover favor direct welfare payments from the federal government to the citizenry.[9]

This combination of drought and economic depression created an unprecedented and rapidly developing crisis for Arkansas in the early 1930s. In the space of only three days in January 1931, Arkansas families requiring and receiving Red Cross aid skyrocketed from 335,000 to over 500,000. A cascade of interrelated calamities, from crashing commodities prices and rising unemployment to the continuing rash of bank failures, caused many Arkansans, as one writer stated, to fall "into a malaise, and the hopelessness was evident as a *New York Times* correspondent reported that the people of Arkansas were 'just sitting and looking.'" Rural areas were hit especially hard. When the Red Cross halted food deliveries to rural England, Arkansas, for example, desperate farmers were moved to take the only action they could to prevent their children from starving: they marched into town and demanded food from the local grocery in what major newspapers across the country mischaracterized as a "food riot," a potential harbinger of more civil unrest to come.[10]

The city of Little Rock likewise struggled with issues of poverty and need during the early years of the Depression as the ranks of the unemployed and the desperate swelled. This moved Ira Sanders to action along several fronts.

In mid-January 1930, Sanders brought to the attention of his temple board "the acute suffering among the poor of Little Rock, and asked that he be permitted to solicit funds for emergency charity [during] Friday evening [services]." The board agreed and appointed a committee to collect these funds.[11] Sanders, along with congregant Samuel Storthz, also created the Jewish Welfare Fund in 1932, a private charity to assist families in need.

In April 1934 Sanders and the four other Reform rabbis in Arkansas joined with Hot Springs rabbi Abraham Rhine in creating the Arkansas Jewish Assembly. For Arkansas Christians, the hardships of the Depression were ameliorated at least in part by the multitude of churches in which people of like faith could congregate for mutual spiritual, material, and community support. The Jewish community, many fewer in number and scattered in small pockets across the state, had no such support system. Rhine, "acutely aware of the plight of these Jews who were isolated from their own community of faith," called a meeting in 1931 to discuss possible solutions to this problem. He suggested that a "real union of communities" would be practical in Arkansas due to the "not too small, not too large" numbers of Jews in the state. He, Sanders, and the other rabbis then created the Arkansas Jewish Assembly "to assist in and promote the activities of all Jewish organizations" and to promote "friendship and brotherhood between the members of all Jewish organizations within the state." For Sanders, the Assembly represented a chance to enhance education throughout the state. He "drilled education into Assembly consciousness," wrote Carolyn LeMaster, suggesting "the Assembly take on a broad educational program that would reach all citizens, not just Jews." In the 1930s, "when the forces of hatred were rampant against the Jews," Sanders said, an educated populace was vital. The assembly and its members also worked diligently during the Depression to help provide what material assistance it could to Arkansas Jews.[12]

From 1927 to 1934, Sanders served on the board of the Family Welfare Agency (FWA), a private Little Rock organization that provided local poor relief in the absence of any federal assistance. However, the blatant race-based inequities of the group's welfare distribution efforts disturbed the rabbi, inequities now exacerbated by the Depression. As was typical in most Southern communities of the era, a disproportionately small percentage of available relief funds went to African American families in need. Sanders recalled that "whenever a black client appealed for help, he received considerably less in aid than the white client." The FWA "was always giving ten cents on the dollar to the black family and to the white family they'd usually give around ninety percent." Bothered over such an unequal distribution of relief, Sanders confronted the other members of the welfare board over this "gross inequality," stating that "the stomachs of the black people were just as important as the stomachs of the white." Sanders told the board he saw no legitimate reason for the monies to be so inequitably distributed. "They're both human beings," he implored, "and they [each] deserve fifty cents [of] the dollar." Moral suasion, though, failed. Sanders followed up with an economic argument: "Do you not realize that if you give the black man the same amount of money you give the white man, your community will benefit economically? The black man will spend as the white man does." This argument seemed more palatable to the board members, as spreading out the welfare payments more broadly did indeed hold out hope for greater spending in their local businesses, which were now hurting due to the Depression; so, through Sanders' efforts, a more equitable distribution of relief funds between black and white welfare recipients was put into place. Funds were disbursed more according to need rather than color. "When you deal with dollars and cents somehow you bring businessmen to their senses. It shouldn't be that way," Sanders later said, "but very often it is that way."[13] The Family Welfare Agency continued to provide assistance to those in need until displaced in 1934 by the federal relief agencies of the Roosevelt administration's New Deal.

With seemingly boundless energy and a deep desire to make a difference in his adopted community, Sanders pressed other organizations such as the American Legion into increased service for poor relief.[14] But those hit hard by the Great Depression also included Congregation B'nai Israel and its members. His first responsibility lay with his congregation, and he took several ameliorative steps on their behalf. As their rabbi, Sanders felt a special responsibility to ease his congregants' suffering.

The Sacrifice

I stand willing to accept a second reduction in my salary.
—IRA SANDERS, 1932

In the summer of 1929 the congregation unanimously reelected Ira Sanders for a new five year term to begin at the conclusion of his initial contract, August 31, 1929, and increased his salary to $12,000 annually.[15] All seemed well at Congregation B'nai Israel in June 1929. But only four months later, with the crash of the economy, the stresses of the Great Depression began to weigh more heavily upon the local community, including the Jewish community. Sanders' generous salary in the face of the economic disaster also weighed heavily on his conscience. In 1930 he volunteered to take a salary cut in order to help with the temple finances; the board, though, initially balked at the suggestion. They dealt with this issue in an October meeting at which everyone spoke "in eulogistic terms" about the rabbi and his contributions over the past four years. The board then "went on record as being thoroughly in sympathy with Dr. Sanders, and voted that his offer of reduction in salary will *not* be accepted; that his spirit of fine work is appreciated, and that in no way must be curtailed."[16] Sanders' salary remained $12,000 per year.

Beginning in the middle of 1930, though, the pressures of the Depression increased even more, and as a result the congregation's finances began to suffer. Month after month, the board dealt with requests from congregants to lower or even excuse their dues and other financial obligations owing to their inability to sustain their pledges and payments. With dues collections and contributions dropping steadily, Congregation B'nai Israel faced a potential financial crisis. In the wake of this increasing financial pressure, one year following the rabbi's offer to take a voluntary pay cut, the board of trustees reversed its former decision. In October 1931, they went on record accepting and "appreciating Dr. Sanders' offer of a cut in salary of $2,000.00 a year." The budget report of September 7, 1931, shows Rabbi Sanders' salary reduced from $1,000 per month ($12,000 annually) to $833.34 per month, amounting to an annual salary of $10,000. By December 1931, dues reductions and accompanying financial strife dominated the agenda of the temple board, and the issue of finance became an increasing source of concern for Rabbi Sanders.

As the Depression deepened the following year, national unemployment more than doubled, rising from the healthy mid-1929 levels of around 4 percent to the more alarming rate of nearly 9 percent in 1931. Arkansas saw disaster levels of unemployment by 1933, at more than 37 percent.[17] Temple finances suffered as congregants lost jobs. By the end of 1931 and for three years thereafter, financial distress dominated the board's agenda, prompting Rabbi Sanders again to step forward and volunteer for a second pay cut: "In view of the present economic situation and the uncertain financial circumstances of our congregation," he wrote temple president Maurice Altheimer in December 1932, "I feel it is my duty to reiterate by letter what I have expressed heretofore by word of mouth to you—namely, that if the necessity warrants, I stand willing to accept a second reduction in my salary of $12,000, with the understanding of course, that as the financial conditions of the congregation improve, my salary shall be restored to the above amount." He added his desire "to cooperate with the board of trustees in solving the problem of congregational finances."[18] The board members, moved by Sanders' offer of a second pay cut, wanted the congregation to know about his sacrifice; accordingly, board member Sidney Kahn moved "that we show Dr. Sanders our appreciation of his cooperation and his services to us, also for his letter to Mr. Altheimer requesting the Board to lower his salary." The congregation should be notified of the letter and the "cut he requested."[19] The minutes of the board's January 1933 meeting show that Sanders' salary indeed had been cut at his own request from $833.34 per month ($10,000 annually) to $700 per month ($8,400 annually), a reduction of $1,600 per year, and an overall reduction of $3,600 from his 1929 contracted annual salary of $12,000.

Sanders would wait decades for the reinstatement of his 1929 salary. Despite the fact that the temple board agreed in writing to a restitution of Sanders' $12,000 contracted salary once the crisis passed, the rabbi's salary was not reinstated even to $10,000 annually until a special meeting of the board of trustees did so on May 27, 1946, fourteen years following his voluntary salary reduction. Full restitution to his contracted 1929 annual salary of $12,000 did not occur until February 1957, twenty-eight years after his voluntary pay cut.[20]

The New Deal and the Pulaski County Public Welfare Commission

The effective rabbi sees his reward only in the changed attitudes and social activism in behalf of just and righteous causes.
—IRA SANDERS, 1978

While the assistance programs and organizations that Sanders founded or participated in successfully provided relief through both jobs and welfare payments during the Great Depression, these groups still could not satisfy the tremendous needs of Little Rock's poor or its neediest citizens. In 1933, the Roosevelt administration's New Deal programs began to provide that assistance both locally and nationwide. In stark contrast to the Hoover administration's policy of addressing the Great Depression though volunteerism and private charities, Roosevelt's New Deal consisted of an ambitious set of federal government programs designed to provide immediate relief through a broad base of welfare and jobs programs for the unemployed, and to bring about economic recovery while reforming those aspects of the economy that had combined to bring about the Depression. In Arkansas, New Deal work relief programs such as the Civil Works Administration (CWA), the Civilian Conservation Corps, the Public Works Administration (PWA), and the Federal Emergency Relief Administration (FERA) provided tens of thousands of jobs for able-bodied Arkansans, jobs that went a long way toward restoring their self-respect and hope. But for "unemployables," whom Ira Sanders defined as "the sick and

the elderly people of the community, and those who were physically handicapped—those who could not physically be and mentally be employed," there
was little federal or local assistance. What aid had been available through the
New Deal was soon to be shut off. Roosevelt believed the states themselves
should handle this aspect of relief; accordingly, in the wake of a 1934 regional
conference held in Louisiana, the administration announced that Arkansas
as well as several other southern states would no longer receive assistance for
"unemployables," who in Arkansas as a whole numbered about forty-one thousand. This news came as a body blow to Arkansas, a poor state now being told
by the Roosevelt administration that much-needed federal monies were about
to dry up.

On top of the issue of how to take care of Arkansas's "unemployables," the
simultaneous cancellation by the Roosevelt administration of a newly introduced
work relief program, the CWA, only served to compound the fiscal problems
and human suffering in Arkansas.[21] On March 30, 1934, Harry Hopkins, one
of the architects of the New Deal and the supervisor of the CWA, announced
the decision at a press conference in Washington, DC. Funded jointly through
the PWA and the FERA, the CWA was a work-relief agency designed to function in the short term only. When Hopkins announced that the relief agency
would cease operations on April 1 after a year of operations, it meant that four
million workers nationwide would be thrown off the relief rolls. The action
hit Arkansas hard, generating much protest. The CWA had been one of the
most effective work relief agencies of the New Deal up to that point, pump-
ing "nearly $1 billion into the economy, augmenting, directly or indirectly, the
buying power of at least 12 million persons and stimulating industrial production."[22] But it was expensive. Franklin Roosevelt had characterized the CWA
as "completely operated and 90 percent financed by the federal government,"
and for poor states such as Arkansas that were unable to provide matching
funds to run the program in the state, the federal government picked up the
whole tab. "It looks as if we are going to have to pay practically all the bills" in
Arkansas, Hopkins lamented. Many Arkansans had jobs because of the CWA.
At its peak in the state, January 1934, the CWA employed about eighty-two
thousand Arkansans. The program was a boon in general to poorer states such
as Arkansas that lacked sufficient funds to provide adequate welfare relief on
their own. When asked in a March 1934 press conference if the cancellation of
the CWA might not mean that states would see more people jobless and "back
on direct relief," Hopkins could only answer, "I hope not." There would be,
he admitted, an unavoidable "period of transition" before the national institution of the CWA's replacement agency, the Works Progress Administration

(WPA) in April 1935. President Roosevelt was joined, ironically, by conservative southern politicians, whose states benefitted the most from CWA jobs, in his fear that a guaranteed government job at the CWA minimum wage of thirty cents per hour might create a class of permanent government dependents, and this affected the president's decision to terminate the program. On April 1, the administration cancelled both the CWA and federal assistance through the FERA for "unemployables," and the onus then fell upon the states and localities to provide stop-gap measures for welfare assistance until such time as the WPA was up and running. For poor Arkansans relying almost entirely upon either the federal government or local community chests to provide welfare relief—and Pulaski County, home of the state's largest metropolitan area, had a high concentration of such people—this precipitated a welfare and humanitarian crisis of significant proportions. Ira Sanders had ideas about how best to address this crisis. His creative response to these federal actions would improve the standard of living for thousands in Pulaski County in 1934.[23]

In April 1934, alongside his work in many other community organizations, and at the behest of Little Rock mayor Horace Knowlton, Sanders organized a local relief agency, the Pulaski County Public Welfare Commission (PWC), to provide a much-needed supplement to the Roosevelt administration's New Deal relief programs. At a luncheon meeting on April 11, 1934, of a citizen's committee created and headed by Sanders, "plans were launched," reported the *Arkansas Democrat*, to organize this "county-city" relief group to assist the poor of the region who "on April 1 were cut off of the federal relief rolls." Sanders served as chair, and community activist Hilda Cornish, businessman Hugo Norvell, and *North Little Rock Times* editor John Pruniski were among its board members. The post of executive secretary was taken by Sanders protégé Ora Nix, who had taken nine sociology courses under him at the now-defunct Little Rock School of Social Work and worked frequently with the rabbi over the years in a variety of social justice causes. Sanders also tapped Brooks Hays for the board, the newly appointed labor compliance officer for the National Recovery Administration in Arkansas.[24]

Sanders creatively addressed the welfare crisis by proposing an ingenious funding device that would provide much-needed relief funds at no cost either to the city or the county. The rabbi proposed that "at [the utility companies'] own expense," a "voluntary tax" of ten cents per month be added to each electric, gas, telephone, and water utility bill for one calendar year in order to raise relief funds to cover the gap between the end of the CWA and the FERA and the institution in 1935 of the WPA and the Social Security Administration (which would not issue its first check until 1940). This funding scheme seemed the "most equitable system of financing this work that can be devised," the Associated Press approvingly reported. As a purely voluntary excise of only one dime, it would not adversely impact or burden already hard-hit Arkansans with an additional tax obligation. Its cost fell only on those who wished to and were able to pay it. Sanders estimated his plan would raise about five thousand dollars per month for the year in which it was collected. Since the utilities agreed to collect the "tax," funds could be raised at no cost to Pulaski County or the City of Little Rock. In April 1934 the Little Rock City Council adopted Sanders' "voluntary tax" proposal.[25]

In the formulation of this idea, Sanders reached out to the various utilities to procure their cooperation and found willing assistance. He contacted the Arkansas Water Company and provided them with an explanatory statement "which we think should be printed on your monthly bills" regarding the voluntary tax, as well as "a list of suggestions to the tellers at your windows for enlightening the public as to the contribution."[26] He also contacted the local telephone company. Southwestern Bell Telephone Company district manager E. N. McCall replied to Sanders' request with a note stating, "We will be very glad to cooperate with your commission in every possible way." The City of North Little Rock also adopted the PWC plan, passing Ordinance 965, which asked "all gas customers, water customers, telephone users and electricity patrons to include ten cents in the monthly payment of their bill." Mayor U. E. Moore reassured his constituents that "every cent of the money will be used for the relief of destitution among the aged and infirm of North Little Rock."[27]

Sanders, hoping to translate the PWC's local success to the state as a whole, sought advice as to how best to bring this issue before the people of Arkansas. Local newspapers "were most cooperative in giving us all the publicity we wanted," recalled Sanders, but he wanted to reach deeper into the community and perhaps induce the state legislature to codify the voluntary relief efforts in order to guarantee the constant flow of assistance statewide to those in need. He sought out Charles Mitchell, president of the County Judges' Association of Arkansas, for help: the Pulaski County Public Welfare Commission, Sanders wrote, "is vitally interested in securing legislation for the state of Arkansas which will enable counties to secure funds by taxation for the vast number of unemployables—the chronic sick, the aged, the paupers, etc. The Commission feels that a one-day conference held in some city in Arkansas might go far towards bringing this matter before the people of the state."[28] That proposed conference never took place; as a result, the PWC relief effort remained localized to Pulaski County. Sanders' idea for the "voluntary tax," his outreach to the utilities, and to the public at large—from whom there had been an overwhelmingly positive response—ensured the flow of aid at the local, city, and county level in and around Little Rock to those hardest hit by the Depression. Such aid began quickly—Sanders reported a "voluntary tax" collection of $378 from the Arkansas Water Company and $350 from Southwestern Bell on June 4, when the entire voluntary collection effort was yet only days old.[29] The local organization gained national attention for the role it played during the worst years of the Great Depression in assisting Pulaski County with its welfare problems prior to the institution of the WPA.

For a time in 1935, the FERA operated concurrently with the WPA, the work-relief agency created to replace it. As the date approached when the FERA would end, the federal government, wanting to delegate more responsibility for welfare to the states and address concerns about possible corruption in the federal program, issued a mandate requiring that those states wishing to continue receiving federal assistance must create their own administrative boards of welfare to provide continuity with much needed assistance. While neighboring states such as Tennessee and Mississippi quickly complied, the Arkansas legislature ignored the mandate and, on the last day of the 1935 legislative session, still had taken no action on it. Ora Nix, now the head of the Pulaski County Public Welfare Commission, was startled to learn that the legislature had done nothing to ensure the continued flow of aid statewide to needy Arkansans. She quickly telephoned Rabbi Sanders and told him of the situation. Within an hour of the legislature's planned adjournment, Sanders and Nix rushed to the capitol. They interrupted the end of the session, and Sanders "made an impassioned plea" to the legislators to act on the federal requirement. Both Nix and Sanders refused to leave until the legislature took up the matter. The impromptu "sit-in" tactic worked. The Arkansas legislature extended the session long enough to pass the necessary relief measures and named Ora Nix as the director of what would be the new state social welfare office. Once again, with Ora Nix's vital assistance, Sanders' actions had a direct and meaningful impact upon the lives of thousands of Arkansans.[30]

The Urban League of Greater Little Rock

Not a white man would sit on the board with me.
—IRA SANDERS, 1963

In addition to his to his work in the community and state in the realms of social justice and social welfare, Sanders continued to seek out means to address racial inequities in Arkansas. His support of the NAACP, his work in the ASWPL, and the other efforts he had made to address racism and racial inequality in

Little Rock acted as a means for him to help facilitate better understanding between black and white Arkansans. In the furtherance of that goal, Sanders helped found the Urban League of Greater Little Rock as another potent weapon in his arsenal aimed at tearing down racial barriers and animosity in the city. As Sanders later said, "Amelia Ives, a schoolteacher, and Bill Nash and I organized the Urban League of Greater Little Rock because we felt the black people of our community were not being given their just due." Amelia B. Ives, an African American public school teacher concerned over too many of her pupils "arriving for classes hungry and poorly clothed," approached Rabbi Sanders to "help her organize an Urban League for the purpose of fulfilling the mandates contained in the National Urban League." Ives and Sanders joined forces with attorney William Nash, dean of the University of Arkansas School of Law, and Erle Chambers, who had earned a law degree at the University of Chicago and served two terms as the first female member of the Arkansas House of Representatives (1923–26). These principal local organizers and an interracial group of about twenty others, including Philander Smith College president M. Lafayette Harris, met in the Little Rock Public Library on February 20, 1937, with Jessie O. Thomas, the southern regional field director of the National Urban League, to establish a branch of the organization in Little Rock.[31]

At the initial meeting of the Urban League of Greater Little Rock, which Sanders missed due to a prior commitment, the organization members elected Nash chairman. As vice chairs, the group named Dr. Fred T. Jones, a pioneering African American physician in the Little Rock community who had helped establish hospitals and insurance companies for the area's black citizens, and noted educator Dr. L. M. Christophe. The league elected Sanders to a leadership position as assistant chairman of the executive committee, and Amelia Ives became the secretary. With more than half of all African Americans in Little Rock employed as domestic laborers and another one-sixth as unskilled laborers, the Urban League focused its early efforts on employment assistance and economic development, working to open more doors for black Arkansans. Sanders served as chairman of the Urban League of Greater Little Rock in 1939 and remained on either the executive board or the advisory board for more than thirty years thereafter. For the rabbi, the Urban League was "a very potent, important, necessary part of the community's life."[32]

Sanders initially had difficulty recruiting other whites to serve with him on the Urban League board. Sanders approached many of his white acquaintances to join him, but "not a white man would sit on the board with me," he recalled in 1963 with frustration.[33] The situation remained that way until several years later, "when it became fashionable for the white citizens of the community to be a part of the board, especially [in later years] when Winthrop Rockefeller sat on the

National Board of Directors." Sanders characterized his purpose in helping create and promote the Urban League as "basic." It was "the creation of a climate
between the two groups through education and understanding."[34] The *Arkansas
Democrat* trumpeted its success early in the league's existence, stating in 1939,
the year Sanders served as chair, that the Urban League of Greater Little Rock
was making "a praiseworthy contribution towards improving the . . . conditions
of Negroes and stimulating better relations between the races."[35]

In order to better understand the African American community and its
needs, the Urban League of Greater Little Rock in 1941 commissioned and
then published a study compiled by the writers' program of the Arkansas Work
Projects Administration entitled *A Survey of Negroes in Little Rock and North
Little Rock*. Ira Sanders, then the Urban League's president, edited the manuscript and wrote the foreword. "No problem," he wrote, "calls for a more careful analysis than that of the Negro. Experts in the field of social science are
beginning to realize that the composite life of any community is improved only
as every ethnic group is granted the opportunity to enlarge and enrich its own
economic, social, and spiritual life, and thus add its contribution to the whole
of the community fabric." Of the study, Sanders stated his hope that "the information within the covers of this volume will aid, at least to a small degree, in the
construction of a serviceable social and economic program for Negroes."[36] The
ninety-seven-page study included sections on aspects of economics, health,
crime, education, housing, and race relations, among others, and acknowledged the racial realities of the era: "The secondary status of Negroes governs
the interracial relationship of the community," as Little Rock–area African
Americans "occupy a position of racial subordination."[37]

The study illustrated some of the problems as well as some of the compara-
tive advantages Little Rock's African American population had in the 1930s.
The report cited statistics from the US Bureau of the Census revealing that
Little Rock's black population, about 24 percent of the total population, had
the highest rates of home ownership among African Americans as compared
to cities of similar size, and ranked second in school attendance. But, black
Little Rock also had the highest infant mortality rate in the study; in 1938, that
number stood at a frightful 48 percent. The report's economic analysis revealed
that about 18 percent of Little Rock's African American population worked
in some aspect of manufacturing, but nearly 50 percent worked as domestic
laborers, and 86 percent of that number were black women. Low—often very
low—wages were the norm; the study pointed out that those low wages translated into a state of "perpetual poverty" that prevented most African Americans
in Little Rock "from bearing their share of the community's burdens—it forces

them into the role of a permanent public liability." This economic reality lay "at the root of virtually all other basic difficulties" of black life in Little Rock. The solution: black Arkansans "must be given a greater share in job opportunities."[38] The Urban League's efforts in the community focused on improved race relations and especially on greater and better job opportunities and salaries.

The report reveals Sanders' editorial influence through its employ of language characteristic of him about the importance of "mutual understanding." "Society has long since learned the lesson," the report begins, "that the physical and mental health of its underprivileged members is a matter of common concern." In many urban areas, the white majority has had a tendency "to forget that the Negro population is an undivorceable element" and that "epidemics know no color lines, and race is no protection from the criminal bred in poverty and nourished by neglect." The report concludes with a hopeful if cautionary note: "Progress is being made," the continuation of which "is dependent upon the further development of the increased mutual understanding between the white and the Negro races." Such progress could be seen in the activities of the Urban League, which the report approvingly states has "fostered improvement of racial relationships."[39]

In 1972 the Urban League of Greater Little Rock honored Ira Sanders both for his formative role and his decades of involvement in the organization by naming him as one of "the ten persons whom we feel deserve the distinction and honor of being selected to the first Urban League Honorary Advisory Board."[40]

In 1940, with the Depression slowly lifting, Ira Sanders and Rev. Jeff Smith, a Little Rock Methodist minister blinded early in life, founded the Arkansas Lighthouse for the Blind, which provided training and employment opportunities for the visually impaired. While Smith was the primary organizer, Sanders raised the initial "start-up money" of one hundred dollars and helped guide the organization as a trustee for decades thereafter. Sanders had a lifelong admiration for Smith, "whose love of life and whose devotion to his fellow man was unparalleled," he later wrote. The Lighthouse for the Blind began as a small workshop behind the Arkansas School for the Blind, with an additional shop on Ninth Street in eastern Little Rock. In 1945, Helen Keller spoke at the dedication ceremony for this facility, and Sanders was also there when the Lighthouse broke ground for a new, more expansive facility in 1965.[41] Sanders retained an affiliation with the Lighthouse throughout his life, serving on the board for more than forty years.

For Sanders, the pursuit of social justice through activities such as those outlined above gave a rabbinate its real meaning. Imbued from childhood with a keen sense of empathy and sense of morality, Sanders believed that the effective rabbi "sees his reward only in the changed attitudes and social activism in behalf of just and righteous causes."[42] Here lies the key to understanding Rabbi Sanders' constant activism throughout his tenure in the Little Rock community on behalf of the disadvantaged, the poor, the sick, and those who suffered under segregation and unequal treatment: his deeply-felt belief that impacting his society by changing people's attitudes and by working for just causes served not merely as a yardstick for success, but *the* yardstick for success—the primary, if not sole, indication that he was fulfilling his rabbinical calling. If, as Sanders believed, the rabbi "sees his reward only in changed attitudes" and in the pursuit of social justice, then his work in the community provided him that reward. This is what he had come to Little Rock to accomplish. It fulfilled him as the source of his professional and personal satisfaction. The law of life, after all, was the law of service.

—4—

Birth Control, Eugenics, and "Human Betterment"

1931–1958

ONE OF THE MOST PROFOUND complications of the Great Depression upon the lives of poor Arkansans, particularly women, involved the most intimate areas of their lives: sexual intercourse, marital relationships, and childbearing, all of which were interconnected with fears of bringing more children into a Depression-era environment wherein adequate care for them could not be provided. During the thirties, this problem was not unique to Arkansas. Almost no one in dire circumstances wanted to have children, but as one Massachusetts woman wrote with frustration, "Ya know down at the Catholic Charities they tell ya your not supposed ta have children if you're on the WPA. An' in the church they tell us you're not supposed ta do anything about it. An' they say you're supposed to live with your man. Now what's a woman gonna do?"[1] For birth control advocates around the country, including Ira Sanders and his allies in Arkansas, the answer to that question lay in ready and affordable access to contraception.

From 1931 forward, Ira Sanders emerged as a driving force in the contraceptive rights movement in Arkansas as a founder both of the Arkansas Eugenics Association (AEA)—later renamed the Planned Parenthood Association of Arkansas—and the Arkansas Human Betterment League. Sanders saw both of these organizations, especially the AEA, which was founded and operating during the worst years of the Great Depression, as potent antipoverty measures and as necessary engines of social reform. During the twin disasters of severe drought and economic depression which befell the region in the 1930s, many Arkansas women feared sexual intimacy lest a child be born for which they could not provide. Smaller families meant fewer mouths to feed. Birth control information, as the key to having smaller families, acted as an antipoverty measure. Sanders believed families and society itself would benefit if the poor had ready access to birth control. Birth control, however, had been and remained a controversial subject. With the 1873 passage of the Comstock Law, federal law banned the sale, possession, or dissemination through the mail of "obscene" materials, whose definition included birth control materials and devices. Most Americans saw birth control movement leader Margaret Sanger as equally controversial. She had coined the term "birth control," had opened America's first birth control clinic in Brooklyn in October 1916, and by 1918 had been arrested multiple times for violating antiobscenity laws in her advocacy for access to reliable contraception. In April 1929, police raided her Brooklyn-based Birth Control Clinic Research Bureau. She lobbied the government to overturn the legal definition of contraceptive information as obscene, and toward that goal in 1932 ordered contraceptive devices from Japan as a means to challenge contraception bans in the courts; as a result of her efforts, a federal appeals court decision in the case *United States v. One Package* (1936) ended that ban.[2]

Rabbi Sanders had an abiding interest in Sanger's work and had done research himself in the field of birth control. In January 1932, Sanders invited sociologist Robert Kelso to speak to the Temple Men's Club on the topic. Kelso had made a public splash with his 1929 work *Poverty*, in which he blasted society's neglect of the poor. "Poverty in the social order," he wrote, "stands out like a fungus upon the surface of decay."[3] Adequate access to birth control would act to ameliorate poverty. Kelso, who at the time directed the St. Louis Community Fund and Council, echoed many of Sanders' beliefs about the social benefits of birth control in his address to the men's club: "Birth control is not a moral issue but a social factor, and the time soon will come when the world will regard it as a social crime to bring children into the world without provision for their well-being."[4] Kelso precisely mirrored Sanders' sociological approach to the issue. Later that year, at the October 1932 meeting of the Arkansas Conference of Social Work, Sanders delivered a paper on the sociological aspects of birth control entitled "Some Population Problems."[5] But more significant was his role the previous year in the founding of the first birth control clinic in Arkansas.

The Arkansas Eugenics Association

Nobody would object to being well-born.

—IRA SANDERS, 1931

On January 28, 1931, Ira Sanders, Hilda Cornish, and Rev. Hay Watson Smith, among others, met in a basement meeting room at Little Rock's Baptist Hospital and founded the Arkansas Eugenics Association (AEA). Four days later, on February 1, 1931, they established the AEA-sponsored Little Rock Birth Control

Clinic, initially located in the same basement rooms of Baptist Hospital in which the organization formed. The clinic provided its services for a nominal fee to any married woman whose family made less than seventy-five dollars per month.[6]

While Ira Sanders played an important and active role in establishing and maintaining the AEA and the birth control clinic, Hilda Cornish played a more significant role; indeed, she was the prime mover. The wife of a successful banker and the mother of six children, fifty-four-year-old Hilda Cornish had been an active presence in Little Rock, an exemplar of the Little Rock upper-class clubwoman through her involvement in a number of civic and charitable groups. She organized the Little Rock Playground Association and served as vice-president of the Community Fund upon its inception. In 1927, Cornish led volunteer efforts to assist those impacted by that year's catastrophic Mississippi River flood. She served as the president of the Central Council of Social Agencies, previously led by Ira Sanders, and was the president of the Arkansas Federation of Women's Clubs. The shattering 1928 suicide of her husband Edward—the result of the failure of his bank—led her to immerse herself even more in community affairs, and birth control became her cause of choice. Cornish met Margaret Sanger in the summer of 1930, and the two quickly developed a friendship in part facilitated by the fact that her son and Sanger's son roomed together at Yale University. Cornish quickly became a trusted Sanger ally as they worked jointly on the National Committee on Federal Legislation for Birth Control and discussed in 1930 the establishment of a birth control clinic in Arkansas.[7] Cornish then invited Ira Sanders and Second Presbyterian Church minister Hay Watson Smith to help her coordinate and organize the first birth control association in Arkansas.[8]

In the five years Sanders had been in Little Rock, he had already become a well-established figure in the area as a social worker, reformer, educator, and champion for social justice, while Reverend Smith, also a noted liberal voice in the community, had been a vocal opponent of Arkansas's 1928 antievolution bill, which almost cost him his pulpit. Other AEA founders included Darmon A. Rhinehart, president of the Arkansas Medical Society; attorney Graham R. Hall, and Dr. Homer Scott, chief of staff of Arkansas Children's Hospital.[9] Raida Pfiefer, a Vassar College graduate whom Sanders knew from Temple B'nai Israel, served as the receptionist for the clinic and from 1933 also sat on the executive board of the AEA. Like Sanders, Pfeifer believed "an increased population would be a runaway problem for the whole world in time unless pregnancies were controlled."[10] The group, on Ira Sanders' suggestion, purposefully avoided the term "birth control" in the name of the organization in order to escape obvious association with the controversial Sanger. The rabbi suggested that "because the movement might evoke criticism on the part of the rather orthodox and staid community, that we call it the Arkansas Eugenics Association on the grounds that nobody would object to being well-born."[11] Sanders proved to be correct. The AEA supported Sanger's ideas and efforts, which elsewhere had met with vocal opposition, but in Little Rock, largely as a result of the work and contributions of known and trusted community leaders such as Rabbi Sanders and Reverend Smith, and aided by support and contributions from local business leaders and well-established clubwomen like Hilda Cornish, there was "no significant organized opposition" to the movement.[12]

Local communities such as Little Rock developed differing strategies to incorporate accessible birth control services into their areas in the face of possible opposition to the national birth control movement. The Little Rock birth control advocates were well aware of what historian Marianne Leung later wrote: "To obtain their goals, community support was crucial, and therefore they shrewdly selected the appropriate context in which to introduce safe and effective birth control into their community." Sanders had suggested they call themselves a "eugenics" association, but in fact, Sanders and the other AEA founders had little interest in the broader eugenics movement, especially its advocacy of forced sterilizations and its targeting of minority women, although they incorporated some of the general rhetoric into their mission statement and some public pronouncements. They camouflaged the Little Rock Birth Control Clinic in the rhetoric of "eugenics" and emphasized its organization as cooperatively operated, like so many other organizations in the Little Rock community, by middle and upper-class "Little Rock clubwomen" and respected local clergy for the benefit of the area's poor. In this way, the AEA founders introduced and sustained birth control services in Little Rock for poor women who desired it "in a context acceptable to an otherwise conservative community."[13] "Birth control," notes historian Cathy Hajo, was "a far more controversial and questionable movement" at the time than eugenics. "Draping birth control in Eugenics robes made it more respectable."[14] "Eugenics" was a term cloaked in the veneer of male-dominated scientific endeavor, while many perceived "birth control" as a radical female-dominated social movement.[15] In Arkansas, then, "eugenics" served merely as a label for what was in fact a contraceptive rights movement, and the name "Arkansas Eugenics Association" provided an acceptable cover for the birth control clinic.

The constitution of the AEA identified the purpose of the organization as "the eugenic development of the human race under favorable physical,

There was an old woman
Who lived in a shoe.
She had so many children
She didn't know what to do.

DON'T BE LIKE THE OLD WOMAN!

Ask Your Doctor for Birth Control Information
or Write to the

Arkansas Eugenics Association

which sponsors the

LITTLE ROCK BIRTH CONTROL CLINIC

THE ASSOCIATION STANDS FOR THESE THINGS

The spacing of children to protect the health of mother and child.

The giving of contraceptive advice in its own clinic by a physician of highest standards to every married woman who requires it, but who cannot afford the advice of a private physician.

A temporary safeguard for families to whom the birth of an additional child would mean, at this time the loss of financial independence, and the beginning of public relief.

An end to the menace to health and life in abortions, especially those self-inflicted, by mothers made desperate at the prospect of the birth of additional children into homes too needy to care for the children already there.

The right of a man and wife to normal, happy marital relations, and to as many children as can be safely carried, safely born and adequately reared.

THE LITTLE ROCK BIRTH CONTROL CLINIC IS
SUPPORTED ENTIRELY BY PRIVATE
SUBSCRIPTIONS

Mrs. Edward Cornish, Chairman of Arkansas Eugenics Association and Director of Birth Control Clinic

Little Rock, Ark.

Flyer for the Arkansas Eugenics Association.
Courtesy Temple B'nai Israel, Little Rock, Arkansas.

economic, and social conditions." In a flyer produced by the AEA, the organization listed its governing principles, which dealt strictly with birth control and not at all with "eugenics," as the organization's name implies:

— The spacing of children to protect the health of the mother.
— The giving of contraceptive advice in its own clinic by a physician of highest standards to every woman who requires it but cannot afford the advice of a private physician.
— A temporary safeguard for families to whom the birth of an additional child would mean, at this time, the loss of financial independence and the beginning of public relief.
— An end to the menace to health and life in abortions, especially those self-inflicted, by mothers made desperate at the prospect of the birth of additional children into homes too needy to care for the children already there.
— The right of a man and wife to normal, happy marital relations and to as many children as can be safely carried, safely born, and adequately reared.

The flyer urged women to "ask [their] doctor for birth control information" or write to the AEA for information about the Little Rock Birth Control Clinic.[16]

The Little Rock clinic was one of only fifty-five birth control clinics in the United States and the first and only birth control clinic in Little Rock for more than a decade. It offered "weekly clinics at which a physician was available to give gynecological examinations and fit women with contraceptive devices such as the diaphragm and spermicidal jelly."[17] The clinic provided advice on family planning and provided access for poor Arkansas women to personal physicians, birth control information, and assistance with birth control devices.[18]

The AEA also looked at the problem from the other side: access for the community's poor to reliable birth control would lessen the local community's future welfare obligations. This argument resonated given the context of the disastrous 1927 Mississippi River flood and its lingering aftereffects, followed in the 1930s by drought, escalating economic depression, and a near-absence of federal aid from the Hoover administration. "Many long time charity cases may not have been a charge on the community had mothers, in their early married lives, been given contraceptive aid," stated the 1931 AEA annual report. "The welfare agencies are now providing care for the third generation of some of these families." Birth control therefore could act as a positive tool for social welfare in that the numbers of the poor requiring future public assistance could be dramatically lessened through fewer births. For a region in the throes of a welfare crisis, this was a potent argument.[19]

The AEA's Little Rock Birth Control Clinic initially offered its service only to poor married white women. A 1934 AEA report noted that "if sufficient funds are available the Association will establish a charity clinic for the Negro women and also arrange for services in the rural section, where the needs are greatest." In 1937, as a result of an anonymous donation the previous year, the AEA clinic began providing poor married African American women the same services and information. Because of the mandates of institutional racial segregation then in place, African American women had access to the clinic at times separate from white women; the services provided, however, were the same.[20]

As a trained social worker and sociologist, Ira Sanders wholeheartedly believed in the benefits of widely available birth control. "Birth control offers the only sane and logical solution to a world over-populated and as a result economically maladjusted," he wrote in a 1933 AEA report. "Fewer and better children would go far to stabilize the economic security of the future, and thus place the ages to come in a more happy and receptive mind to receive those blessings that civilization will have in store for them."[21] His beliefs, though, did not extend to "negative eugenics"—that is, racially targeted sterilizations, or indeed forced or coerced sterilizations of any kind. His was the approach of the sociologist concerned about the positive impact ready access to voluntary birth control could have on Arkansas and on American society. Making birth control easily accessible to the poor who desired it, he reasoned, would be beneficial to those families unable to care for additional children and to society as a whole, which would be relieved of the necessity of providing ever more public assistance to care for poverty-stricken children.

The many letters received by the AEA attest to its value and significance in the lives of poor Arkansas women during the Depression years. "We are terribly poor," wrote a woman from Mt. Olive, Arkansas, in April 1941. "We have four children, oldest 8½ years, baby 13 moths [sic]. I live in terror that I will become pregnant again. I honestly believe that I will die if I give birth again." She tells of her family's poverty and her husband's unemployment. "Life is just a dull, drab ache of fear." She concludes with a plea for help: "Will you please tell me where, if possible I can buy whatever contraceptives that are safe and how much they cost. My doctor says he does not know. I do not think it fair to all concerned to have more children." For desperate Arkansas women of limited means such as this, the AEA and the information and doctor referrals they provided acted as a lifeline. The AEA "was there to help families that were financially unable to find help elsewhere."[22]

In 1938 Arkansas governor Carl Bailey, concerned about the fact that the University of Arkansas Medical School had "lost its ratings" from the American Medical Association, approached Thomas Fitzhugh, the chair of the State of Arkansas Department of Public Utilities, to discuss whether the school's lack of instruction regarding birth control might be the cause for the loss of accreditation. Fitzhugh raised "the possibility of including instructions to the students in birth control practices as a part of the new curriculum," and Bailey "was very much interested." The governor suggested that Fitzhugh ask the AEA's Hilda Cornish to prepare a memo for him on the matter, one that he could then present to the university board of trustees. Fitzhugh requested such a memo from Cornish, who in turn contacted Dr. Clarence J. Gamble, a Massachusetts physician, eugenics advocate, and noted birth control expert, for assistance. Gamble agreed with Governor Bailey in believing the UA Medical School's change of rating was related to its failure to "disseminate authoritative information" regarding "thorough instruction in contraceptive techniques." Gamble wrote a second letter to Cornish that same day, stating his belief that "birth control is at the present time the most effective and most neglected portion of public health work." He recommended that Cornish obtain "whatever political backing is available to be used, for the present, to encourage the Arkansas State Board of Health to undertake such a contraceptive program." He cited North Carolina as a successful model for Arkansas to emulate: "Thus far 46 counties have begun giving the service to underprivileged families."[23] Cornish acted on all of these recommendations and by 1940 "was successful in convincing the University of Arkansas Medical School to include birth control methods in its curriculum and provide services at the University Hospital. With the addition of these new services, the Little Rock Birth Control Clinic closed," henceforth providing only doctor referrals and educational materials and no longer offering weekly clinical services. In its years of operation between January 1931 and January 1940, the clinic served over 1500 white women and 150 black women, assisting women with diaphragms and their use and distributing literature on birth control, sex, marriage, and parenting. In 1942, when Margaret Sanger's Brooklyn-based American Birth Control League changed its name to the more palatable, less controversial Planned Parenthood Federation, the AEA likewise became the Planned Parenthood Association of Arkansas (PPA).[24] Sanders and Hilda Cornish continued their deep involvement in the organization, which continued to provide physician referrals and educational materials; however, financial problems wreaked havoc on the group's mission.

Planned Parenthood Struggles

We feel that Planned Parenthood is the basis of
all intelligent and wise social planning.
—IRA SANDERS, 1951

For Ira Sanders the struggle on behalf of women's reproductive rights remained a central goal of his fight for social justice, and his work in this area continued unabated through the 1940s and into the postwar era. Sanders agreed to assume the PPA chairmanship in 1951.[25] He fervently believed in the organization's mission to provide family planning advice to poor Arkansas women who might otherwise never have access to it. His lifelong interest in the sociology of population and birth control contributed to his passion on the topic, likely reinforced by his reading of Albert Maisel's landmark article of October 1951 in *Look*, "The World's Exploding Population." As PPA chairman, Sanders tried to address the key stumbling block for the group during this time: a crippling lack of sufficient operational funding. There was never enough money to support the activities of the organization. On one occasion in 1951, the lack of available funds forced Sanders to return to the national organization a bundle of one thousand informational pamphlets he had requested, incorrectly believing the New York office would provide them *gratis*. The cost of the bundle was only thirty-five dollars, but the Arkansas group simply did not have available even that modest sum. "I hope you will understand our financial embarrassment which compels me to return the package unopened," a chagrined Sanders wrote.[26]

In dire financial straits, the organization reached out in many disparate directions for assistance. Sanders and Cornish wrote to state senator and juvenile court president Max Howell in January: "We feel that Planned Parenthood is the basis of all intelligent and wise social planning, and to this end we are soliciting the best minds in the community to assist us in formulating our future program." They asked Howell to name someone from his juvenile court board who might serve with Planned Parenthood, believing such a connection would aid in developing future plans and especially in fundraising efforts.[27] PPA also wrote hundreds of targeted letters of solicitation to former AEA and PPA donors, signed by Sanders and Cornish. Because of the necessity of informing the public as to "intelligent family planning and population problems," they wrote, and because "we are the only agency prepared to undertake such a program," the letter reminded former donors of the necessity "of making medical contraceptive advice accessible to all low-income family groups, thus saving these families from stark tragedy." Each letter asked its recipient to give anywhere from ten to one hundred dollars, based on records of previous donations, but in the short term the fund raising drive could not save the foundering Arkansas organization. By October 1955 circumstances forced Sanders to inform the national organization, "Inasmuch as we have had no means to carry on the work of the Planned Parenthood Association of Arkansas for the past years, the Board of Directors have decided to dissolve this organization and to refer all cases that might come to the organization to Mrs. Ed [Hilda] Cornish. We regret this exceedingly but in the absence of financial means, we are unable to carry on a program of activities."[28] Thereafter, the PPA ceased to function as an organization, not to return to the state for more than thirty years.

For a time leading up to its financial collapse, and certainly after PPA's 1955 dissolution, Hilda Cornish continued the work of the PPA with assistance from Ira Sanders. She almost single-handedly dealt with the correspondence of all those desiring birth control information and devices, and she referred those in need to doctors in the area who had been a part of PPA's network of affiliated physicians willing to provide services, including birth control devices. The letters Cornish received from poor and working-class Arkansas women asking for help with family planning are often heartbreaking, revealing the desperation of women who, often physically as well as financially, could not afford to bear another child. "At this time," wrote one Arkansas woman in July 1951, "I am now recuperating from a miscarriage which will be my second. In June 1949 a child was born too early (6 months) and died the following day after birth. Under these circumstances I feel that I need some kind of control until at which time my body will be better able to withstand pregnancies." As was her standard practice in response to letters such as this, Cornish provided the woman with the names and addresses of nearby physicians within the network of participating doctors created by her and Sanders who could help her both with information and services. In another case, in stilted but earnest prose, an eighteen-year-old Arkansas woman wrote Cornish in September 1952 to ask for "a birth control and I would like for you all to send me one and the price of it." She told Cornish her age, and said, "I am soon to be the mother of 3 children. So let me know at once can you all send me one. I'll be willing to pay a reasonable price for it." Cornish sent her the names and addresses of four physicians in her general area to whom she could go for assistance.[29]

The PPA sometimes faced resistance from local doctors whom Cornish could not recruit into her network because they believed birth control information was already common knowledge. She wrote in anger to Sanders over one such case: "It is not fair . . . to say that everyone knows about birth control. It is not true as we well know when we receive letters such as Mrs. Griffin's, the very mother we should be reaching." Cornish's reference is to a letter she had received only four days earlier, a plaintive cry for help: "I'm the mother of 5 children and looking for my 6th. I've done all I could to avoidance [*sic*] it but haven't had any luck yet. I wish you could help me please. Poor me I've tried all I new [*sic*] how and just can't help myself at all please."[30] Desperate pleas such as this evinced the great need for the work Cornish and Sanders carried on for birth control and reproductive rights, even after the collapse of the PPA in 1955.

The Arkansas Human Betterment League and "Eugenic" Sterilization

I don't think there was any vasectomy at all performed.
—IRA SANDERS, 1978

In 1941, the Arkansas legislature considered legislation to enact forced surgical sterilization of "undesirables" in the state. In attempting to do so, they followed the lead of the eugenics movement in other states that had targeted those deemed "undesirable" or mentally incompetent. In neighboring Mississippi, for example, a total of 683 forced sterilizations took place after 1928, the year that state's legislature passed its law affecting "persons who are afflicted with hereditary forms of insanity that are recurrent, idiocy, imbecility, feeble-mindedness, or epilepsy." Mississippi was the twenty-seventh state to pass such a law, while Virginia had led the way in forced sterilization, with over seven thousand such cases following the passage of its Eugenical Sterilization Act in 1924.[31] A challenge to the Virginia statute provided an opportunity for the United States Supreme Court to legitimate such procedures in the infamous 1927 case *Buck v. Bell*, wherein associate justice Oliver Wendell Holmes, writing for the Court, upheld the forced sterilization of a "feeble-minded" young Virginia woman named Carrie Buck with the unfortunate phrase "three generations of imbeciles are enough."[32] The proposed Arkansas bill would create an agency, the Arkansas State Board of Eugenics, staffed by the superintendent of the Arkansas State Hospital (founded in 1873 as the Arkansas Lunatic Asylum, then in 1905 renamed the Arkansas State Hospital for Nervous Diseases), the dean of the University of Arkansas Medical School, and a selected group of advisors from various institutions and prisons responsible for recommending subjects for the procedure. This proposed legislation would go well beyond the work of the AEA or Planned Parenthood, which provided for and advocated access to voluntary birth control only and performed no surgical procedures.

The bill also contained a provision to provide for publicly funded contraception. The proposed forced-sterilization bill failed to pass the state senate not because of its threat of coerced sterilizations or taxpayer-supported birth control, but because the public deemed the bill an example of "socialized medicine." Accordingly, unlike many other states during the heyday of the eugenics movement, Arkansas created no state-sanctioned sterilization agency and performed no "eugenic" sterilizations.[33] The movement remained in Arkansas as Sanders and Cornish had envisioned it—a voluntary reproductive rights movement designed both to aid poor Arkansas women and families and ameliorate overall poverty in the state.

Sanders and Hilda Cornish had founded the AEA as an antipoverty measure, a way to provide access to birth control and contraceptive information for "the poorer elements of the community."[34] Surgeries were never a part either of the AEA or the PPA agenda, and the legislature's 1941 attempt to pass such a law had failed. However, another Sanders-led organization, the largely ineffectual Arkansas Human Betterment League (AHBL), was established without meeting such opposition. Sanders founded the AHBL in 1951 with an avowed mission uncomfortably close in some of its aspects to the broader eugenics agenda of sterilization. It is important to note that, in the case of the AHBL, this meant not coerced, state-sanctioned, racially targeted, or clandestine surgeries, but voluntary access to what the group termed "permanent birth control"—that is, surgical sterilization procedures such as vasectomies or tubal ligations—for lower-income Arkansans who desired them. In many ways, then, the Arkansas Human Betterment League acted as an extension of the ideas behind the Arkansas Eugenics Association in that both groups concerned themselves with access to birth control measures for those ordinarily unable to afford it. However, Rabbi Sanders and the AHBL veered dangerously close to the more sinister aspects of eugenics as the sterilization of the "feeble-minded" became a particular target for the organization.

The goal of the AHBL's national parent organization, the Human Betterment Foundation, founded in Pasadena, California, in 1929, was "the constructive, practical advancement and betterment of human life, character, and citizenship in such a manner as to make for human happiness and progress in this life." For this organization, eugenic sterilization represented "only the first of a series of major problems that will from time to time be taken up." The organization's publicity material makes plain, however, that the HBF's "first major problem" was "the investigations of the possibilities of race betterment by eugenic sterilization."[35] This original incarnation of the HBF disbanded, and the organization reformed some years later in Des Moines, Iowa, sponsoring and encouraging the growth in several states, including Arkansas, of affiliates known as Human Betterment Leagues.

The Arkansas Human Betterment League formed at the Hotel Marion in downtown Little Rock on April 19, 1951. Rabbi Ira Sanders called and chaired this meeting of "a group of persons interested in an educational program on selective sterilization." During the course of the meeting, the attendees nominated him both for a seat on the board of directors and for the presidency of the organization, positions to which he was later elected. The AHBL drew up a constitution detailing the group's purposes and objectives: "the study of the care of the physically or mentally handicapped, economically deficient or socially inadequate in Arkansas; the encouragement of the best teaching and training of such patients; the promotion of measures which will prevent such handicaps; an educational program in this field in order to assure the best possible care of such cases and of the children involved."[36] The group agreed to meet twice annually.

The generic description of the AHBL goals does not mention or refer to sterilization, except in the vague phrase "the promotion of such measures which will prevent such handicaps." In this benign phrase lay the true and potentially problematic purposes of the AHBL. The availability of voluntary sterilization procedures for poor Arkansans desiring them, which the group often referred to as "permanent birth control" in order to make it more palatable, in and of itself was not problematic, as "voluntary access" always remained the group's focus. Poor married women desiring tubal ligation or men desiring a vasectomy would now have access to those procedures despite their ability to pay. The much more problematic aspect of Rabbi Sanders' work with the AHBL lay in his desire to promote the sterilization of the institutionalized or mentally incompetent if so approved by their families or legal guardians. This second provision presented a minefield of issues, any of which might explode under the feet of the organization, and which brought both Sanders and the AHBL perilously close to the broader, more insidious forced sterilization procedures common to the practice of eugenics in many other states. Who speaks for the institutionalized absent a spouse or parent? Does the institution have the right to recommend and then perform such a procedure on a patient or resident who has no family and is otherwise incapable of giving consent? These difficult questions posed potential moral as well as legal dilemmas.

Despite its broad statement of principles, the AHBL quickly made human sterilization its primary focal point, as demonstrated during the group's first meeting after its formation, on November 1, 1951. At this meeting, the members present selected Rabbi Sanders, already chosen as president and a member of the board of directors of the organization, to represent the Arkansas group on the board of the National Federation of Human Betterment Leagues.[37] Sanders then introduced special guest Dr. Clarence J. Gamble, a Massachusetts physician, birth control and eugenics advocate, and heir to the Proctor and Gamble company fortune, to address the luncheon meeting. Gamble spoke to the initial gathering of the AHBL on the topic of the sterilization of the mentally deficient in Arkansas, as reported by both major Little Rock newspapers: "Sterilization was cited today as a means of decreasing the number of feeble-minded persons in Arkansas." Gamble "explained the benefits to the families as well as the communities received by having the mentally ill permanently sterilized."[38] The AHBL would focus on providing access to sterilization for poor, married, competent adults requesting it and also vigorously promote the sterilization, with family or institutional consent, of the mentally incompetent. Race and ethnicity were never considerations for the Arkansas group.

Dr. Gamble also acted as the prime benefactor of the AHBL, providing both loans and grants to the organization. He donated twenty shares of Proctor and Gamble stock to the AHBL in order to provide the start-up funding. The proceeds from the sale of that stock were to "fill the treasury" and provide funds from which the group could repay a cash advance Gamble had loaned to the group earlier in the year.[39] In operation for six years "under the subsidizing through Dr. Gamble," as Rabbi Sanders later put it, it seems no sterilization procedures of any kind were ever actually performed. "The main purpose" of the AHBL, recalls Sanders, "was to sterilize," but, he adds, "the doctors gave advice only when requested to, and to my knowledge while we had the association, I don't think there was any vasectomy at all performed. I don't think there was ever any case records available where we had to perform any sort of vasectomy or done nothing more than merely to educate the public for — to give knowledge to those who may want to perform the operation."[40] While the AHBL disseminated much information about sterilization and recommended the "voluntary" sterilization of mentally deficient individuals as a positive social good, in practice it was primarily an advocacy group that apparently never actually oversaw or subsidized even one sterilization procedure.

The AHBL's most prominent activity involved the mailing of informational pamphlets on sterilization. In March 1952, the group mailed 5,419 copies of *Why Fear Sterilization?*, a three-page flyer reprinting Clarence Gamble's January 1948 article of the same name in *Hygeia*, the health magazine of the American Medical Association.[41] By December of that year, the Arkansas group also had mailed 3,436 copies of *Speaking of Sterilization*, an eight-page pamphlet produced by the Human Betterment League of North Carolina, and 1,200 copies of the pamphlet *Human Sterilization* directly to nurses, attorneys, state and county officials, social workers, and doctors in Arkansas. In the December 1952 meeting of the AHBL, Rabbi Sanders led a discussion on the "need for sterilizations in the state and available facilities." Dr. Willis Brown of Little Rock volunteered office space to interview candidates for the procedure, noting "there are that many requests," and Dr. Harlan Hill also noted that "space was available at Baptist State Hospital for women in childbirth to be made sterile, if they so desired and were not financially able to pay for the service." Ira Sanders and a committee of two others made plans to visit the Arkansas attorney general "to obtain his unofficial backing as soon as he is in office."[42]

The sterilization of the mentally ill remained a focus of the group. In May 1954, Phoebe Marousek of the national Human Betterment Foundation spoke in Paragould, Arkansas, on the benefits of sterilization legislation for Arkansas. The objectives of the HBF, she said, were providing "a voluntary protection plan for those for whom parenthood would be permanently unwise or dangerous; . . . alleviating succeeding generations of hereditary diseases or defects; and . . . safeguarding children from unsatisfactory upbringing by mentally handicapped parents." Marousek took care to state that the program would be limited "to one of strict selection thus avoiding the possibility of its abuse through possible wholesale sterilization or becoming a political instrument."[43] After the presentation, Mrs. Jamie Newsome of Paragould wrote to the AHBL requesting five hundred *Speaking of Sterilization* pamphlets to distribute in an effort to help her gain support for a proposed sterilization bill: "I am preparing legislation for the introducing of a bill, which will authorize the sterilization of Arkansas' mental defectives, at state expense, in the 1955 meeting of the State Legislature."[44] The Arkansas group forwarded the letter to Marousek in Iowa, who responded with an already-completed sample draft of a sterilization bill "to use as a springboard from which to write your proposed bill." Marousek then told Newsome of the AHBL's program of mailing pamphlets to state and local officials: "I feel quite sure they will be willing to accelerate their program of mailing to this group if it is determined that the time is right to introduce such a bill." However, to AHBL secretary Ida Ruth Atkinson, Marousek expressed a different sentiment: "When the league was formed in Arkansas we were told by several community leaders that no law was needed for the sterilization of the mentally defective and for the time being they preferred to operate just as the law stood."[45]

Atkinson replied by explaining the sterilization process as it then stood in Arkansas absent state laws on the matter: "Persons desiring sterilization, but need[ing] investigation, are sent to Miss Nell Reed [of the Family Service

Agency]. After a thorough case study, the history is sent to a hospital Committee on Facilities that passes judgment. Medical consent forms accompany the recommendation of the committee to the University Hospital. Then when the family can make arrangements for the care of children in the family, the parent is entered into the hospital for sterilization."[46]

Clarence Gamble explained the primary thrust of the AHBL agenda to Winthrop Rockefeller, member of the advisory committee to the new University of Arkansas Medical Center. The Arkansas Human Betterment League, Gamble wrote, is "concerned with the need and value of surgical sterilization, in other words permanent birth control, particularly for the mentally handicapped." The AHBL encouraged the "use of sterilization only voluntarily. The Human Betterment groups, of which the Human Betterment League of Arkansas is one, are conducting an educational program aimed at more effective use of sterilization for the mentally handicapped, particularly the mentally retarded and others for whom it is needed but not now available because of economic insufficiency."[47] Gamble stressed the voluntary nature of the procedure in Arkansas, but the prickly problem of who could legally or morally give such consent for those patients without relatives remained unasked, to say nothing of being answered.

By May 1954, as Ira Sanders proudly reported at the biannual meeting, the AHBL had mailed over twenty thousand copies of different sterilization pamphlets to various groups and individuals across the state. In January 1955, the AHBL met with Arkansas state representative Hayes Triplett of Paragould to discuss his plans to introduce House Bill 330, "An Act Authorizing Voluntary Limitation of Parenthood," a sterilization bill Ira Sanders and the AHBL enthusiastically supported. The group thanked Triplett "for his genuine interest in one of our state's most basic social problems."[48] The bill, though, failed to pass, given that Arkansas already had voluntary sterilization provisions in place through cooperation between hospitals and the Family Service Agency.

The AHBL membership unanimously reelected Ira Sanders president in its November 1955 meeting and gave him another three-year term on the board of directors. By that time, as had been the case with Planned Parenthood of Arkansas, a lack of money became the critical concern of the organization. AHBL secretary Ida Ruth Atkinson, who had not been paid in months, noted that the group had "not received a contribution since October 1954," functioning instead on a $300 loan from Clarence Gamble and the remains of the start-up funds made available through the sale of Gamble's stock contribution some years before. "At present," she wrote in February 1957, "we have a balance of $74." All of the group's expenses went toward the dissemination of educational materials. They had funded not a single sterilization procedure. Gamble, eager to see the AHBL remain a viable organization, addressed the financial crisis by loaning the group an additional $400 (the earlier $300 loan from Gamble to the AHBL remained unpaid). He also instructed HBF executive director Phoebe Marousek to make a $1200 tax-deductible donation from the HBF to the AHBL "as a contribution for their educational and charitable work in that state. This will permit them," he wrote, "to repay the $700 loan and retain an additional $500 for their future work." He also requested that Marousek submit a report as to the future viability of the Arkansas organization.[49] Gamble's loans and grants were almost single-handedly keeping the AHBL operational.

Marousek's progress report was bleak, and the HBF director placed the blame squarely on Ira Sanders. The AHBL barely functioned, its "work seriously handicapped by a lack of funds" so severe, Marousek told Gamble in May 1957, that "Mrs. Atkinson has not written a salary check during this current calendar year." She believed the problem was due to the ineffectual leadership of Rabbi Sanders, though she offered no specifics as to why, and suggested a change at the top of the Arkansas organization. "The league would be well-served by a new president," she told Gamble, though she also deemed it important that both Sanders and Hilda Cornish be shown "some particular courtesy in recognition of their interest and assistance with the work and also to keep their interest in the organization." In other words, they felt the organization needed to get rid of Sanders without alienating him. Accordingly, in the November 19, 1957, meeting, Ira Sanders presided over the election of a new slate of officers, including a new president. They named Sanders to the national HBF board but removed him from the presidency a full year before the scheduled end of his tenure.[50] The organization did not survive the change in leadership or its prolonged financial instability, folding in 1958.

Throughout the years of the Great Depression and World War II and well into the postwar era, Ira Sanders played an important role in working to provide access to birth control and family planning for Arkansas families. Working with Hilda Cornish, he approached the question of birth control from the perspective of the sociologist, viewing family planning as a means to ameliorate poverty and improve society. His work as a birth control and reproductive rights activist did not hamper his involvement in many other social causes, especially during the war years, when events presented many other challenges for Sanders.

—5—

World War II, Zionism, Cold War

1933–1954

THE WORLD WAR II YEARS and the immediate postwar environment presented significant challenges to Ira Sanders and gave him the opportunity to influence events at a number of levels. His work during the war to help Jewish refugees escape the Holocaust and perhaps to make a small difference himself in the flow of events in Europe came up short, which haunted him throughout his life. Conversely, Sanders' work in cofounding and leading the Urban League of Greater Little Rock to assist African Americans in securing their fair share of wartime jobs saw much greater success. The war and the Holocaust also dramatically changed his views regarding the establishment of a Jewish state, which Sanders had opposed before the war. Like many other Reform Jews in America, Sanders became a committed Zionist primarily as a result of the events of World War II. Finally, as the United States entered the postwar world as the preeminent power in the world, Sanders often tied his calls for racial justice to the threat of international communism: an egalitarian, color-blind America presented the most potent challenge to communism.

Ira Sanders' world changed rapidly during these years. The Second World War and the immediate postwar period saw numerous economic and social changes to the status quo in Arkansas generally and in Little Rock specifically. Wartime production facilities in neighboring Jacksonville, Maumelle, and elsewhere in and around Little Rock brought much needed jobs with good pay, and the influx of prospective workers created a need for extensive housing construction, creating even more jobs. By war's end, Little Rock had the highest population density of any southern city. Change came on the civil rights front as well. The 1944 US Supreme Court decision *Smith v. Allwright* eliminated the so-called white primary, and early disorganized local attempts in Arkansas to circumvent the court's decision foundered. Ben Johnson notes that "the double-primary system [in Arkansas] fell of its own weight" after twin sets of primary elections in 1946 stretched on for a month. Other signs pointed to a concerted amelioration of Jim Crow in Arkansas. "Democratic [Party] mandates requiring

oaths of fealty to segregation were not enforced at the precinct levels," and in
1950 the state Democratic Party convention "repealed the provision limiting
the vote to white electors." The Arkansas poll tax, while still in place, was, at
one dollar per year, the lowest in the South and, as Johnson points out, while
the tax "excited the ire of white reformers," by the 1950s it was not a "principal
impediment" to black voting to anywhere near the degree it had been in earlier
decades. Additionally, the University of Arkansas School of Law desegregated
with little fanfare in 1948, and with no interference from segregationist governor Ben Laney. In January of that year, the University of Arkansas board
of trustees "formally approved a policy desegregating the graduate and professional schools." The law school saw its first African American graduate in
1951.[1] Progressive Democrat Sidney McMath won the governorship in 1948 and
instituted further programs to modernize Arkansas, especially in the realm of
education, and to bring in new business investments. A populist and a racial
progressive, McMath supported and promoted both antilynching legislation
and an end to the poll tax. He also oversaw the desegregation of the University
of Arkansas Medical School and increased funding for black schools and salaries of black teachers.[2] The harsh climate of race relations characteristic of the
prewar decades gave way to reform, amelioration, and egalitarian change. Little
Rock began to develop a much more moderate environment concerning race
and race relations than its southern neighbors. As Sanders later put it, this new
postwar atmosphere "undoubtedly helped to make Little Rock a much more
involved community, involved in the whole question of the dignity of human
rights, of human personalities, and the war undoubtedly served to make men
more strongly attached to each other in bonds of sympathy and understanding and fulfillment of their own dreams of what a democracy should be like."[3]
These changes began in the war years, years which presented Ira Sanders both
challenges and opportunities he had never seen before.

Ira Sanders and the Holocaust

The ashes of the hundreds who could have been saved have
haunted [me] through the years as a nightmare.
—IRA SANDERS, 1978

In the years prior to World War II, Sanders worked with Stephen S. Wise, the
influential rabbi of New York's Free Synagogue, and became acquainted with
Joseph T. Robinson, United States senator from Arkansas and Senate majority
leader. Both relationships gave Sanders important inroads to power and influence during the 1930s.

Wise and Sanders were friends and shared an affinity for dynamic social action. While both were active in the Palestine Foundation Fund (Wise served as chairman in 1925, and Sanders was the chief Pennsylvania organizer while serving as rabbi in Allentown), they held disparate views. Wise was an avid political Zionist who promoted the creation of a Jewish state, and Sanders was a promoter of Jewish religious life in the Holy Land absent a political state.

Sen. Joseph T. Robinson had already earned the admiration of Ira Sanders by the time of the Second World War. The rabbi had controversially and publicly supported the Al Smith–Joe Robinson Democratic presidential ticket from the pulpit in 1928. The senator further impressed Sanders by being among the first statesmen to take strong and public anti-Hitler stances; in March 1933 in New York and Chicago, Robinson, along with a few fellow senators including New York's Robert Wagner, expressed outrage at Nazi Germany's newly codified anti-Jewish policies.[4]

Stephen Wise took note of Robinson's activities as well, and in early June 1933 he wrote to Sanders asking for help in persuading Senator Robinson to introduce a Senate resolution regarding the Nazi regime's treatment of German Jews. If Robinson would introduce such a resolution, Wise told Sanders, they would be "almost sure to be able to get the right kind of support of both sides of the House for Senator Robinson, because of his popularity and authority in the Senate." He asked Sanders to line up "half a dozen" friends, Jew and non-Jew, to wire Robinson in support of such a resolution. "Dear Ira," Wise concluded, "I have the feeling that you will be very glad to take this step. I dare say you know the Senator well, and you surely know whom to approach who has connections in the Senate."[5] Sanders followed through with Wise's request, and one week hence, on June 10, 1933, on the floor of the US Senate, Robinson "immortalized himself," as Sanders later wrote, by becoming one of the first American statesmen to speak out against the German state's treatment of Jews. He stated that the "Nazi administration has startled and shocked mankind by the severe policies enforced against the Jews." Robinson called Nazi persecution of the Jews "sickening and terrifying" and hoped "wholesome world opinion [would] influence sentiment in Germany so that in time—a short time—the iron grip of racial hatred [would] be relaxed and the Jewish people again be permitted to enjoy fair freedom."[6]

When in the summer of 1934 Ira and Selma Sanders took a vacation trip through Europe, Senator Robinson, at Sanders' request, armed the rabbi with a letter of introduction addressed to Italian leader Benito Mussolini, who Sanders believed "was gradually veering towards Hitler's anti-Semitic agenda," and with whom Sanders planned to meet to discuss the plight of Italian Jews and thus help improve the growing Jewish crisis in Europe "in some small way."[7]

Sanders presented his letter to an Italian official who informed the rabbi that Il Duce could not see him, as the Italian leader presently was out of the country in Germany visiting Adolf Hitler. Mussolini's absence frustrated Sanders' personal mission in Europe, but the rabbi continued to do what he could to influence events once he returned to the United States, both through the pulpit and by speaking in the community. With Robinson's death in 1937, though, Sanders lost a critical connection to the Washington power structure. "With this avenue of communication gone," Sanders wrote, he "became stymied in the pursuit of a well-organized plan to halt Hitler's campaign" of anti-Semitism.[8] Prior to leaving for Europe, Sanders had been granted an audience with Pope Pius XI, scheduled to take place June 5, 1934; however, the rabbi could not take advantage of this opportunity as he and Mrs. Sanders' travel itinerary did not have them arriving in Europe—Naples, specifically—until June 30.[9]

Throughout the 1930s, Sanders received many letters from European Jews hoping to immigrate to the United States, a prospect made all the more difficult due to the draconian restrictions placed on immigration as a result of the Immigration Act of 1924. This act instituted a rigid quota system, limiting the immigrant pool for each year after its passage to 2 percent of any given nationality or group already living in the United States as of the US census of 1890. The law used the early census as a base in order to limit dramatically the numbers of southern and eastern European immigrants—especially Jewish, Catholic, and Eastern Orthodox—who had begun to arrive in large numbers only after 1890. Nativists of the era believed these immigrants were less able or willing to assimilate, and American organized labor generally agreed, viewing these new immigrants as a threat to jobs and wages. By tying the quota to the 1890 census, legislators could reduce this most recent wave of nontraditional immigrants that had begun after 1890 to a trickle. The side effect of the law during Hitler's rise was of course to trap most European Jews in place, making escape from the Nazi pogroms to the United States very problematic.[10]

Sanders provided affidavits for a number of European Jews seeking asylum in the United States, and he beseeched his congregation to do the same, pleading with friends and congregants to sign affidavits in support of immigrating individuals and families. However, Sanders later noted, "Signatures were few and most of these requests for immigration were unanswered—a tragedy that well-nigh destroyed [my] soul throughout the years."[11] Sanders lived the rest of his life with deep regrets over his failure to help more people escape Nazism. In his journal, he wrote, "The ashes of the hundreds who could have been saved have haunted [me] through the years as a nightmare. Perhaps [I] could have been more militant in procuring signees for affidavits. For any sin of omission," Sanders ruefully concluded, he asked for forgiveness. Throughout the war years, he continued to speak out strongly against Nazi totalitarianism, which he termed "the very antithesis of democracy" and "Germany's substitute for democracy and religion." In one wartime sermon, Sanders warned, "The exaltation of the state is destructive to progress. It overthrows the concept of liberty. . . . The individual becomes an unthinking cog in the vast machinery of the State. Life is interpreted in terms of power and might. The nation is supreme—a monster which crushes and destroys men."[12]

Sanders referred to November 9, 1938—Kristallnacht, or the Night of Broken Glass, a wave of violent attacks upon hundreds of synagogues and Jewish-owned businesses throughout Germany and Austria—as "the saddest day" of his life. Following the tragic events, temples and synagogues across the country, including Congregation B'nai Israel, held special services, as did churches of many denominations. In a sanctuary "crowded to capacity," Sanders preached a heartfelt and hopeful sermon that right would yet triumph in Europe—a message some disheartened congregants openly questioned at the time.[13] The tragic events of Europe before and during the war caused discouragement and crises of faith for many in his congregation. Sanders responded throughout the World War II era by often sharing hopeful messages from the pulpit about the connections between Judaism and democracy; the inappropriate aggrandizement, as seen in the totalitarian nations, of the state over the ideals of freedom; and the materialism of the fascists compared to the religious and spiritual freedoms of America. "In a time when nations are ready to lock in armed conflict with each other, and tyrannical governments such as Germany, the Italian, and the Japanese are still binding thousands of their citizens to the shackles of bondage, the voice of God again reverberates: 'Send forth my people, that they may serve Me.' This voice of God—the voice of freedom, right, and justice—will always be heard, and freedom from modern bondage of the exaltation of the state will always triumph among men and nations." The world at war stood at a crossroads, Sanders said, and would "be redeemed from the curse of modern slavery only through the rediscovery and the reassertion of the worth of personality and of the dignity of the individual," a tenet Sanders applied in his community throughout his life.[14]

Eloquent and inspirational as a rabbi, Sanders could also light fires of righteous indignation when appropriate. On one occasion, Sanders railed against those who called World War II some kind of manifestation of God's will. In a blistering Yom Kippur sermon on the evening of September 30, 1941, Sanders said, "Religion is based on the idea of justice." Humanity must not hide its own failures behind excuses. "Mankind is using a shabby device to make God a

scapegoat of its failure! Man himself has transformed the world into a wilderness of desolation, and conditions today are the result of man's choice between
good and evil."[15]

The War, the Urban League, and
Defense Jobs for African Americans

They will tell you, you know, [you qualify only] for maid work,
but you tell them that you don't want this [type of work].
—IRA SANDERS, 1941

Beginning on September 1, 1939, World War II raged in Europe and stood
looming on the American horizon. Though technically a neutral power, the
United States had taken cautious steps to move toward a more overtly anti-
Nazi, pro-British posture. President Franklin Roosevelt's 1939 Cash-and-Carry
program amended the 1936 Neutrality Act by allowing the sale of armaments
to combatants on a cash-and-carry basis, while his "Arsenal of Democracy"
fireside chat on December 29, 1940, and the passage of the Lend-Lease Act
in March 11, 1941, foreshadowed a much greater level of American industrial
production in the service of an allied victory and an approaching involvement
by the United States itself in the Second World War. Lend-Lease had a particularly significant impact both domestically and in the course of the allied efforts
in the war in that it promised stepped-up production in the United States of
military materials for the allied powers, especially Great Britain, then desperate
for assistance.[16]

In the United States, more production meant more manufacturing facilities
and therefore more jobs. War production profoundly affected national unemployment numbers, and after the US entry into the war in December 1941, the
combination of defense jobs and military service caused the numbers of jobless
to plummet from 14.6 percent in 1940, to 4.7 percent in 1942, and then to an
astounding low of 1.2 percent in 1944.[17] War production facilities and employment opportunities soon came to Arkansas, but racist hiring practices threatened to lock thousands of black Arkansans out of these jobs.

World War II–era defense work created many thousands of jobs in the Little
Rock area. Two defense and munitions plants and several proposed housing
projects required the significant use of labor. The Urban League leadership,
however, saw "evident plans to limit the use of Negro workers" and confine
them to unskilled jobs; accordingly, the league "launched an all-out effort to
gain access for blacks to these jobs," skilled as well as unskilled.[18]

Sanders acted in important capacities with the Urban League during the war years, helping black Arkansans gain access to well-paying defense jobs, but he did not act alone; as usual, Sanders worked with dedicated colleagues and associates.

In his capacity as a leader in the Urban League of Greater Little Rock, Ira Sanders worked to assist African Americans in securing a fair share of the new employment opportunities created by Cash-and-Carry and Lend-Lease during these last years of the Great Depression. One such effort involved Sadye Allen Thompson, the African American woman Rabbi Sanders had been forced to oust from the Little Rock School of Social Work years before, and her efforts to secure a position after the opening of a defense plant in Pulaski County on the eve of American entry into World War II.

On June 4, 1941, a few months after the adoption of the Lend-Lease program, the War Department announced that a $33 million ordnance plant would be built in Jacksonville, twenty-one miles northeast of Little Rock. Arkansans of all races welcomed the news, as such a plant would provide the area with thousands of much-needed jobs at higher than average wages. Initially, however, it was plain that opportunities for African Americans at this facility would be much more circumscribed than those for whites. As was the practice in the Jim Crow South, black men and women eager to get a job in the forthcoming defense facility were overlooked or pushed aside in favor of whites, or found themselves being considered only for custodial work. Once word had gotten out about the construction of the plant, Sanders and others within the Urban League, most notably Clifford Minton, who succeeded Sanders as director in 1940, tried to move beyond the well-established racial barriers and, Sadye Thompson later recalled, "talked to [the plant officials] and asked if they could not employ Negroes on the [production] lines to do work. Of course they did not."[19]

Sanders tried generally to help African Americans secure the same employment opportunities as whites enjoyed, but he also wanted specifically to assist Ms. Thompson, then unemployed, after she had been forcibly turned out of the Little Rock School of Social Work against both their wishes some years earlier. Sanders encouraged Thompson to apply for a job on the Jacksonville plant production line, and not to settle for maid work. For some, janitorial work was acceptable, but Sanders urged Thompson to aim higher. Thompson recalled,

[Sanders] was there but he was getting others [in the Urban League] to do this too. If I would apply at the employment office to work at Jacksonville, he said 'Now they will tell you, you know, [you qualify only] for maid work, but you tell them that you don't want this [type of work].' So, I

applied and I told them I wanted to work on the line. They did tell me
that I could just get work as a maid, and I said no, I'd rather work on the
assembly lines. They said they had nothing for Negroes to do.

The plant initially successfully rebuffed Sanders, Minton, and the Urban
League in their efforts to ensure black Arkansans had an equal chance at
these plum jobs. The opportunity would come to fruition only with a harder,
more concerted push from the Urban League, with Pres. Franklin Roosevelt's
Executive Order 8802 on June 25, 1941, prohibiting racial discrimination in
defense plants, and with the establishment of the Fair Employment Practices
Commission ensuring equality of opportunity at such facilities. A presidential executive order now supported the promise of equal opportunity in the
workplace. Backed by the mandates of the order, which Roosevelt issued just
three weeks after the announcement of the Jacksonville plant's construction,
the Urban League later proudly noted that through a redoubled effort they
had "succeeded in opening up thousands of jobs for blacks in both construction and production operations" in the Little Rock–area facilities during the
war years. These jobs by no means came solely as a result of FDR's executive
order, which was spottily enforced in the South: the Roosevelt administration
lacked the political will to challenge southern segregation and white supremacy,
remaining reluctant to address the southern racial status quo and fearful of
losing the region's support for domestic New Deal policies.[20] The local Urban
League, most notably Minton and Sanders, worked hard to ensure that the
promise of the president's executive order became reality. Minton worked well
with Sanders, made great use of the press, especially Little Rock's black-owned
Twin City Press, and both men "cultivated community support for civil rights
activities."[21]

Sadye Thompson numbered among those employed at the Jacksonville
defense facility. She got a job on the production lines of the Arkansas Ordnance
Plant in Jacksonville shortly after its opening, making primers for 155 mm how-
itzers. A national first, the efforts of the Urban League of Greater Little Rock
received well-deserved attention from figures in Washington, DC, including
Dr. Robert C. Weaver of the Federal Housing Authority and the National
Defense Advisory Committee and Dr. Mary McLeod Bethune, both key advisors to President Roosevelt as members of the so-called Black Cabinet.[22] By
the end of 1944, about three thousand African Americans worked on four production lines set aside for black workers at the Jacksonville facility, making
up 24 percent of the overall plant workforce. The plant closed in early 1946.
Ms. Thompson later attended Philander Smith College in Little Rock and went

on to earn a master's degree in social work from the University of Arkansas. She and Sanders worked together in the Urban League for eleven years, and Thompson later worked in the Pulaski County welfare office for fourteen years. As for her career choice of social work, Thompson said, "The inspiration came from Rabbi Sanders."[23]

Zionism and the American Council for Judaism

We cannot but believe that Jewish nationalism tends to confuse our fellow men about our place and function in society.
—IRA SANDERS, 1942

In the unpublished memoir that Sanders began late in his life, the rabbi reflected upon "the prized possession of [his] family," a particular framed image that he had much admired where it hung in his boyhood home in Missouri after being passed down to his father from his grandfather. The "pictorial representation of some of Judaism's most sacred values" depicted a pair of large columns representing the Temple of Jerusalem, a robed Moses clutching the Tablets, symbols of the Twelve Tribes, and in the center pious Jews standing and praying at the Wailing Wall, which was left in ruins after the destruction of the temple in 70 CE. "This one picture," wrote Sanders, "alone inspired [me] at an early age to espouse the cause of Zionism, and to work for the restoration of the land of Israel."[24]

As this passage suggests, Ira Sanders considered himself a lifelong supporter of the creation of the State of Israel; in fact, the evidence suggests otherwise. While the picture he describes no doubt held deep meaning for him, Sanders' ideas involving Jews and the Holy Land evolved over time and were neither tethered to nor dependent upon the creation of a Jewish state. Once created, there is no doubt that the State of Israel found in Ira Sanders an avid advocate and vocal supporter, but like most in the Reform movement, Sanders focused first not on the creation of a political Jewish state in the Middle East but on Jewish life here in America. In his inaugural sermon following his installation as associate rabbi of Manhattan's Temple Israel in September 1924, Sanders called for "a distinctly American Jewish culture, grounded in and hewn from an American environment." In a true reflection of Reform Judaism's non-Zionist tenets, he emphasized "a new Jewry upon these American shores." Again, in an April 1925 sermon praising Reform Judaism founder Isaac Meyer Wise, Rabbi Sanders called Wise "Israel's modern Moses, leading Jewry into its promised land—America!"[25] Sanders' attitudes and outlook on Zionism evolved over time and were shaped and clarified by his involvement in a series of meetings held during the war years, from 1942 to 1944, by the horrific events of the Holocaust, and then also by the postwar creation of the State of Israel in 1948. In June 1942, Sanders became an original member of the non-Zionist group later known as the American Council for Judaism (ACJ), which was established in response to the growth of Zionism within the Reform movement. But internal struggles and disagreements transformed the group from one "promoting a revival of the ideology of classical Reform Judaism" into a strongly anti-Zionist organization. As a result of those changes, Sanders quickly came to regret his involvement and—though he was a founding member of the group—vocally denounced the organization. On April 14, 1944, following a tumultuous two years, he resigned.[26]

"From the beginning," writes Eli Evans in *The Provincials*, "the issue of Zionism plagued the Reform movement, trying earnestly to forge a new Judaism in America." In the years following the issuance of the so-called Balfour Declaration in 1917, a British white paper stating that the British government would "view with favour the establishment in Palestine of a national home for the Jewish people" and would "use their best endeavours to facilitate the achievement" of that goal, Reform Judaism remained institutionally opposed to the establishment of a political Jewish state. Going back to 1890, well prior either to this British diplomatic statement or the 1922 creation of the British Mandate for Palestine, Isaac Meyer Wise spearheaded the effort to place on the record the opposition of the Central Conference of American Rabbis (CCAR) to "any attempt toward the establishment of a Jewish state." In the view of Reform Judaism, "Israel remained a religious community, not a nation." In a dramatic softening of that opposition posture, a 1935 follow-up CCAR resolution stated that the organization would adopt a neutral posture on the question of Zionism. Then, at the 1942 annual meeting held in Cincinnati, the CCAR for the first time adopted what many considered a pro-Zionist resolution, one supporting the formation of a Jewish army in Palestine, in effect nullifying the earlier resolution of neutrality.[27] The practices and policies of Nazi Germany toward the Jews of Europe provided an obvious motivation for this change of policy.

The 1942 CCAR resolution and the group's apparent move toward a pro-Zionist position displeased Louis Wolsey, the former rabbi (1899–1907) of Congregation B'nai Israel in Little Rock who was now based in Philadelphia, and the man who in 1926 helped convince Ira Sanders to move from New York to Arkansas. Wolsey called for a meeting of non-Zionist rabbis to be held in early June 1942 in Atlantic City, New Jersey, to "discuss the problems that confront

Judaism and Jews in the world emergency."[28] Rabbi James Heller, an ardent Zionist and, like Wolsey, also a former rabbi of Little Rock's Congregation B'nai Israel (1920), had become the CCAR president in 1941 with an agenda that included putting "the Conference solidly behind Zionist objectives." Heller worked hard to prevent the Atlantic City meeting from taking place, to no avail. Fearing that a potential schism could be developing within the Reform movement, Heller backed off his pro-Zionist initiative and instead offered a platform compromise on Zionism. He proposed that a "permanent by-law" be added to the CCAR constitution that would establish a neutral position for the organization on the question of Zionism, and he called for an admission that the resolution to form an army had been a mistake. His compromise was rejected.[29]

At the Atlantic City meeting and afterward, eighty-nine rabbis including Ira Sanders signed the "Atlantic City Statement of Principles" that affirmed support for Jewish life in Palestine as well as for Jewish life in other parts of the world. The signatories declared that they could not "subscribe to or support the *political* emphasis now paramount in the Zionist program." The statement put forth that the primary reason for the Atlantic City gathering lay in the rabbis' concerns over "the growing secularism in American Jewish life, the absorption of large numbers of Jewish nationalistic endeavors, and the tendency to reduce the religious basis of Jewish life to a place of secondary importance." In addition, the statement spoke for the rabbis who supported it: "We cannot but believe that Jewish nationalism tends to confuse our fellow men about our place and function in society and also diverts our own attention from our historic role to live as a religious community wherever we may dwell."[30] In short, the rabbis were concerned about the future of Reform Judaism in the face of what they saw as an increasingly political Zionism.

In fact, though, most of the group's discussion in Atlantic City did not even address Zionism per se. Rather, it focused on the problems facing the Reform movement and fears of its shrinking influence in the wake of the vastly increased eastern European Jewish immigration of 1880–1920, whose numbers afterward made up fully 85 percent of the American Jewish population before being choked off by the restrictive quotas of the Immigration Act of 1924. This wave of incoming eastern European Jews swelled the ranks of the secular and unaffiliated as well as the Orthodox and Conservative branches of American Judaism as the Reform membership numbers concurrently declined. By 1940, the Reform movement "only claimed approximately 200,000 dues-paying members out of an estimated total American Jewish population of 4.7 million." These were the primary fears motivating the rabbis to meet. Zionism was more of a "keyword for all that is non-Reform." By the end of 1942, this group became known as the American Council for Judaism (ACJ). It originally promoted a point of view that was not "anti-Zionist" but "anti-nationalist," with the purpose of representing "a religious opposition to political Zionism."[31]

Ira Sanders also numbered among the thirty-three rabbis who signed the ACJ's strongly worded council statement of August 30, 1943, formally opposing the creation of a political Jewish state. Sanders and the other signatory rabbis stood united in their belief: "We consider ourselves no longer a nation. We are a religious community, and neither pray for nor anticipate a return to Palestine nor a restoration of any of the laws concerning the Jewish state." The statement also read in part that the ACJ appreciated Palestine's role in "providing refuge for a part of Europe's persecuted Jews" and hoped it would "continue as one of the places for such resettlement." The statement continued:

> We oppose the efforts to establish a National Jewish State in Palestine or anywhere else as a philosophy of defeatism, and one which does not offer a practical solution of the Jewish problem. Palestine is a part of Israel's religious heritage, as it is a part of the heritage of two other religions of the world. We look forward to the ultimate establishment of a democratic, autonomous government in Palestine, wherein Jews, Moslems [sic] and Christians shall be justly represented; every man enjoying equal rights and enjoying equal responsibilities; a democratic government in which our fellow Jews shall be free Palestinians whose religion is Judaism, even as we are Americans whose religion is Judaism.[32]

But even by the time Sanders signed this statement, he had growing concerns that the ACJ's message had become too focused on anti-Zionism at the expense of the original mission of bolstering the tenets of Reform Judaism, a concern that evolved and played out over the course of the next three years.

Rabbi Sanders feared that the increasingly strident anti-Zionism of the ACJ might facilitate the development of a pro- and anti-Zionist schism within Reform congregations. He proved prescient in this concern, as the beginnings of precisely such a schism began to manifest in Texas in November 1943 when the board of Houston's Congregation Beth Israel, one of the South's oldest, largest, and wealthiest Reform congregations, adopted what it called "Basic Principles" that professed to seek "to safeguard at least a segment of the Jewish people of this nation against indictment before the Lord for worshipping a false god, ZIONISM." More broadly, the Houston Basic Principles sought to purge non-Reform beliefs and practices from the temple by stripping away the voting rights of Zionist members, of those who observed the kosher laws, and of congregants who wanted more Hebrew to be used during services. Sanders found particularly offensive the Basic Principles' rejection of Reform Judaism's historic commitment to racial justice. This ideological purge triggered a process by which the Houston congregation broke apart, splitting into pro- and anti-Zionist factions: the associate rabbi and 142 members resigned in order to form a new congregation outside the restrictions of the Basic Principles.[33]

Many of the ACJ rabbis feared the spread of such a dramatic development might threaten the entire Reform movement, and Ira Sanders in particular harbored fears over this possibility. The Houston Basic Principles supporters actively encouraged other Reform congregations to join them and to adopt similarly stringent anti-Zionist guidelines. The contagion the ACJ had inadvertently set loose now threatened to spread to Little Rock, which Congregation B'nai Israel member Alan Thalheimer remembered being at that time "a hotbed" of ACJ activity. Rabbi Sanders faced the issue himself when several members of his Little Rock congregation approached him in his office and proposed to him precisely such a split as had occurred in Houston, with the establishment of a separate anti-Zionist congregation for those who opposed the creation of a Jewish state and any non-Reform practices. Sanders' stern and angry reply—"over my dead body"—laid that issue to rest in Little Rock, though not without consequences, as some members of the temple resigned over the controversy.[34]

ACJ members such as Sanders and Baltimore rabbi Abraham Shusterman harbored increasing concerns that the organization had become "so anti-Zionist that we have forgotten our original pro-Reform platform."[35] The rapid evolution of the ACJ into an overtly anti-Zionist organ led member rabbis in ever-increasing numbers to reassess their involvement; they then began resigning in large numbers. Those leaving the group included former Little Rock rabbi Louis Witt, who resigned over what he saw as "the Council's negative attitude toward Palestine and the refugees."[36] As the non-Zionist rabbis—a camp to which Ira Sanders belonged—engaged in a large-scale exodus, a core of ardent anti-Zionists remained firmly in place within the leadership of the organization, helping to accelerate the ACJ's transformation into an ever more strident anti-Zionist group.

By April 17, 1944, Sanders too had seen enough, and he resigned from the ACJ. It was becoming clear by this time that the ACJ's increasingly zealous anti-Zionism worked at tragic cross purposes with the urgent need to get European Jews out of harm's way. Sanders' deep regrets over his inability to assist more Jews from escaping the ongoing Nazi extermination policies also influenced his decision to leave the ACJ. The Jews needed a safe haven during the war, and the United States did not provide that haven. His position on Jewish life in Palestine and the creation of a Jewish state profoundly shifted as a result of these events. Sanders welcomed the establishment of the State of Israel when it occurred in 1948. This event settled the question and sent the American Council for Judaism into irrelevancy.

Rabbi Sanders expressed concerns about the freedom of his pulpit as another factor in his resignation. He feared that the Council might, as had happened in Houston, "make use of prominent laypeople in the synagogue" to further an overtly anti-Zionist agenda, thus threatening the authority and autonomy of the rabbi. "I need not tell you," Sanders wrote his friend and ACJ founder Louis Wolsey, "these absurd principles [adopted by Houston's Beth Israel and which ostracized Zionists] are far from intellectual, coming as they do from untutored laymen who know little or nothing about Judaism and less about drawing up principles to guide a congregation."[37] Essentially, Sanders resigned for several reasons. First, he believed the ACJ, in its growing anti-Zionist zeal, tacitly encouraged schism within congregations like the one that happened in Houston and the one that was threatened in Little Rock. Second, he tenaciously protected his right to control his own pulpit. And third, he fervently stood by Reform Judaism's mission of social and racial justice. While he was a supporter of Jewish life in the Holy Land, he personally had opposed the establishment of a Jewish state, even though he had chosen never to broach the topic in sermons. For him, the establishment of such a state had to be opposed "outside of the Synagogue, which is sacred soil."[38] He rejected as illegitimate any attempts to influence his right to an unfettered pulpit.

Sanders feared his ACJ resignation might adversely affect his long-standing friendship with Wolsey. Sanders told him, "I trust that our friendship of over 20 years will, in no wise [sic], be impaired because of the position I am forced to take after three months of mental anguish and struggle." Wolsey responded, "Please be assured that nothing you do will interfere with our personal relations. I am altogether too fond of you."[39] Several months later, in January 1945, with the ACJ rapidly morphing into something he had neither intended nor envisioned, Wolsey himself resigned from the organization he had established only three years earlier. He chose the Friday evening of May 14, 1948, the date of the establishment of the State of Israel, to explain this resignation and speak about his disillusionment with what had occurred inside the ACJ. In a sermon entitled "Why I Withdrew from the American Council for Judaism," reprinted in the Philadelphia *Jewish Exponent*, Wolsey charged the group with "abandoning the 'unexceptionally religious' mission he had envisioned for an all-out battle with the Zionist movement." Now among the ranks of the many Reform rabbis who had preceded him in resignation from the ACJ, Wolsey received many congratulatory messages from them, including one from his old friend Ira Sanders.[40]

Rabbi Sanders' journey toward Zionism reveals the evolution of his overall position in support of Jewish life in the Middle East and in eventual support of the State of Israel. But the record also reveals that, in order to sustain his later self-narrative in the years following his resignation from the ACJ—that of a life-long supporter of Zionism—he seems to have erased his involvement in the formative history of the group from this personal narrative. For example, in a 1982 interview (in part about the ACJ) with Carolyn LeMaster for her book *A Corner of the Tapestry*, a comprehensive work on Arkansas Jewry, Sanders never mentions his involvement with the group. He tells LeMaster only that the ACJ "gained a few adherents in Little Rock, and a group functioned there for a while."[41]

It is absolutely clear that Ira Sanders always had a deep interest in supporting Jewish life in the Holy Land, but this interest changed by degrees and over time. During his years in Pennsylvania in the 1920s, Sanders had been a pivotal figure in the Palestine Foundation Fund, and he took great pride in his activity within this organization, which had been created in 1920 to raise funds to assist Jews in immigrating to Palestine. He saw that organization, though, as one that supported and helped finance Jewish immigration to the region, not as one that bankrolled the creation of a political state. He joined the ACJ in 1942, but as detailed above, in 1944 he resigned when it became a strident anti-Zionist group rather than a benign non-Zionist group. With the establishment of the State of Israel in 1948, Sanders came full circle and became a committed supporter. By the late 1950s, when Sanders addressed a group of recently ordained rabbis at a symposium, he gave his audience the impression that he never had any connection with the ACJ. As he spoke concerning the role of the rabbi in relation to the congregation, he held out his own experiences as examples for the young rabbis, recounting the differences in the early 1940s between his support for Jewish life in Palestine and the desire of many in his congregation that Zionism not emanate from the pulpit. In doing so, he rewrote his past: the Little Rock Jewish "community was divided on the subject of [Houston's] Basic Principles and the American Council for Judaism, and the rabbi [referring to himself] took the attitude that while he was unalterably opposed to these principles and this organization," he nonetheless felt "that the [anti-Zionist] members of his congregation had the right to disagree with him." He made no mention of his own early ACJ support or involvement or his contemporary non-Zionist point of view. The ACJ's quick evolution from a society that reaffirmed the primacy of Reform Judaism's non-Zionist principles to one that zealously opposed the establishment of Israel served in many ways as a kind of reverse mirror image of Sanders' own evolution from a supporter of Jewish religious life in Palestine to a supporter of the State of Israel. In his remarks to the young rabbis, he added, "In the years to come the State of Israel will add immeasurably to the cultural and religious status of our people. It will give increasing stature and dignity to your calling. How privileged you are!"[42] By 1967, Sanders' numerous activities in support of Israel were such that he was honored in a ceremony celebrating his contributions: his leadership in nineteen separate Israel bond drives, one per year every year following the 1948 creation of the State of Israel. In 1970, he visited Israel for the first time, his "most exalted hour," as he grandiosely referred to it in his memoir. "On that memorable day," Sanders wrote, he "remembered the years when [his] congregation could have been split into two factions because of the anti-Zionistic attitude of many members" had he "not taken a quick but determined stand against those who wanted to force members of the congregation to accept a regimented Anti-Zionistic Reform Judaism." He added, again with no mention of his own formative involvement, "Little Rock Jewry regrettably had been the victim of the anti-Zionistic forces organized under the aegis of the local chapter of the Council of American Judaism [sic]."[43] Nowhere in his memoir does Sanders discuss or even mention his ACJ involvement. As the ACJ deepened its anti-Zionist radicalization in the years following his resignation, and as the political State of Israel continued to exist beyond its creation in May 1948—with him as an avid supporter—Sanders explained away or simply ignored his involvement in the founding of the non-Zionist ACJ.

Postwar, Cold War

Unless the prejudices confused with pretexts are challenged and repulsed,
a divided America will become ripe for a Communist America.
—IRA SANDERS, 1959

In the immediate aftermath of the war and the horrors of the Holocaust, Rabbi Sanders' messages about the evils of racism and his related work in the community increased. He worked to resettle World War II refugees in Arkansas and warned of the dangers of international communism. The broad embrace of cultural pluralism and racial acceptance offered the greatest hope for America in the postwar world. In an address shortly after the war, Sanders said, "Racially, the world must realize that every human group possesses worth." He called the doctrine that there are superior and inferior races "scientifically unsound," continuing, "There is no master race. Mankind is one, and if there are differences,

Rabbi Sanders, 1947. Courtesy of Temple B'nai Israel,
Little Rock, Arkansas.

it does not mean superiority or inferiority, but variety. Out of the mingling of the various races there must come that cultural pluralism necessary to mankind's progress. Political, economic, and racial justice! These are the foundation stones upon which we must build the new international order."[44]

Sanders chaired the Arkansas Committee of the Displaced Persons Commission (DPC), created in the wake of the passage on June 28, 1948, of the Displaced Persons Act, which "administered [the] selection and resettlement

in the United States of certain European displaced persons."[45] The act had
come about largely as a result of Jewish activism; specifically, of the actions
of the Citizens' Committee on Displaced Persons, a lobbying group created
by the American Jewish Committee, an international human rights organization founded in 1906 (not to be confused with the American Jewish Congress,
founded in 1918 upon the belief that the Committee was antidemocratic and
dominated by conservative elites). The American Jewish Committee had great
concerns about the special problems European Jews faced after the war, especially in Poland, where some two hundred thousand Jews who had fled to the
Soviet Union ahead of the Nazi onslaught were now returning to their homes,
only to face overt acts of anti-Semitism, persecution, and hostility. To implement
the specifics of the bill, Pres. Harry Truman appointed a Displaced Persons
Commission, headed (as a symbolic gesture) by a Catholic, a Protestant, and a
Jew. The national DPC worked with state bodies and volunteer groups to help
settle displaced persons in the United States. Between the act's 1948 implementation and the year 1952, more than 446,000 displaced persons were admitted to
the United States: 47 percent were Catholic, Protestants and Orthodox made up
35 percent, and Jews accounted for 16 percent of those resettled. Most settled in
the northern and northeastern United States.[46]

Rabbi Sanders, the leader of the resettlement efforts in the state, noted in
a 1951 report to Gov. Sidney McMath that 794 displaced persons had been
admitted to Arkansas.[47] The act required applicants to present guarantees from
American sponsors that both employment and housing were waiting for them
in the United States, and it was up to the Arkansas DPC to help find those
in the state willing to accommodate the refugees. Sanders led in that initiative. In a related effort, Governor McMath had been among those who peti-
tioned the US Senate Foreign Relations Committee in 1950 to approve the
United Nations Convention on the Prevention and Punishment of the Crime
of Genocide, which denounced "mass murder because of race, nationality, or
religion." McMath invited Rabbi Sanders and a small group of religious dignitaries to his office to witness his signature on the petition.[48]

Following the defeat of the Axis powers in 1945, the Cold War—a political,
economic, and sociological struggle for postwar power and influence between
the United States and the Soviet Union—rapidly emerged as America's primary foreign policy concern. Fears of communism, its international spread,
and its domestic influence began to dominate the American conversation. For
Sanders, both fascism and communism involved the aggrandizement of the
state at the cost of the intrinsic worth of the individual. The key to success in
the struggle against the encroachment of communism involved highlighting

Gov. Sidney McMath (*seated*) signs a 1950 petition to the US Senate Foreign
Relations Committee to approve the United Nations Convention on the Prevention
and Punishment of the Crime of Genocide. *Standing, left to right:* Rev. James Workman,
Monsignor John J. Healy, Rev. Marion Boggs, Rev. William Oglesby, Rabbi Ira Sanders,
Daniel Lichtenberg (regional director of the American Jewish Committee of Dallas).
Courtesy of the UALR Center for Arkansas History and Culture,
Arkansas Studies Institute, Little Rock, Arkansas.

the same ideals he promoted in the struggles for racial and social justice in
Arkansas: adherence to moral law and the inherent value of the individual.
Speaking before the Little Rock Rotary Club in February 1951, Sanders warned,
"A vicious Communist cult has been extended into many parts of the world and
many democratic principles have been sacrificed on the altars of that creed.
In such a world, America must reaffirm the principles of brotherhood" and
racial acceptance.[49] In a University of Arkansas baccalaureate address at the
mid-year commencement ceremony in February 1952, he offered these same
principles as a prescription for battling the influence of communism and "the
trials through which men and nations are now passing." For Sanders, religion
could restore "the lost values, the forgotten ideals, the neglected principles and
standards of the moral life." Most significantly, Sanders said, religion could

aid in "establishing that spiritual authority which is higher than the arrogance and tyranny of the state." He told the graduates, "The menace of this exaltation of the state is obvious and threatens the loss of everything for which men have fought and died." Without this moral law, he concluded, "we perish."[50] During the anxiety-beclouded 1950s, the phrase "under God" was added to the Pledge of Allegiance, attendance nationwide at religious services nearly doubled, Catholic bishop Fulton J. Sheen's *Life Is Worth Living* was one of television's most popular programs, and the motto In God We Trust became an official part of the currency. Like many living in this time, Sanders issued a call to faith as a primary weapon in the arsenal of anti-communism.[51] Widespread religious expression stood in stark contrast to Soviet atheism, and Sanders saw it as among the best ways to differentiate the values of American republicanism and Russian communism.

The conquest of racial prejudice stood at the heart of that call. "Unless the prejudices confused with pretexts are challenged and repulsed," Sanders told his congregation in a January 1959 sermon, "a divided America will become ripe for a Communist America. Unless we fight for peace in the spirit of teamwork and with the same enthusiasm for brotherhood and unity as we fought for war, we will lose the peace and freedom we fought to win."[52] A universal moral law that values and protects the rights of the individual lay at the heart of both his wartime and his Cold War messages, the same ideals he had stressed and would continue to stress in his battle for racial and social justice in Arkansas.

The quest for social and racial justice in Arkansas and the personal fulfillment Ira Sanders derived from that quest marked all aspects of his life and did not go unnoticed by others. He frequently talked about these issues to his family, to numerous civic and community groups, and of course to his congregation. His inspirations for lectures and sermon topics, which he recalled were so often "linked with sociological issues of the day," often came to him just before he dropped off to sleep. "Many are the times I get out of bed," he told the *Arkansas Gazette* in 1952, "and jot down notes to be used in the week's sermon," frequently on topics such as "inter-racial problems" or other social concerns.[53] In 1951 the University of Arkansas awarded Rabbi Sanders an honorary doctorate, with the citation accompanying the honor singling out for merit his work in the field of racial justice: "You have worked consistently for the betterment of race relations. You have striven long and hard to better the conditions of all our people and to promote understanding of race relationships."[54] The occasion marked his twenty-fifth anniversary as rabbi of Congregation B'nai Israel. Sanders received congratulations from many people on the honorary doctorate, on his rabbinical anniversary, and on his efforts to improve the Little

Rabbi Sanders (*fourth from the left*) receives an honorary doctorate from Hebrew
Union College, March 27, 1954. Courtesy of UALR Center for Arkansas History
and Culture, Arkansas Studies Institute, Little Rock, Arkansas.

Rock community. Among them was M. Lafayette Harris, president of Little
Rock's historically black Philander Smith College, who recalled their halcyon
days together in the Depression-era struggle for racial justice: "I can remember
personally," he wrote, "the inspiration you were to me as we struggled to get the
Urban League organized. I also have in mind the great spiritual lift you have
given to our college community from time to time. We regard you as a friend
to all men." Jacob Blaustein, president of the American Jewish Committee,
thanked Sanders for "his devotion" to the "task of eliminating racial and religious prejudice," a task that will succeed "because to people like you com-
batting prejudice is an everyday, living practice and not merely an exercise in
dialectics."[55] Three years later, Hebrew Union College bestowed on Sanders the
honorary degree of doctor of divinity. HUC president Nelson Glueck emphasized Sanders' "dedicated work in furtherance of better race relations. Your
consecrated efforts have made you a symbol of the truth and of the dignity and
the nobility of the faith which you have so brilliantly preached."[56]

One such "consecrated effort" Sanders had made involved the desegregation of the Little Rock Public Library. Rabbi Sanders had joined the board of
the public library shortly after his arrival in 1926, beginning five decades of
service in that capacity. In 1948, Sanders and fellow board members Adolphine
Terry, a longtime community activist responsible for the formation of the
Little Rock Housing Association, and John N. "Ned" Heiskell, library board
president and publisher of the *Arkansas Gazette*, began advocating for African
American access to the main library in Little Rock. Adolphine Terry was the
prime mover, and she found a strong ally in Sanders and, to a lesser degree, in
Heiskell. However, the other members of the library board had reservations.
Some, displaying their own prejudices, suspected that African Americans
would not, or perhaps could not, comport themselves properly in the facility.
Indeed, one board member suggested that, prior to desegregation, the library
board should send notices to African American churches and ministers in the
area, instructing the clergy to inform the potential library customers among
their congregants that they must act and dress appropriately while in the
library. Dismayed and deeply offended by the very prospect of such an action,
Adolphine Terry asked him "who on earth he thought was coming, and what
people were coming for." Who made this suggestion is not known, but in fact it
may have been library board president Heiskell himself, who earlier had gone
on record opposed to the naming of a black board member.[57]

Prodded by Terry and Sanders, the board reluctantly relented on the desegregation issue and agreed in 1948 to an extremely limited integration. At first,
admission was granted to adults only, and only in small numbers, and only to
the main library — a small victory, but a victory nonetheless, and a platform on
which to build greater access for African Americans more quickly. The board
formally and more broadly desegregated the main library on January 15, 1951,
with a resolution passed five days earlier: "Resolved, first that the adult department of the main library be open to Negroes beginning with students of the
seventh grade and to all Negroes over the age of sixteen. Second, that Negroes
be required to make application for a library card in the same manner as white
patrons."[58] Thereafter, the main library opened its doors widely to adult black
patrons for the first time.

Community support such as that provided by newly hired Philander Smith
College history professor Georg C. Iggers in a November 1950 *Arkansas
Gazette* letter proved helpful and demonstrated community support for the
library's desegregation. In his letter, Iggers eloquently argued that the "only
solution" to the severe imbalance in the black and white branches of the library
lay in "opening the doors of the main library to all readers" regardless of race.

"The admission of our Negro fellow citizens to the Little Rock public library would be a meaningful expression of the adherence of the citizens of Little Rock to democracy and to American ideals."[59] But Professor Iggers was late to the party: the desegregation of the library was a years-long gradual process nearing completion by 1950. His letter is best seen as an example of the support for the overall moderate progression of racial acceptance then ongoing in Arkansas and in Little Rock particularly, and not as the cause of the library's desegregation.

After the library's initial desegregation, African Americans above the age of sixteen and students from the seventh grade forward were eligible for library cards and unfettered patronage of the main library. During the first seven months of integration, over 250 black patrons registered for cards and gained borrowing privileges.[60] Sanders also continued his work in a variety of community organizations, including his lobbying efforts on behalf of the Pulaski County Tuberculosis Association, an organization he had helped lead since 1927. As a result, in 1955, the city's highest-profile Jewish leader found himself in the somewhat unusual circumstance of urging contributions to the 1955 Christmas seal drive in order to reach the association's goal of $35,000.[61]

Sanders' role in the desegregation of the public library represented another successful challenge to the established racial hierarchy of Arkansas. His pursuit of color-blind welfare policies before and during the Great Depression, his activism in defying segregation and pursuing racial justice through organizations such as the NAACP, the Association of Southern Women for the Prevention of Lynching, and the Urban League of Greater Little Rock all helped set the stage for the momentous changes to come in the 1950s and 1960s. Having labored for social justice in the Little Rock community since 1926, Sanders had positioned himself to be a quiet yet powerful voice in support of the dramatic changes still to come. The civil rights movement would provide as yet unseen challenges for Ira Sanders, southern rabbis, and the southern Jewish community as a whole.

—6—

The Southern Rabbi Meets the Civil Rights Movement

1950–1957

OVER HIS LIFETIME, Rabbi Ira Sanders' outreach to the Little Rock African American community took on many forms. Sometimes it came in bold and controversial efforts to assist the community at large, such as when he attempted to integrate the Little Rock School of Social Work or when he played a role in creating the Urban League of Greater Little Rock. Others came as singularly personal one-to-one connections. An example of the latter occurred on a hot summer day in Little Rock in the mid-1950s. Mrs. Dorothy Woods Mitchell had come downtown to pay her water bill. An African American domestic worker who was both visibly pregnant and uncomfortably hot, she stood alone waiting for the bus at the corner of Fifth and Broadway in front of Temple B'nai Israel. Rabbi Sanders saw her as he approached the Temple, noticing her discomfort. He paused to speak to Mrs. Mitchell, checking on her well-being and asking if she'd like to come stand with him under the shade of a large bush next to the temple until the bus arrived. The two struck up a conversation. Sanders then invited Mrs. Mitchell into the temple "to look around" and cool off from the summer heat. He ended up giving her a personal guided tour of the synagogue as the two began a cordial friendship that lasted the rest of Sanders' life. Decades later, when Sanders, now an elderly widower, lived at the Riviera apartments, Mrs. Mitchell, who coincidently worked in the building, frequently would come by to visit. "Every time I'd see him, we'd have a conversation," she recalled. "He was so nice." She made a point always to visit on his birthday, and sometimes brought him homemade matzo ball soup.[1] She never forgot that simple act of kindness on that hot summer day. For Sanders' part, his desire to connect and to understand the lives and concerns of black Arkansans motivated his work in civil rights, whether through very public acts to challenge the status quo, or through quiet, personal acts of friendship and understanding.

By the mid-fifties, Sanders had already established a solid record of civil rights activism; indeed, in the decades prior to the US Supreme Court's 1954 landmark decision in *Brown v. Board of Education*, writes historian Clive Webb, "no southern rabbi had campaigned more rigorously against segregation than Ira Sanders of Little Rock." The 1950s mark the beginning of the most active years of the modern civil rights movement, and Ira Sanders' activism in the community continued as he took public steps to combat social and racial injustice. But his was not the typical response of the southern rabbi during the years of the civil rights struggle. Two hundred or so rabbis lived and worked in the South during the civil rights decades, with Reform rabbis making up a little more than half that number. Like Ira Sanders, several of these Reform rabbis played important roles in their communities to advance the cause of racial equality, acting in accordance with Reform Judaism's "prophetic mission to combat social injustice." But these rabbis, scattered across the South, never acted in concert; rather, they worked alone or where possible in ecumenical cooperation with ministers and clergy of Christian faiths. The rabbinic struggle for racial justice during the heyday of the civil rights movement, then, was often a solitary endeavor rife with dangers. The rabbis frequently faced resistance from within their own congregations and from the southern Jewish community at large, both of whom feared the potential for reprisals for their rabbi's works or, as members of a minority group themselves, the loss of their sense of security in the region. This congregational and community resistance sometimes cost rabbis their pulpits. There also lurked the frightening possibility of segregationist violence directed against the rabbi, his home, his synagogue, possibilities that became horribly real on a number of occasions throughout the civil rights struggle. These rabbis, then, had little to gain and much to lose in exchange for their fight against racial injustice.[2]

Well aware since the late 1920s of these pitfalls and the dangers of his activism on behalf of racial and social justice, Ira Sanders nevertheless stepped forthrightly into the struggle, leading not through protests or direct action campaigns, but through moral suasion, public addresses, newspaper interviews, community outreach, and pulpit offerings on the topic of racial and social justice. For Sanders, the civil rights movement represented the logical continuation of a struggle he had waged along a number of fronts in Little Rock since 1926. He had always been a champion of the dispossessed and of social and economic justice in general, but the struggle for racial equality held special significance for him. Of the many causes for social justice Ira Sanders championed, and of the many fights he quietly or publicly waged on behalf of others, none seemed more just and righteous to him than the fight for racial equality that raged across the South and the nation during the mid-twentieth century. His belief in the basic and essential equality of all people was grounded in his upbringing and in the tenets of both Reform Judaism and the profession of social work as well as his deep sense of personal empathy for the plight of others, and this belief came to the fore as he became more active for the cause. "I have always been a champion of the dignity of man. To me, the thing that counts most is your character. That's been my philosophy through the years. I've always championed the cause of those who are entitled to the same privileges of living as I am entitled to, and that in the sight of God, and certainly in the sight of our fellow man, we're all equal."[3] The cause of justice, of fair play, he wrote, quoting Jeremiah, "flamed in my heart," like "burning fire shut up in my bones."[4] He dedicated himself to furthering the cause. No southern rabbi matched Sanders' activism prior to *Brown*, and few would match his determination in fighting Jim Crow in the civil rights era. But he knew he could not wage this fight alone. Rabbi Sanders always maintained a steadfast belief in the values and virtues of interfaith alliances, and his affiliation with Little Rock clergy of all denominations served him well in the civil rights era. However, early in the struggle, Sanders found that he would have to sacrifice his participation in one such alliance in order to facilitate the cause of African American rights.

Ecumenicalism and Interfaith Alliances

I resign.
—IRA SANDERS, 1950

For years Sanders was a proud member of the Greater Little Rock Ministerial Alliance; he was the only Jewish clergyman in this otherwise all-Christian organization of local religious leaders. The alliance was also an all-white organization. In 1950, a proposed merger between that organization and its all-black counterpart, the Christian Ministerial Alliance, led to a meeting of the two groups to discuss the possibility of a single alliance. They met at the Phyllis Wheatley Young Women's Christian Association building, one of the only facilities where black and white Little Rock citizens could meet. Among the members present was Rabbi Sanders and a young seminarian from Yale Divinity School, Donald K. Campbell, an intern with Rev. Marion Boggs at Second Presbyterian Church in Little Rock. Campbell recalls that during the merger discussion, some of the more fundamentalist and conservative ministers among the black clergy objected to the merger solely on the basis of Rabbi Sanders' participation; in their view, the combined alliance had to be a Christian-only organization. As the discussion progressed, Campbell recalls, it became clear that no merger would take place if Sanders remained a member of the group. Sanders had long been affiliated with interfaith alliances in his years in Little Rock, and he found that being part of a larger group of interdenominational clergy made his work for racial and social justice more successful as well as more readily accepted in the Little Rock community. However, in order to promote the critically important goals of interracial dialogue and cooperation, Sanders decided in the moment to sacrifice his position in the group for what he perceived to be a greater good. "If my presence is blocking this [merger]," the rabbi told the gathering, then "I resign." Campbell later said this "selfless action made a great impression" on him.[5] The rabbi's resignation helped pave the way for the eventual creation of the Interracial Ministerial Alliance (IMA) in 1956, headed by Presbyterian minister Dunbar Ogden Jr. Sanders held Reverend Ogden in very high esteem, calling him "the finest example of Christian ideals that [he had] ever known."[6]

The IMA had a brief and shaky history. "It was the tension of the early integration days" that initially held that group together, writes Dunbar H. Ogden, son of IMA leader Reverend Ogden. "Within this biracial association a group of white ministers and a group of black ministers exchanged ideas, and from it they issued statements and exerted pro-integration pressure."[7] Sanders' act of voluntary exile from the group made possible both the merger of the associations and the IMA's subsequent work on behalf of racial justice.

The promotion of the ideals of equality and racial justice became the dominant theme of Sanders' activism in the 1950s, and he used his position as a respected community leader and frequent public speaker to great effect in promoting these ideals. It would not go unnoticed. "There is a gentleman," opined the *Arkansas Gazette* in 1950, "whose good works come to our attention ever so often. They come without benefit of a publicity chairman or a photographer—which is unusual in our existence. He is Dr. Ira Sanders. Somehow, his spirit of brotherhood pervades the area of our community with which we have to deal more than any person we can think of at the moment."[8] Then in February 1951, the Little Rock Rotary Club honored Sanders for his twenty-five years of service and community contributions. Sanders used the occasion to stress themes of racial equality which he couched in nonconfrontational and religious terms he believed would find wider acceptance: "All that is non-conformist and all that is democratic has gone into the making of this America," he said. "There is one law for the strong and weak, the rich and poor, alien and citizen, all races and creeds. It is important," he continued, "that we reaffirm the rights of man under God. We are responsible for the welfare of others, although this age seems to reject this principle. Many nations reject brotherhood for a blown-up racial philosophy — in such a world, America must reaffirm the principles of brotherhood." He drew sharp distinctions between the concepts of racial tolerance, a phrase he disdained, and racial acceptance: "We must not say 'tolerance,' looking down from superior heights. We must remind ourselves that brotherhood means for us to accept the wide differences in humanity and ask ourselves if we are always right and the others are always wrong."[9] Here, on the cusp of the modern civil rights movement, Sanders was laying the groundwork for the white community to accept the changes in the racial status quo to come. His messages of racial acceptance and equality, suffused with widely accepted Judeo-Christian principles, cloaked in dearly held traditions of democratic ideals, and delivered with unassailable logic, gravity, and eloquence, were designed to change attitudes and to create an atmosphere wherein change could occur peacefully and with general principled acceptance.

Southern Jews and the Civil Rights Movement

If we deny human rights, you might as well not live.
—IRA SANDERS, 1978

Being an outspoken Jew in favor of African American civil rights in the American South of the 1950s carried with it a large measure of risk. Many southern Jews, and most southern rabbis, worried that the protests and confrontational tactics of the civil rights movement might threaten traditional Jewish-gentile relations and Jewish acceptance within the larger southern Christian community. Southern Jews were well assimilated, and as a result the American South "boasted the lowest rate of anti-Jewish discrimination in the country." And because southern Jews were small in number — less than 1 percent of the overall population of the South — good relations with the larger community were essential.[10] In order to protect this standing, rabbis in the South such as Ira Sanders generally favored the use of moral suasion rather than direct action protests as their prime tool to move minds on the question of racial equality. This tactic, though, should not be confused with or interpreted as timidity; rather, because southern rabbis had the safety and standing of their congregants always in mind, they sought to influence change while simultaneously insulating and protecting their congregations and southern Jewry in general. Reform rabbis in the South remained mindful of the potential dangers of their activism to their congregants. Several among their numbers were eager to enlist in the civil rights movement, but their dual responsibilities — to their congregation and the larger Jewish community and to the struggle for black equality — tempered their actions.

Even so, a few southern rabbis — Sanders among them — took courageous steps beyond moral suasion and toward greater public challenges to segregation.[11] Sanders never feared the exposure of his racially progressive ideas. His long years of community service had made him a familiar figure to Arkansans, who regarded him as much a civic father as a rabbi. He also frequently spoke out alongside like-minded Catholic and Protestant clergy in order both to present a united religious front against prejudice and to help insulate the Jewish community from any potential backlash from his activism. This interfaith cooperation helped provide that measure of insulation; for example, his February 1951 remarks about cultural pluralism and racial equality appeared in the *Arkansas Gazette* alongside equally progressive remarks from Catholic bishop Albert Fletcher and Greater Little Rock Ministerial Alliance president Rev. Eulis Hill.[12]

The fact that many southern Jews outside the rabbinate were merchants and retailers made them particularly sensitive to majority public opinion, perhaps more so than other members of the community. After all, their livelihoods depended in large measure upon community good will. Jews feared community-wide reprisals as well; that is, if an individual member of the Jewish community held a widely unpopular or publicly-challenged opinion, the fear was that the entire Jewish community might be targeted for retribution.[13] The hostile reaction on the part of many southern whites to the US Supreme Court school desegregation decision *Brown v. Board of Education* in 1954 created deep-seated concerns for southern Jews, many of whom feared an erosion of their standing and relationship with the white Christian South. Would those white southern Christians who opposed integration see their Jewish neighbors primarily as white, like themselves, or primarily as Jews — like African Americans, a perceived "other" among them?[14] The *National Jewish Post and Opinion* reported in October 1958 that while the Jewish children in Little Rock public high schools "to a man" supported integration, many feared saying so in public because of potential retaliation.[15]

Anger and resentment about a perceived "Jewish position" favorable to racial integration could easily spill over into overt acts of anti-Semitism. Indeed, these were exactly the circumstances surrounding the bombing of a Reform temple in Atlanta, the Hebrew Benevolent Congregation, also known simply as "the Temple," on October 12, 1958. Segregationists bombed that facility, its rabbi Jacob Rothschild later said, "because I was so obviously identified with the Civil Rights Movement."[16] From November 1957 to October 1958, eight southern synagogues were bombed, some in areas of outspoken Jewish support for civil rights, and others in areas where Jews had remained relatively silent on the issue. Many southern Jews also feared for themselves when northern Jewish civil rights workers came to their areas to work in the movement, in their eyes potentially endangering the local Jewish community. Locals often implored them, "Please, do not endanger us, do not get our synagogue bombed."[17]

A sharp rise in anti-Semitic literature in the early fifties sought to draw a link between black civil rights and an imagined Jewish-communist-Zionist conspiracy. Many white obstructionists trumpeted such a connection to promote views of the civil rights movement through the lens of Cold War paranoia as nothing more than a communist-directed plot against the United States, in which Jews provided the connection between the movement and the Kremlin. The segregationist Capital Citizens' Council of Little Rock employed this very tactic against Sanders and the Little Rock Jewish community, cloaking their anti-Semitism and support for segregation in the veneer of anticommunism.[18] Louisiana judge Leander Perez provides perhaps the most vivid example of the tactic of intersecting the anti-Semitic argument with the anticommunist and segregationist arguments. Perez labeled the *Brown* decision "Communist trash" and saw the civil rights movement as a Zionist-communist conspiracy to force miscegenation in order to "breed an America too lazy and weak" to resist the encroachment of international communism. American Jews, he insisted, were the link between the Kremlin and the movement.[19] Admittedly, Perez is an extreme example, but his views were nevertheless held by many white southerners either as genuine beliefs or, more often, as rationalizations to maintain the existing racial hierarchy of the South and halt the advance of the African American freedom movement by tying that movement to the nearly universally dreaded specter of communism.

Well before the Supreme Court's *Brown* decision of May 17, 1954, Ira Sanders had taken a public stand for racial justice. Unlike many southern rabbis, he did not fear his photo or his comments on the topic appearing in the newspapers, as they frequently did. His 1951 speech to the Little Rock Rotary Club, largely reprinted in the pages of Little Rock's progressive-minded *Arkansas Gazette*, had warned that "flouting moral law brings disaster." No class should dominate another, nor should inequality be manifest in the law. Sanders had stressed not tolerance, which implies hierarchy, but racial acceptance and equality. Three years before *Brown*, then, he was moving minds on the race issue and hoping to inspire people to action. After *Brown*, which the rabbi approvingly said "unquestionably" caused "the greatest social upheaval in the twentieth century," he redoubled his efforts, arguing that "if we deny human rights, you might as well not live because everybody has a right under the sun." Americans regardless of race "must be given the privilege of fulfilling [themselves] through human rights, through the justice and the brotherhood which are necessary for the preservation of the human race."[20] He spoke again about equality and acceptance before the Rotarians in November 1954, six months after the Court's landmark school desegregation decision, in the midst of the growing uproar about it. Little Rock school board member Louise McLean commended Sanders on his strong comments in favor of racial and social justice: "I am particularly conscious at this time of the very few persons courageous enough to speak out for the truth. I would be very proud if any spokesman for the church with which I am affiliated had the brains and the fortitude to make such a talk in this our 'Bible Belt.' Count me in the camp of followers of liberal intelligent leadership like yours."[21]

The Southern Rabbi

The Jewish leaders . . . were committed to the status quo.
—IRA SANDERS, 1963

Ira Sanders' activism is better understood when laid side by side with the experiences of his fellow southern rabbis of the era. Concerns over segregationist reprisals against the Jewish community for the activism of its rabbis constrained many southern rabbis during the civil rights movement. Like Ira Sanders, most southern rabbis supported racial desegregation, but unlike Sanders, most also took either no public stand on the issue or very careful, controlled measures. Deep South rabbis showed a greater degree of trepidation than their Upper South colleagues. For example, Rabbi Martin Hinchin of Alexandria, Louisiana, explained how he protected the local Jewish community: "[While] I have my own ideas [on the subject], I don't foist them upon my own congregation." Rabbi Eugene Blachschleger of Temple Beth Or in Montgomery, Alabama, also remained silent, including throughout the 1955–56 Montgomery Bus Boycott and the other momentous activities involving desegregation in his city. He said, "[I] made no public pronouncements on [desegregation] either from my pulpit or in the columns of our daily press."[22]

Blachschleger's was a tortured and imposed silence. His congregation and community would not tolerate his speaking out. "When I shave in the morning," he confessed to Albert Vorspan, director of the Commission on Social Action of the UAHC, "I cannot look at myself in the mirror because I know as a Jew what is right and what is wrong, and I cannot say it."[23] His silence was a source of consternation for Southern Christian Leadership Conference

(SCLC) leader Dr. Martin Luther King Jr.: "The national Jewish bodies have been most helpful [in the civil rights movement], but the local Jewish leadership has been silent. Montgomery Jews want to bury their heads and repeat that it is not a Jewish problem." King said he wanted them "to join with us on the side of justice."[24] Blachschleger offered Rabbi Sanders moral support during the 1957 Little Rock Central High School desegregation crisis, writing in a letter to Sanders that he understood his "position and anxiety" over the situation, having gone through similar community traumas the previous year, a clear reference to the upheaval in Montgomery over the bus boycott of 1955–56.[25] But Blachschleger's experiences veered very far from those of Sanders; for years, the Little Rock rabbi had taken very public stands for integration and had spoken out with regularity on the issues of race and equality, while Rabbi Blachschleger, in a much more hostile segregationist environment, had done none of these things.

Years later, another Sanders colleague, Rabbi Charles Mantinband of Hattiesburg, Mississippi, perhaps unaware of the Montgomery rabbi's inner turmoil, was still taking Blachschleger to task. He sternly criticized Blachschleger as part of the "sorry spectacle" of inaction he saw around him among southern rabbis during the civil rights movement. In a 1963 letter to *Carolina Israelite* publisher and writer Harry Golden, Mantinband singled out Blachschleger as having "remained conspicuously silent not only at the time of the Montgomery bus boycott but throughout the entire desegregation crisis."[26] The risks involved in the actions taken by the activist rabbis of the South such as Ira Sanders are all the more striking when considered alongside the inaction of many of their colleagues.

A 1961 survey found that while 97 percent of northern Jews supported the *Brown* desegregation decision, a full 40 percent of southern Jews called it "unfortunate." Like many white Southerners in general, many southern Jews believed the pace of integration was too quick. Memphis rabbi James Wax wrote with disapproval in 1959 that Southern Jews in general "neither express integrationist sentiments nor identify themselves with an integrationist movement."[27] Accordingly, only a handful of Southern rabbis stepped forward publicly and forcefully to combat Jim Crow in the South after World War II, and since fully 75 percent of southern Jewish congregations were Reform, the rabbis engaged in the civil rights movement were almost all Reform rabbis. Conservative and Orthodox rabbis played a much smaller role both in interfaith activities and in publicly supporting racial integration.[28] Many rabbis, Reform, Conservative, and Orthodox, however, agreed with Louisiana rabbi Martin Hinchin, who, while personally supporting a measured and gradual form of integration, did

not take a public position on the issue: "I don't want to harm the Jewish community in any way, shape, or form." One cannot "legislate sociology," he stated.[29]

The actions of rabbis working for the cause of racial desegregation did at
times directly incite reactionary segregationist violence or reprisals. However,
a rabbi's or a congregation's level of support or nonsupport for civil rights
reforms did not seem to correlate much at all with incidents of anti-Semitic
violence in the South. According to a 1958–59 study by Albert Vorspan, chair
of the UAHC Commission on Social Action, almost all southern Reform rabbis
supported civil rights, though to widely varying degrees of intensity. Though
some Southern rabbis faced opposition to their activism from within their own
congregations, few were constrained by their temple or synagogue boards, as
"most rabbis will not stand for a controlled pulpit."[30] However, the acts and
threats of violence against Jewish communities, according to Vorspan, "reveal
a crazy-quilt pattern" not at all reflective of the actual level of Jewish pro-civil
rights activism. Vorspan reported that while an unnamed outspoken rabbi in
Mississippi was not threatened with violence due to his activism, a synagogue
in Jacksonville, Florida, "in which there had never been a discussion of the
segregation issue was ripped by a bomb." Segregationists also bombed two
North Carolina synagogues, though neither their congregations nor their rabbis played any role in desegregation issues. Meanwhile, the synagogue of vocal
civil rights advocate and Rabbi William Silverman in Nashville, Tennessee, was
left untouched. The attacks seemed more related to the local segregationists'
latent anti-Semitism and the general and evolving atmosphere of defiance of
the law that bred violence than to the overt actions of the Jewish community
or their rabbis.[31]

Ira Sanders' work on behalf of racial justice in Arkansas did not occur in
a vacuum. It occurred amidst the valiant struggles of pioneering civil rights
organizers ranging from Dr. Martin Luther King Jr. and other ministers of the
SCLC, to the activists of the Student Nonviolent Coordinating Committee and
the Congress of Racial Equality, to civil rights workers of every race and background across the South. A handful of southern Reform rabbis including Ira
Sanders joined in this civil rights activism in the 1950s and 1960s, also working
for social and racial justice and often advocating different strategies for success
largely dependent upon their various and diverse local social and political cli-
mates. William Silverman of Nashville, Tennessee; Emmet Frank of Alexandria,
Virginia; Perry Nussbaum of Jackson, Mississippi; Charles Mantinband of
Hattiesburg, Mississippi; and Jacob Rothschild of Atlanta, Georgia, all took
stands for civil rights that resembled that of Ira Sanders of Little Rock. Each
faced unique challenges brought by their local circumstances.[32]

Although Nashville rabbi William Silverman's temple escaped bombing, he received multiple death threats for himself and his children, and the city's Jewish community center was bombed. As a result, Silverman began carrying a handgun for protection, earning the nickname "Pistol-Packing Rabbi" as a result. He served Nashville from 1950 to 1960, remaining the object of near-constant harassment. In addition to the community center bombing, Nashville suffered from other acts of segregationist violence including school bombings and the painting of swastikas on synagogues and homes. The city saw more violence than Little Rock, despite its moderate white leadership; indeed, Nashville was a key center of the civil rights movement, and some of its most noteworthy achievements, including the successful sit-ins leading to the integration of the department store lunch counters in 1960, among the earliest such direct action protests in the South. Like Ira Sanders, Rabbi Silverman regularly spoke out on racial equality. "I always spoke on the question," he told Allen Krause in 1966. "I spoke very bluntly from my pulpit and some members of the congregation didn't like it, others loved it." Like Sanders of Little Rock, Silverman did not have to face many congregants who tried to restrain or muzzle him.[33] But unlike Sanders of Little Rock, Silverman was rarely quoted in the press, even though he was quite forthright in his views on racial egalitarianism: "I have been called a 'nigger-lover.' This is true. I love Negroes and those who are yellow, brown, and white. Isn't that what religion teaches? The Negro is my brother, a child of God, created in the divine image."[34]

As in Arkansas's capital city of Little Rock, Mississippi's capital city of Jackson had a highly assimilated Jewish community "indistinguishable in ideology," a local rabbi reported, from the larger community. The difference between the two cities lay in what "assimilated" meant in these disparate communities. For Little Rock, it meant acclimation to a racial atmosphere that had become dramatically more moderate in the years after World War II. Gradual public desegregation measures and progressive change had been quietly and successfully underway for some years, for the most part leaving behind the harshest aspects of Jim Crow typical of the nadir of race relations. In Jackson, though, the local racial atmosphere was a static and toxic mix of segregationist intimidation and overt white supremacy. In 1956, Jackson rabbi Perry Nussbaum described a much more hostile local milieu than that which faced Ira Sanders: a community environment producing a "steady diet of viciousness and vituperation," wrote Nussbaum, was met by a local Protestant clergy largely offering either overt support for segregation or, at best, "silent acquiescence," and a Mississippi state legislature determinedly "churning out laws guaranteed to insure the purity of the white race." Such a severe environment with little or no meaningful community or interfaith support constrained Rabbi Nussbaum in what he could accomplish. Given this acute lack of support, he might have been expected to be publicly more cautious—both for the sake of his personal safety and for the safety of his congregants—than some of his contemporaries.

Yet Nussbaum chose to act for racial and social justice in a variety of ways, including his many visits in 1961 providing food and spiritual comfort to jailed Freedom Riders being held at Parchman, Mississippi's notorious state penitentiary. Nussbaum's continued activism within the larger vacuum of community support resulted in eventual bombings by segregationists, only months apart in 1967, of both Temple Beth Israel and the rabbi's own home. Nussbaum believed southern rabbis needed help in the form of strong interfaith cooperation. In 1956 he wrote, "If there were some public Christian leadership [in Jackson], even toward moderation, this would have been a different report."[35] Probably the greatest difference between the Jackson and Little Rock situations was the degree to which interfaith cooperation aided Ira Sanders' cause, while the profound lack of such solidarity hampered Rabbi Nussbaum.

Nussbaum's activism drew stern criticism from some concerned southern rabbis who feared a change for the worse in the largely positive status quo of Jew-gentile relations in the South. Birmingham rabbi Milton Grafman, an advocate of more measured civil rights reform and a critic of the SCLC's Birmingham protest campaign of 1963, was not pleased with Nussbaum's support of the Freedom Riders, many of whom were northern Jews and whom Grafman condemned "for upsetting the balance between [southern] Jews and their white neighbors." Likewise, Cleveland, Mississippi rabbi Moses Landau "condemned Nussbaum for his violation of the South's unwritten rules on issues of race," believing his actions threatened his congregation. The bombing of Jackson's Temple Beth Israel six years later seemingly confirmed Landau's concerns. "I am paid by my congregation," Landau wrote, "and as long as I eat their bread, I shall not do anything that might harm any member of my congregation without their consent." Allan Schwartzman, a rabbi in Greenville, Mississippi, among others, fully agreed with Landau.[36] Many other southern rabbis, despite personal feelings favorable to equal treatment and desegregation, nevertheless publicly remained quiet for reasons such as these.

Nussbaum emphasized a lack of interfaith cooperation as a critical factor in his difficulties in Jackson, and Atlanta's Jacob Rothschild also emphasized such cooperation as a key to success. "I do not believe that the rabbi in today's South will serve any good purpose in leading crusades." Instead, wrote Rothschild, "let him labor alongside others of like mind and dedicated purpose."[37] Like Sanders, Rothschild also never shied away from public pronouncements in favor of desegregation. He had expressed disappointment in Pres. Dwight Eisenhower's tepid response to the *Brown* decision. The president had personally and privately hoped the court would uphold the "separate but equal" precedent of *Plessy v. Ferguson* and had pulled chief justice Earl Warren aside at a White House dinner prior to the *Brown* decision, telling him of white southern segregationists, "These are not bad people. All they are concerned about is to see that their sweet little girls are not required to sit in school alongside some big overgrown Negroes."[38] Eisenhower's belief that "you can't legislate the hearts of men" led Rabbi Rothschild to retort "laws do not wait for general acceptance—they stimulate and coerce a way of life that is better."[39] Both Sanders in Little Rock and Rothschild in Atlanta spoke out in a variety of settings regarding integration and racial justice. Active in a number of civic organizations, Rothschild used his oratorical skills to great effect. But though his approach differed in many ways from that of Jackson's Perry Nussbaum, the same outcome resulted. On October 12, 1958, segregationists armed with fifty sticks of dynamite blew apart Rothschild's Temple in Atlanta, causing an entire wall to collapse and partially destroying the facility. Atlanta's was the fifth such bombing incident in the South over an eight-month span.[40]

In Hattiesburg, Mississippi, Rabbi Charles Mantinband had great difficulties with both his congregation and his congregational board, who told him "in no uncertain terms that they would prefer their rabbi remain silent, if not neutral, on the segregation issue." Mantinband would not remain silent, and he told the board as much, but he and his temple board did find it possible to coexist for a time, only because they agreed "in principle, if not in method."[41] That coexistence did not last, however. By 1964, Mantinband had tired of his congregation's constant efforts to censure him anytime he manifested any activism regarding race. He found the challenges to his authority, the persistent criticism, and his congregation's attempts at censorship unacceptable. The pressure of such a constrained rabbinate finally forced Mantinband out. "They made it so miserable for him," one temple member recalled. The Hattiesburg rabbi accepted an offer from a congregation in Longview, Texas, and then resigned.[42] Arthur Levin, southern regional director of the Anti-Defamation League (ADL) from 1948 to 1962, had proudly pointed to Charles Mantinband as an "example of a rabbi who was outspoken and who made no compromises with his conscience and his congregation."[43] In his local environment, though, such courage and outspokenness had cost Mantinband his pulpit.

Both personally and professionally, Mantinband and Sanders were alike in many ways: they were virtually the same age, both came from the Upper South (Sanders from Missouri, Mantinband from Virginia), both had spent time as students in New York universities, both pointed to that educational experience as transformative, and most importantly they shared a deep sense of the "oneness" of people despite the seeming barriers of race. Both men absorbed the concepts and practice of social justice and activism present both explicitly and implicitly in Reform Judaism. The two rabbis differed in that Sanders was raised from the age of six in Kansas City and then from adolescence in Cincinnati, while Mantinband's formative years were in the more racially conservative Norfolk, Virginia. Mantinband "grew up with an unquestioning acceptance of the racial [segregationist] teachings he received both at home and in the classroom." He overcame those teachings, however, once he had experiences with African Americans outside the oppressive strictures of the Jim Crow South: "After considerable struggle I learned to exercise control in my attitude and make no distinction between one man and another."[44] Ira Sanders' experiences going "to school with all peoples" in Kansas City and in Cincinnati, as well as in the integrated classrooms of Columbia University, both reflected and helped mold his attitudes regarding racial equality. In Mantinband's case, racially integrated classes at the City College of New York helped shape his egalitarian attitudes and dispel the racial propaganda of his youth.[45]

In Little Rock, Ira Sanders faced some of the same obstacles and overt dangers presented to Jacob Rothschild, albeit to a lesser degree, but he faced nothing approaching the difficulties presented to Rabbis Silverman, Nussbaum, and Mantinband. There are several reasons for this: for one, regarding the question of racial integration, Sanders lived and worked in a moderate city within a state that was becoming more moderate. Little Rock's city fathers and business leaders favored compromise over confrontation with the civil rights movement. The postwar reforms such as those of the Sidney McMath administration, coupled with the general acceptance of a measured integration, had by the early 1950s created a much more racially moderate atmosphere than the harsh Jim Crow climate that marked Arkansas and Little Rock in earlier decades. The city had adapted gradually to the changing racial dynamics of the era. Jackson, Hattiesburg, Birmingham, Montgomery, and even Atlanta, along with the states they belonged to, represented much harsher, more overtly racist environments in the 1950s than did Little Rock or Arkansas. In addition, by the time of the *Brown* decision in 1954, Sanders already had labored in the state for nearly thirty years to build strong interfaith alliances. He had established himself as a trusted, constructive, and familiar presence in the community—as a social worker and civic father known as much for his work in education and social welfare as for racial acceptance. Rabbi Sanders enjoyed a much higher degree of interfaith cooperation from both Catholic and Protestant clergy than did Mantinband or Nussbaum when they sought such assistance. Regarding his congregation, Sanders' own recollection was that, unlike Rabbi Mantinband of Hattiesburg, he had little to no objections from his congregation or board of trustees over his activism: "practically no one in the congregation," he said, protested his civil rights activities.[46] These factors gave Ira Sanders advantages and inroads to greater activism that many other southern rabbis simply did not enjoy.

Other factors worked in Sanders' favor to create a more moderate atmosphere within which the rabbi could effectively pursue social justice goals in Little Rock. In many other rabbis' cities, campaigns of transformative, community-disrupting direct actions of civil disobedience often triggered violent reactions. The participants in the 1955–56 Montgomery Bus Boycott faced a year of violence and intimidation. In 1960, sit-ins in Nashville badly disrupted the downtown area and resulted in violence against student demonstrators. In 1961, Freedom Riders faced bombing and brutalization. Birmingham segregationists met the 1963 freedom struggle in that city with fire hoses, bombings, and murder. Yet these types of confrontational direct action campaigns either did not occur in Little Rock or did not produce the same violent results when they did occur. Although the 1957 Central High crisis in Little Rock precipitated large crowds and some violence around the school, the desegregation of the school was neither a direct action campaign nor an act of civil disobedience in the same mode as a sit-in or a protest march, but rather an action in fulfillment of a federal mandate. Additionally, what violence did occur did not spill over into the city at large. The Freedom Riders' arrival in Little Rock in 1961 precipitated neither violence nor large-scale community resistance because, as John Kirk relates, city leaders intervened, fearful of negative press in the face of potential racial violence, and facilitated the riders' peaceful departure from the state after their arrests.

When several nonviolent sit-ins occurred in downtown Little Rock department store lunch counters from 1960 to 1962, led in large part by Philander Smith College students, the result was the peaceful desegregation of those lunch counters in January 1963 after negotiations and efforts by the city leaders to keep racial division out of the headlines. Almost no public confrontation or violent reaction occurred, primarily because the downtown businesses and community leaders did not want to suffer the economic consequences of racial unrest. They formed the Downtown Negotiating Committee to meet with local African American leaders in order to peacefully resolve the conflict by agreeing to a gradual integration of downtown businesses and lunch counters. Bill Hansen, a veteran of the Student Nonviolent Coordinating Committee who came to Little Rock to assist the sit-in movement, observed as much. He said that based on what he had seen, "There would be no widespread consternation among the white community if Negroes were served at the lunch counters."[47] This event represented the moderate path to racial progress to which Sanders subscribed. It avoided the potential collisions that polarized other southern cities, made compromise more difficult, and shut down many southern rabbis, such as Eugene Blachschleger of Montgomery, for fear of violent retribution against the local Jewish community. By the end of 1963, with little fanfare, Little Rock had for the most part desegregated all its public facilities and many of its private ones a year before the mandate to do so was presented by the 1964 Civil Rights Act. Without the violence that precipitated the hardening of positions and often blocked effective compromise or negotiation, Ira Sanders had an easier, more moderate path open to him than did Reform rabbis and activists in many other southern cities. Less racial confrontation created a gentler atmosphere, which in turn facilitated compromise, which enhanced Sanders' ability to lead through persuasion in Little Rock.

Sanders shared certain traits with another Southern rabbi, Emmet Frank of Alexandria, Virginia, who was most widely known for his vociferous assault on segregation and on one of its greatest champions, US senator from Virginia Harry Byrd, an architect of southern white resistance to integration. In October 1958, Rabbi Frank took the pulpit of his temple in Alexandria, Virginia, for the Kol Nidre service on the eve of Yom Kippur, the Day of Atonement, one of the holiest nights of the Jewish year, and ripped into the segregationist senator and his cause. The seriousness and solemnity of the occasion lent additional gravity to his remarks. "Let the segregationists foam at the mouth. There is only one word to describe their madness—Godlessness, or to coin a new synonym—Byrdliness. Byrdliness has done more harm to the stability of our country than McCarthyism."[48] More than a year before Frank's headline-making blast against Byrd and segregation, Ira Sanders himself would take center stage in the chambers of the Arkansas General Assembly in Little Rock in order to mount a titanic verbal assault of his own against segregation and the politicians that defended it amidst the most significant civil rights crisis in Arkansas history, the integration of Little Rock Central High School.

— 7 —

The Central High Crisis and Beyond

1957–1963

SOCIOLOGIST S. I. GOLDSTEIN wrote in 1953 that in America, the rabbi must be "teacher, scholar, educator, preacher, prayer leader, pastor, organizer, administrator, and — most important for our present purposes — ambassador of good will to the non-Jewish world."[1] When Arkansas governor Orval Faubus took obstructionist actions to prevent the desegregation of Little Rock Central High School, plunging the city into tumult, Rabbi Ira Sanders of necessity played all of these roles and more. The rabbi's boldest stance for social and racial justice came with the Little Rock Central High School crisis of 1957–59. Governor Faubus' actions at the beginning of the 1957 school year garnered international attention, and the crisis atmosphere lasted two full years, beginning in February with legislation designed to circumvent the US Supreme Court's desegregation orders, and culminating in Faubus' decision to block the integration with military force and the accompanying mob violence around the high school. This led the president to order a federal military presence to uphold the Supreme Court mandate and restore order to the situation, and finally the governor ordered the closing of the public schools in 1958, an action made legal by newly-adopted acts of the Arkansas legislature. Throughout this tumultuous period, as Little Rock quite unexpectedly became the face of defiance of court-ordered school desegregation, Ira Sanders provided dramatic leadership on behalf of racial justice. Although the Little Rock Jewish community at large acted with caution and reticence during the crisis, Sanders and a few others within that community took public stands for desegregation. But this leadership came at a cost. More than once, Sanders endured threats against his life; in addition, segregationists angered by his actions targeted Jewish businesses with boycotts and economic pressure, and radical factions opposed to integration made bomb threats against Temple B'nai Israel.

Following the Central High School crisis, Rabbi Sanders returned to the problem of segregation in general and to housing inequality specifically. The Greater Little Rock Conference on Religion and Human Relations, later called the Greater Little Rock Conference on Religion and Race, which Sanders cofounded in 1963, worked diligently for several years to end segregation in religious life as well as put an end to housing discrimination and the ghettoization of some Little Rock neighborhoods. The year 1963 also marked the end of Ira Sanders' rabbinate at Congregation B'nai Israel, potentially the end of an era in Little Rock and Arkansas history.

Standing before the Legislature

The dignity of the individual must never be destroyed . . . .
—IRA SANDERS, 1957

In early 1957, the Arkansas General Assembly stood poised to vote on four proposals designed to frustrate and circumvent the US Supreme Court's desegregation orders handed down in the *Brown v. Board of Education* decisions of 1954 and 1955. State representative Lucien Rogers of Rogers, Arkansas, introduced the bills: House Bill 322 would allow for the creation of a "state sovereignty commission" ostensibly to protect Arkansans against the encroachments of the federal government. House Bill 323 would allow parents to keep their children out of integrated schools. House Bill 324 would force "certain organizations"—that is, the NAACP—to register with the state, thereby forcing the organization to divulge the names and addresses of its membership, making them vulnerable to segregationist retribution. House Bill 325 would provide state-funded legal assistance to Arkansas school districts for the purpose of retaining legal counsel to fight the integration orders.[2] These four measures taken together would erect a formidable barrier against desegregation in Arkansas. The house adopted all four measures without debate and with only one dissenting vote, but public furor over the rapid adoption of the measures forced the state senate to approve, albeit by a margin of a single vote, an open hearing at which the public would be invited to speak on the measures.[3] Rabbi Sanders determined to speak at that session in opposition to the obstructionist laws.

The public hearing convened in the chambers of the Arkansas General Assembly on the evening of February 18, 1957. Nine hundred people packed the house chamber, with many others on the steps outside where they could hear, if not see, the proceedings. The six hundred people crowding the gallery were mostly African American, while the three hundred or so on the floor were almost all white. The large-scale opposition to the four measures had shaken the confidence of the supporters of the four measures. For three hours and ten minutes on that cool February evening, the senate heard impassioned arguments both for and against the measures. The first to take the speaker's platform, attorney R. B. McCulloch of Forrest City, Arkansas, the author of House Bill 322, spoke in favor of that bill, and the crowd on the floor "applauded loudly several times." Dr. Hoyt Chastain, the pastor of Second Baptist Church of Malvern, Arkansas, was one of several clergymen there to speak on the fate of the four bills. Chastain supported their passage: "One of the principle reasons I am *for* segregation," he stated, "is that Communists are *against* it." Ben Laney of Camden, who had been Arkansas's thirty-third governor (1945–49) and was a staunch supporter of "states' rights," also voiced his support of the bills, despite his visceral personal dislike of the grandstanding Orval Faubus.[4]

Joining Sanders in speaking out against the four measures were ministers and pastors from Baptist, Methodist, Presbyterian, Catholic, and other churches from around the state as well as several laypersons including labor leaders and politicians. Even the editorial page of the progressive *Arkansas Gazette* opined, "The real issue is not segregation but basic individual rights."[5] Although not necessarily acquainted one with another, most of the clergymen who spoke at the special session stood united in their opposition to the anti-integration bills. Rev. William Byrd of Pine Bluff's First Methodist Church and Rev. William L. Miller of the First Christian Church (Disciples of Christ) in Rogers, Arkansas, spoke against the bills. Miller, president of the Arkansas State Convention of Christian Churches, warned of "dark days of inquisition ahead" if the bills, especially House Bill 324, passed the Senate. Already on record as a strong opponent of the proposed state sovereignty commission, he had earlier characterized it as "so similar to those which prevail in certain fascist and communist nations today." Odell Smith of Little Rock, president of the Arkansas State Federation of Labor, agreed with Miller and characterized the bills as having more in harmony with fascism and communism than democracy.[6]

Rev. Roland S. Smith of Little Rock's historic First Missionary Baptist Church, founded in 1845 as First Negro Baptist Church, was the only African American to address the gathering, and he spoke defiantly in opposition to the bills. According to both the *Arkansas Gazette* and Arkansas NAACP leader Daisy Bates, who was in the gallery to hear the speeches, Reverend Smith's was one of the "most impassioned" speeches of the session. Smith noted that "Negroes had been 'separate but equal' for more than sixty years, during which time they had demonstrated love and loyalty to the United States." Faith in God, he stated, would bring justice and righteousness between the races.[7] Already well known in the Little Rock area as an outspoken advocate of desegregation, Smith had led a group of local ministers to meet with Governor Faubus in February 1956 in an ultimately unsuccessful attempt to move him on the question of integration. His appearance in the legislature, reported the *Arkansas Gazette*, caused "a perceptible softening of the noise on the floor and in the gallery." Later, the Reverend V. O. Wright of Little Rock's Immanuel Baptist Church said the bills would set up "a political gestapo," while Monsignor James E. O'Connell, rector of St. John's Seminary in Little Rock, also compared the measures to those of Hitler's Germany. He stated that "the dominant principle of Nazism was its subscription to segregation and the cardinal principle of the master race."[8]

Rabbi Sanders, the only Jewish speaker of the evening, ignored the advice of several friends who asked him not to speak lest his life be in jeopardy. Sanders recalled the evening as "so intense." He said, "The chambers were jammed with all sorts of people, a tremendous crowd."[9] The hundreds of people who had packed into the chambers to hear the speeches had been quite vocal, applauding and booing various speakers. When his turn to speak came, Sanders took his position behind the microphone. With eyes fixed on the senators and in a bold and resonant voice, the rabbi used all the moral suasion at his command in an attempt to kill the bills. Hecklers and taunts frequently interrupted his address, but Sanders plowed through the dissension, determined to make his points. He had crafted a careful yet powerful message tailor-made for this overwhelmingly Christian audience of lawmakers before him. Accordingly, his address stressed three themes: the moral, "Christian" aspect of racial justice, the "pocketbook" issues related to the potential loss of business, investment, and tax revenues should the state be perceived as having a hostile environment or taking steps backward, and the legal principles of federalism and state acquiescence to the rulings of the United States Supreme Court, the US Constitution, and federal law in general.

Standing before the assembly, Sanders began by attempting to insulate the local Jewish community from any backlash his comments might produce. He had served as the rabbi of Congregation B'nai Israel for nearly thirty-one years and was well-known as its rabbi, but he began by stating that he spoke only for himself: "Tonight I speak as a private citizen [representing] no organization and no group." He continued, "The state of Arkansas is very dear to me. It has provided me the opportunity to serve many causes in social welfare, touching both colored and white citizens, Jews and Christians alike." He told the lawmakers of his fears regarding the negative impact of the four laws both on the state and more broadly on the foundations of American freedom. "Our

Rabbi Sanders addresses the Arkansas Senate and a standing-room-only crowd on February 18, 1957. Photo courtesy of the *Arkansas Democrat-Gazette*.

nation," Sanders said, "must be based on liberty and justice for all peoples," whose "contributions to the cultural pluralism of our land" have been great. The "dignity of the individual must never be destroyed by granting the state those powers which would deny anyone the liberty and the freedom guaranteed by the Constitution." The four anti-integration measures, he stated, were "all concerned with the thought of circumventing the highest legal authority of our land. They will never stand the test of time, for higher than the legal law of the land stands this moral law of God. It operates slowly, but surely, and in the end justice will prevail." Like the prophet Isaiah he had so diligently studied, Sanders portended an ominous future for his fellow Arkansans should the legislature choose this path.[10]

Sanders turned to the legislature's recent passage of a package of tax measures and other economic incentives designed to lure businesses to Arkansas. He warned, "What you have done to bring industry into the state will be overwhelmingly nullified" by the enactment of the bills. From his previous experiences with Pulaski County welfare agencies in years past, where he had successfully used this "pocketbook" tactic to address the question of equitable distribution of money between black and white recipients, Sanders knew that the financial consequences of the loss of investments and business revenue in Arkansas might register with those unmoved by his moral or his legal arguments. Since World War II, civic and business leaders in Little Rock had worked in tandem to attract jobs and new business investments to the state. Sanders knew that businesses in general were very leery of investments in communities experiencing the instability and violence that might accompany massive resistance to public school integration. He used this information in his attempt to move the senators on the question of the four bills, calling them measures that denied "America's traditional guarantees of individual freedom and liberty." He warned, "The state you and I love will lose first an increased economy coming from new industries, and secondly it will be held morally in just opprobrium before the country."[11]

Finally, aware that he stood before a nearly universally Christian audience of legislators and spectators, Sanders tried to persuade them with a concluding appeal based on their faith. "When Jesus died on the cross," said Sanders, approaching his crescendo, "he repeated those immortal words 'Father forgive them for they know not what they do.'" Now rousing himself to his full oratorical glory, Rabbi Sanders thundered, "Legislators! May future generations reading the statute books of Arkansas NOT be compelled to say these words of you!" He implored the senators, "For the sake of the glorious heritage Arkansas may yet give to our beloved America, *defeat*, I pray you, *in toto*, the four measures, and the God of all men will bless your handiwork." During the cacophony of applause and cheers mixed with jeers and heckling that accompanied his conclusion, Sanders was asked to leave the legislative chambers immediately. The reason, he later stated, was "the fear that somebody might assassinate me."[12]

Courageous though his efforts had been, Sanders' plea fell upon deaf ears. Each of the four measures easily passed the state senate: House Bill 322, creating a state sovereignty commission, passed by a vote of 21–12; House Bill 323, allowing parents to keep their children out of integrated schools, was adopted unanimously, 32–0; House Bill 324, forcing "certain organizations" to register with the state, passed 20–14; and House Bill 325, providing state funds to school districts fighting integration, passed by a vote of 29–3.[13] Now that the four measures had passed both houses of the state legislature, on February 26, 1957, Gov. Orval Faubus, a previous racial moderate who believed an appeal to segregationists would fend off primary challengers from the right and lead to his reelection, signed the anti-integration measures into law with little fanfare, blithely stating, "The laws would not jeopardize the rights of anyone." Three of the measures had so-called "emergency clauses" attached to them, making them effective immediately, while the remaining one, creating the Arkansas State Sovereignty Commission, became effective after ninety days.[14]

Sanders' speech elicited many responses. Former governor Sidney S. McMath, a progressive Democrat elected to the statehouse in 1948 (and afterward one of the nation's top trial attorneys) commended Sanders' address in opposition to "these means of infringement upon basic constitutional rights." McMath had won the governorship riding a wave of postwar reform in the South. As a progressive on matters of race, he had helped integrate the University of Arkansas Medical School, pushed for increased funding for black schools and teachers, and supported both federal antilynching legislation and the elimination of the Arkansas poll tax. He lost his bid for a third term in a contentious 1952 Democratic primary election against Francis Cherry, the eventual gubernatorial victor, amidst unproven charges of fraud in the highway department. "Your statement was clear, convincing, and courageous," McMath told Sanders.[15]

The Reverend Charles C. Walker, African American minister of Little Rock's First Congregational Church, called the speech "great," "courageous," and "scholarly and truthfully put." Walker wrote, "Ever since I have been located here, you have been assiduously working toward a more humane approach for all our citizens." Sanders' courage and determination to speak up publicly for civil rights, Walker told his associate, had helped the reverend "encourage others to 'stand up and be counted.'"[16] The rabbi's performance before the legislature had set an example others would emulate in taking their own stands for equality.

Sanders' speech before the legislature of course did not prevent either the passage of the anti-integration bills or the community disruption to come. The violent opposition that accompanied the desegregation of Little Rock Central High School was in many ways unexpected.

Mobs at the Schoolhouse Door

I spoke freely against the evils of segregation.
—IRA SANDERS, 1978

"It was bound to happen sooner or later," writes *The Fifties* author David Halberstam in relation to segregationist violence, "but no one thought it would happen in Little Rock."[17] The violence, disruptions, and international spotlight that accompanied the Central High desegregation efforts came as a surprise to most Arkansans, especially residents of Little Rock. On the issue of civil rights, Little Rock had since World War II enjoyed a reputation as a moderate city unlike Birmingham or Montgomery. It boasted a moderate mayor in Woodrow W. Mann, who, while not a personal advocate of classroom integration, was nonetheless fully prepared to implement the Supreme Court's orders and the school board's plans, and it was he who would request that Eisenhower send in troops to keep order.[18] Additionally, Little Rock had a progressive newspaper in the *Arkansas Gazette* under the editorship of Harry Ashmore, a moderate Democrat, Brooks Hays, in Washington as its representative, and a governor, Orval Faubus, who was not known for race-baiting, at least not yet. Indeed, in his January 1955 inaugural address, Faubus did not even mention segregation. Arkansas also had been the first former Confederate state to comply with the court's 1954 *Brown* decision, when public schools in Arkansas towns such as Fayetteville, Charleston, and Hoxie integrated, if only in small numbers. By 1957, writes Ben Johnson, "about 940 African American students out of a total black student population of 102,000 were attending integrated public schools in Arkansas."[19] The state and its capital city even before 1954 had already made many advances toward racial integration without major incident, as proudly related by the Little Rock Council on Education in its 1952 report. The University of Arkansas had, without court mandate or compulsion, opened its doors to racial integration in 1948, and other campuses around the state were in the process of following suit; by 1957, black students attended all seven predominantly white state colleges. The Little Rock Public Library, with Ira Sanders and Adolphine Terry as driving forces, already had quietly desegregated. The report added, "No segregation was practiced at the opening of the first Little Rock Community Center, all major department stores have removed drinking fountain segregation signs, and the Rock Island RR has abolished segregation on its trains." The report proudly concluded, "All this seems to indicate the increasing understanding of Arkansas for a peaceful and gradual solution to the problem of segregation." An NAACP field secretary in mid-1955 agreed, calling Arkansas "the bright spot of the south."[20] All of these factors suggested that Arkansas represented the very picture of moderate racial progress and placed the state in stark contrast to other southern states such as Alabama and neighboring Mississippi.

Add to these factors the relatively small numbers of Arkansans associated with white citizens' councils, segregationist organizations that in other states had real political power and were successfully massing coordinated resistance to civil rights progress. The Capital Citizens' Council of Little Rock (CCCLR), the most prominent opponent of school integration, organized in April 1955, but neither it nor its statewide affiliate claimed more than a few hundred members. In Arkansas, the stalwart segregationists existed in factions, unable to cooperate to win elections, coordinate obstructionist tactics, or exert much influence on Governor Faubus.[21] This factor combined with all the others to make the events leading to and surrounding the Central High School affair all the more surprising.

The passage of the four obstructionist bills, coupled with the critical factor — Orval Faubus' fateful and cynical political calculation that a staunch segregationist stood a better chance of election in 1958 than a racial moderate — set the stage for the events of September 1957 at Little Rock Central High School. The story is often told and has been well chronicled.[22] The nine young African American students who set out to integrate Central High instead found themselves at the center of a crisis of international scope. Governor Faubus chose his actions based upon the political reelection dividends they would pay. On September 2, he dispatched the Arkansas National Guard to the school, ostensibly to keep order, but in fact to block the students' entry. In the process, he set the State of Arkansas against the United States government by providing a very public challenge to the authority of the US Supreme Court.

Winthrop Rockefeller, chairman of the Arkansas Industrial Development Commission since 1955, echoed some of the economic themes raised by Ira Sanders in his address before the legislature as he tried to reason with Faubus, fearing the governor's actions would adversely impact efforts to bring jobs and investments to Arkansas. "I'm sorry, but I'm already committed," Faubus told Rockefeller. "I'm going to run for a third term, and if I don't do this, [segregationist candidates] Jim Johnson and Bruce Bennett will tear me to shreds." The Central High Crisis, then, rested on the basest of foundations: personal political ambition. The actions Faubus took in furthering his ambition, through his deployment of the state's armed forces in an effort to block the implementation of federal law, precipitated the Central High crisis and triggered perhaps the greatest constitutional challenge to federal authority since the American Civil War.[23]

Faubus' defiance of federal law forced Pres. Dwight Eisenhower, himself no advocate of the *Brown* desegregation decision, into action. Arkansas congressman Brooks Hays arranged a meeting between Faubus and Eisenhower, and the president received reassurances after meeting with the governor that the guardsmen would be removed from the school and the situation resolved. A federal court also ordered Faubus on September 20 to cease interference with the school's desegregation. Faubus did remove the National Guard but took no other action. Thus, when on September 23 the nine children returned to school, they were essentially defenseless against the growing, angry, menacing white mob shouting obscenities and hurling racial epithets. It was more than the Little Rock Police Department could handle.

National and international press covered the shocking events at Central High in September 1957 and its scenes of intimidation, threats, and violence against the nine children, reporters, and bystanders alike. On September 24, on the request of Little Rock mayor Woodrow Mann, Eisenhower federalized the Arkansas National Guard and sent in elements of the 101st Airborne Division to Little Rock to establish order and protect both the children and the integrity of the court desegregation order. He acted in defense of the principles of federalism and Supreme Court authority, but he also acted out of concern that the crisis would badly tarnish America's international image in the charged atmosphere of the Cold War era. In a televised address on September 24, 1957, announcing his intervention in the Little Rock crisis, Eisenhower said, "It would be difficult to exaggerate the harm that is being done to the prestige and influence . . . of our nation and the world. Our enemies are gloating over this incident and using it everywhere to misrepresent our whole nation."[24] The crisis, in addition to its international implications, boiled down to the question of state authority versus federal authority, and while the outcome was never really in question, the damage done in achieving that outcome would be considerable. In the eyes of the world outside Arkansas, the obstructionist actions of its governor and the actions of "a few hundred frenzied men and women" around the Central High campus, recalls *Arkansas Gazette* publisher Harry Ashmore, seared into "the consciousness of the world" the city of Little Rock as the symbol "of brutal, dead-end resistance to the minimum requirements of racial justice." The "psychic damage" was heavy as the world saw "the naked face of hatred" on display in the capital city.[25] Arkansas's moderate and peaceful recent history of desegregation made the events surrounding Central High all the more surprising. In addition to the obvious concerns created for the Little Rock African American community, the ferocity of the protests also created concerns for Little Rock's Jewish community.

Few Jewish children actually attended Central High; out of a total enrollment of around two thousand students, there were but six Jewish children. Despite that fact, Ira Sanders and other Little Rock Jews, including a significant number of women, played important roles in the crisis. After Governor Faubus ordered to close the schools rather than desegregate them for the 1958 year, Sanders later wrote, "I spoke freely against the evils of segregation. I met openly and often secretly with the liberal forces of the community, to help lay the strategy that reopened the schools with practically no one in the congregation protesting." Likewise, attorney and Congregation B'nai Israel president Henry E. Spitzberg, a strong and public advocate of the Supreme Court's *Brown* decision, remained "hopeful," he said, "about its implications for changing race relations in the South," and he worked closely with school superintendent Virgil Blossom in formulating strategies to respond to Faubus' actions.[26] The tandem of Sanders and Spitzberg received strong assistance from a number of women in the Little Rock Jewish community as well.

The Women's Emergency Committee to Open Our Schools (WEC), an organization of hundreds of Little Rock–area women, played a significant part in the effort to reopen the schools on a desegregated basis. Jewish women made up a disproportionate number of the group's leaders, including Josephine Menkus, Ruth Kretchmar, Jane Mendel, Carolyn Tenenbaum, Rosa Lasker, and Alice Back, who with nearly sixty other Jewish women provided key leadership. Most significant was Irene Samuel, the non-Jewish wife of Dr. John Samuel, a Jewish Little Rock–area physician who had opened both his practice and his waiting room to African Americans on an equal basis and had suffered for it. Even Rabbi Sanders' wife Selma, normally a somewhat private person and not at all a clubwoman, volunteered with the organization. Had it not been for the significant participation and leadership of the Jewish women, Irene Samuel later said, the WEC "would not have been as effectual."[27]

The Ministry of Reconciliation

If ever there was a time when we ministers are called upon to
reaffirm the dignity of the individual . . . that time has come.
——IRA SANDERS, 1957

President Eisenhower suggested that members of the Little Rock clergy might aid in ameliorating the Central High crisis. In a letter to Little Rock Episcopal bishop Robert Brown, Eisenhower wrote, "Religious leaders have an especial opportunity" to keep government "strong and vital and continuously devoted to the concepts that inspired the signers of the Declaration of Independence." As to the Central High crisis, Eisenhower said, "The real question is whether we shall respect the institutions of free government or, by defying them, set up either a process of deterioration and disruption or compel the authorities to resort to force to obtain that respect which we all should willingly give." He continued, "All of us realize that not through legislation alone can prejudice and hatred be eliminated from the hearts of men." The president said he was calling upon the Little Rock clergy to "play its part" to help the Little Rock situation. "I am convinced," Eisenhower concluded, "that if all of us work together . . . we should eventually be able to work out all our problems, including those of race, and as a consequence, our beloved country will be greater, stronger, and more secure."[28]

In response to the president's request, Brown and five other Little Rock clergymen and religious leaders—Ira Sanders, Rep. Brooks Hays, at that time the president of the Southern Baptist Convention, Dr. Marion Boggs of Second Presbyterian Church, Dr. Aubrey Dalton of First Methodist Church, and Dr. Dunbar Ogden of Central Presbyterian Church, who was also the president of Little Rock's newly-formed Interracial Ministerial Alliance—met preliminarily to outline. a basis of approach to the charge Eisenhower had given them. The broad goal of the group, Bishop Brown wrote, was to "reopen all lines of communication through love."[29] Rabbi Sanders suggested that the group take some action, such as a collective moral pronouncement, in order to reaffirm the dignity of the individual and proclaim aloud justice for all. The group followed Sanders' lead and collectively agreed on a few as yet ill-defined ideas. First, a city-wide day of prayer would be held during which a clergy-authored and clergy-led common prayer would be recited simultaneously by participants at houses of worship all over the region. This day of prayer would be held—again, at Sanders' suggestion—on Columbus Day, Saturday, October 12. Sanders chose Columbus Day, he said at the time, as an "appropriate

Rabbi Sanders passionately addresses his fellow clergy at a planning session of the
Ministry of Reconciliation, 1957. Courtesy of the UALR Center for Arkansas
History and Culture, Arkansas Studies Institute, Little Rock, Arkansas.

time to reiterate the principle of equality, justice, and liberty on which the country was founded." Second, the group agreed that the governor and the Little
Rock school board would be informed. Third, the ministers agreed to hold
another preparatory meeting, this time inviting clergy from all over the city, in
order to specify and then coordinate their actions prior to the Columbus Day
activities.[30] Finally, the group agreed to limit the invitations to the upcoming planning session to white ministers and clergymen only because of the
fear that African American participation in the endeavor at this stage might
further incite violence directed against the black community. Potentially, the
churches or homes of those African American ministers involved in the planning might be targets for segregationist bombings or other reprisals. So, while
African American ministers, pastors, and congregants became participants
in the Ministry of Reconciliation's Columbus Day events, black clergy were
not invited to participate directly in the planning of those events so as not "to
heighten tensions and deepen divisions," *Time* magazine reported, though they
were "kept informed."[31]

The larger planning meeting convened on October 4, 1957. More than forty white clergymen from all over the city gathered at Trinity Episcopal Church in Little Rock; there, they drew up the details for the Ministry of Reconciliation to assist the community in coming together in the midst of the crisis. Notable additions to this meeting included Methodist bishop Paul E. Martin and Presbyterian minister Richard Hardie. The meeting produced a remarkable degree of unity. Monsignor James O'Connell said he could assure everyone present "that the Roman Catholic Church will be pleased to cooperate" with them in what he termed a "great spiritual effort to cast out the devils of prejudice and violence." Hardie said the group "is going to have to stand up and give the right-thinking people the encouragement and help they need to stand firm." Rabbi Sanders added, "If ever there was a time when we ministers are called upon to reaffirm the dignity of the individual to which all faiths in the world subscribe, that time has come. By means of prayer we should fulfill our Ministry of Reconciliation with God and our fellowmen." Sanders continued by characterizing for the clergymen the significance of the gathering: "We are not concerned this afternoon with integration versus segregation; we are not concerned this afternoon with state versus federal rights; but we are concerned today with the great moral and spiritual truths which echo down through the ages. I wish to reaffirm first the dignity of the individual and secondly, proclaim aloud justice for all people, of all races, and all creeds that the words of the poet may be fulfilled: more things are wrought by prayer than half the world dreams of."[32] The strategy for the Ministry of Reconciliation included a city-wide day of prayer and the immediate organization of discussion groups so that the community as a whole could grapple with the moral and religious implications of the desegregation question. The ministers left the meeting, Bishop Brown recorded, "with a feeling of accomplishment and unanimity." Announcements in the Little Rock newspapers advertised the upcoming Columbus Day meetings, as did an October 10 press conference held by Sanders, Brown, Ogden, and Martin, representatives of the Jewish, Episcopal, Presbyterian, and Methodist faiths.[33]

Both the governor and the Little Rock school board supported the Ministry of Reconciliation and its goals. In a somewhat self-serving letter, Faubus told the ministers, "Your attitude of seeking to bring about reconciliation, rather than attempting to place blame, is, I believe, the proper approach. It is not a time now for recrimination or blame-placing." Through school superintendent Virgil Blossom and Little Rock Board of Education president W. G. Cooper, the school board offered their unqualified support of the clergy's plan: we "would like to join in asking the people of Little Rock to pray for divine guidance . . . during this serious and far-reaching crisis."[34]

On Columbus Day, October 12, 1957, a Saturday, the meetings took place in eighty-five separate houses of worship in the Greater Little Rock area, twenty of them historically African American, with the clergy who planned the event themselves questioning whether their actions would have any significant impact: "At least," wrote Robert Brown, the participants could "witness love by their own example and pray that their witness would inspire a response." To the press, an optimistic Rabbi Sanders reiterated "more things are wrought by prayer than we have ever dreamed."[35] Participating clergy led those attending in common recitation of a six-point prayer for "forgiveness for having left undone the things that ought to have been done; the support and preservation of law and order; the leaders of the communities, state, and nation; the youth in the schools of the community; the casting out of rancor and prejudice in favor of understanding and compassion; and resistance against unthinking agitators."[36] In the crowded sanctuary of Congregation B'nai Israel, Ira Sanders—in order to better hammer home the message he wanted delivered—added specific points about race and racial equality to the otherwise generic prayer the clergy had all agreed to recite in common. To the six points, he added three more: "For that blessed day when all peoples and all races shall live side by side in tranquility and in good will; to remove hatred and malice from the hearts of those who would destroy the right of Thy creatures; and to show them that men of all colors are Thy children, each a pattern to help establish the whole vast fabric of society in which all men shall dwell in unity and accord."[37] Both Bishop Brown and Rabbi Sanders were pleased with the higher-than-expected level of participation in the day of prayer. Brown said that such numbers indicated "a desire on the part of citizens to want God's guidance in matters of law and order," and Sanders added that Jewish participation "went far beyond expectations."[38] More than five thousand people attended the eighty-five meetings. Governor Faubus was not among them.

Despite some concerns to the contrary, the Ministry of Reconciliation did aid in ameliorating the situation. Bishop Brown wrote that "following the Day of Prayer, Little Rock witnessed an observable lessening of civic tension and an increase of frankness in discussing the integration issue."[39] The event generated some badly needed positive news coverage of the Little Rock situation in the local and national press, even though it inevitably also engendered segregationist counter-responses. Just prior to the Columbus Day meetings, the anti-integrationist Mother's League of Central High School put a quarter-page ad in the local newspapers opposing the clergy's effort. Addressed to "the Clergymen, Catholic, Jewish, and Protestant, who are promoting the Prayer Meetings Saturday," the ad asked rhetorically "How can you advocate race-mixing and pray to escape the fruits of race-mixing? Is it proper for those who have for years advocated race-mixing to come forward as peacemakers?"[40] Likewise, the evening before the Columbus Day meetings, October 11, 1957, thirty-five independent Baptist ministers hosted a community gathering of about 660 segregationists opposed to the ideals of the Ministry of Reconciliation, instead offering up prayers for a very different kind of solution to the crisis, imploring the "Almighty" to "have the Negro pupils go back to the all-Negro high school."[41] The fact that liberals and moderates who favored desegregation outnumbered the segregationists at these competing sets of meetings by more than a ten-to-one margin offered hope for the situation in Arkansas.

In the wake of the day of prayer, Rabbi Sanders, Bishop Brown, and the other ministers, wanting to go further than symbolic measures to resolve the crisis, devised a strategy designed to bring the moderate and progressive students of Central High into a more proactive role. They reasoned that the sons and daughters of the segregationist Capital Citizens' Council and Mothers' League members "had been thoroughly indoctrinated by their parents" into leading "a campaign of abuse," harassing and intimidating the black students at Central High. Aware that these students represented a relatively small minority of the overall student body, Sanders, Brown, and the other four original organizers of the Ministry of Reconciliation introduced a controversial counterstrategy campaign involving the Central High students. The idea was to have student leaders such as the student council president, the captain of the football team, and the head of the honor society, among others, lead an effort to counteract the "troublemakers" in the school. The plan called for them to write letters to President Eisenhower, Governor Faubus, and other dignitaries, including "stage and screen personalities," in the hopes that the recipients might be induced to visit the campus and speak "on the issues at stake" and, by inspiring students and garnering media attention, positively influence the entire community. As Brown described it, the "real leaders" at Central High were not the children of the segregationists but "the children of moderate parents." This student-led campaign would "prove that the majority were not consenting to harassment and were setting up their own affirmative program to confine the tactics of the aggressors." Though Sanders and the other ministers recognized that this plan might be problematic—in proposing this approach, the clergymen knew they were placing a great deal of responsibility on the students—they pushed ahead anyway and approached school superintendent Virgil Blossom and the school board with the strategy. The board quickly rejected the plan on the bases that the responsibility to improve the situation at Central High should fall to the adults, not the children, and that such a plan inevitably would thrust specific students into the spotlight, possibly making them and their families targets for segregationist retribution. As a result, though many students at Central High apparently were keen on the idea, the ministers abandoned the plan.[42]

Rabbi Sanders enjoyed remarkable support from his congregation and the public for his activities both in the Ministry of Reconciliation and within the community on behalf of racial justice. An indication of that support can be seen in the five hundred participants in the Columbus Day activities at the temple, with substantially more Jewish attendees than a typical Friday evening or Saturday morning service. Of his own congregation, Sanders told the *Jewish Daily Forward* that he "was unaware of any" congregational dissent regarding his civil rights activities. But had there been any, Sanders continued, it would not have influenced him. "How can a Jew be a segregationist?" he asked. "Didn't we suffer enough from restrictive measures for the Jews?"[43] Strong congregational support at least in part allowed Sanders to play the role he did, for unlike many of his fellow southern rabbis, he was restrained by neither his congregation nor his board of trustees in his civil rights activities and his pursuit of racial justice.

On Sunday, December 1, 1957, the ABC Radio network broadcast the UAHC-sponsored program *Message of Israel* to a nationwide radio audience, as it did every Sunday morning. This particular installment, coming as it did in the very midst of the Little Rock Central High School crisis, featured an address by the program's guest, Ira Sanders, who presented a message of inclusion and acceptance across racial lines, a remarkable document emerging from the national focal point of the fight against racial segregation. For those listening in the national audience, Sanders' resonant voice, reiterating themes he had emphasized in many previous addresses, represented the voice of racial acceptance and a path to progress in Little Rock:

So many of us tolerate our neighbors. Tolerance is a destructive force in life. It presupposes the superiority of one group over another. We must learn to understand and accept each other. By heredity and environment we are each different. It is our duty to understand these forces, and to respect those whose skin is of a different color from ours, whose religion differs from the faith we profess. It is in the home that we must lay the foundations for this racial and religious understanding and acceptance. If America stands for any one thing, it must maintain that, in understanding and accepting our fellow man of all races and creeds, we build for cultural pluralism. Like the rainbow which contains all the colors of the spectrum, so do we need to know and to appreciate each other, so that through interdependence one upon the other we can create a new mentality here in

America. .... A high challenge has therefore come to all of us as we face the greatest social revolution of our times—the problem of desegregation. It is a difficult and vexing question affecting the future of our country. And yet arduous as is the problem, and perplexing as are the times, we must learn to be patient, understanding, and sympathetic as we seek to build the finer America we are called upon to establish. In the new America we must give equal opportunities to all our citizens. The great Judeo-Christian tradition is built upon the acceptance of all men as children of God, created equal in His image, to whom rich and poor, black and white, Christian and Jew are alike. As Washington's Monument is fashioned out of stones sent from every state in the union, so the genius of America must be molded from contributions made by every group.[44]

ABC Radio beamed Sanders' powerful statement of racial acceptance and social justice to listeners all over the nation, a voice of reason emerging from the cacophony surrounding the Central High Crisis.

Boycotts and Bomb Threats

We are made of sturdier stuff than to let intimidation or fear frighten us.
—IRA SANDERS, 1960

In his memoir of the Little Rock Central High School crisis, school superintendent Virgil Blossom wrote of his experiences as a favorite target of harassment by segregationists. During the crisis, Blossom wrote, he also became "keenly aware" that the bigotry on display went well beyond his personal harassment, and even beyond the immediate circumstances of Central High, cutting in many directions. For example, he saw "propaganda of an anti-Semitic character" dramatically increase in an "outpouring of hatred and venom, with all kinds of crackpots and hate peddlers trying to horn in." Threats of deadly violence against the Little Rock Jewish community accompanied this propaganda.[45]

About fourteen hundred Jews lived in Little Rock in 1957–58, constituting about 1 percent of the city's overall population. Though small in number, they wielded significant civic and economic influence. Many Jewish business and retail figures in Little Rock feared that threats to the status quo created by the civil rights movement could potentially upset that influence. Some of the significant business and retail leaders in the city included Hugo Heiman, president of the Blass Department Store, the largest department store in the city; Louis Rosen, who served as president of the Rotary Club; and Henry Spitzberg, one of the city's leading attorneys who worked closely with school superintendent Virgil Blossom during the crisis. Some of the most prominent businessmen in Little Rock were Jewish, but four Jewish families in particular—Pfeifer, Blass, Kempner, and Cohn—were "associated with large, prestigious department stores" whose success depended a great deal upon community good will. Garment manufacturers Gus and Leonard Ottenheimer were significant employers of labor in the city, having built an industrial complex in Little Rock in 1955. Sam Peck was a respected hotel owner, while Julius Tenenbaum and Sol Alman ran substantial scrap and metal companies. The Jewish economic presence in Little Rock was also well integrated into the larger community and had been for decades. Abe Tenenbaum had established his company in 1890, while the Gus Blass Company dated to 1867. James Kempner, son of department store founder Ike Kempner, helped establish the Little Rock Urban Progress Association while participating in a number of other civic and business organizations.[46] These are a few of numerous examples. These businessmen, particularly the retail department store owners, depended upon the support and patronage of the community at large for the success of their businesses. The question of racial desegregation in general, and the Central High crisis in particular, put them and the rest of city's Jewish population in a potentially precarious position. As a result, with few exceptions, Little Rock Jews as a whole acted with great caution and restraint during the crisis, and the men much more so than the women. One civic leader reportedly stated that the great economic power of the Jewish community may "have compounded the tendency toward inaction in crisis which characterizes any business group." In essence, "the Jews were afraid to act."[47]

Despite the activism both overtly and behind the scenes of some Little Rock Jews such as Ira Sanders, Henry Spitzberg, and the Jewish women of the WEC during the Central High crisis, there existed in fact a fear of retribution, particularly among the Jewish-owned retail businesses in the city. While some worked quietly and behind the scenes with Christians of like mind, others established a kind of informal censorship committee that "exerted social and economic pressure within the Little Rock Jewish community to keep the Jews from becoming involved in the crisis" and worked to keep certain things out of the press in order to protect the larger Jewish community. As one Jewish department store owner stated at the time, "The Jews could not take the lead in desegregation activities." The threat of anti-Semitic retaliation, which often went hand-in-hand with racist and segregationist sentiments, always loomed. This "censorship group" also took some proactive steps, such as quietly working with the "more sensible" elements within the segregationist Capital Citizens' Council of Little Rock to halt the "radicals" among the CCCLR from distributing ten thousand copies of the anti-Semitic magazine *Common Sense*. Rabbi Sanders lamented the generalized lack of action among the broader Jewish community with this rather harsh assessment: "The Jewish people have always been lacka-daisical when confronted with a social problem. The Jewish leaders, as well as other community leaders, were committed to the status quo. Although the Jewish community knew that segregation was wrong, the only Jews that took the lead were outside the local Jewish community."[48]

The Jewish community for the most part had deep and substantial roots in the larger community, which they believed offered them a degree of insulation. Nevertheless, Jewish-owned retail businesses suffered as a result of the deseg-regation crisis. The CCCLR targeted Jewish-owned Little Rock businesses and instituted a boycott of the pro–civil rights *Arkansas Gazette* and the big department stores that advertised in its pages. They also sent volunteers to the large downtown department stores demanding, under threat of boycott, that the owners, all Jewish, sign proclamations against racial "mongrelization" and "race-mixing." Episcopal bishop Robert Brown noted that the CCCLR campaign also involved "anonymous telephone calls" and "abusive letters and mailings." Like other white citizens' councils in the South, the CCCLR veered deeply into anti-Semitism as well as racism. In addition to their efforts to pre-serve segregation, the group also distributed anti-Semitic literature and spon-sored talks by prominent anti-Semites such as Gerald L. K. Smith acolyte Rev. J. A. Lovell of Texas, who addressed the Little Rock group in July 1957 with a talk entitled "Must America Sell Her Birthright to Appease the Internationalist and Communist?"[49]

The CCCLR met on September 24, 1957, and organized a group of about five hundred segregationist women to write letters to the Jewish presidents of the three premier Little Rock department stores, Cohn, Blass, and Pfeifer, "stating they would not buy any more merchandise from the stores until these stores stopped advertising in the *Arkansas Gazette*." The CCCLR timed the release of the letters to coincide with the December holiday buying season. This caused headaches both for the *Gazette* and the three retailers, as newspaper sales fell by over twenty thousand, translating into far fewer readers of department store advertisements and a moderate retail slump. Death threats accompanied some of the letters.[50]

While violence did accompany the events of September 1957, it was localized around Central High. Segregationists did not target Jewish-owned businesses for picketing or other direct-action protest demonstrations or for extralegal

Temple B'nai Israel, 1958. Courtesy Temple B'nai Israel,
Little Rock, Arkansas.

reprisals such as vandalism. The downtown retail areas quickly returned to normal activities, though the Capital Citizens' Council did continue its attempts
to exert economic pressure on the Jewish-owned stores from time to time. One
such attempt to boycott Jewish merchants, planned to coincide in 1959 with the
reopening of Little Rock Central High School (after its closing by the governor during the 1958–59 school year), was a failure. A segregationist-promoted
"buyer's strike" failed to have any impact whatsoever.[51] The segregationists,
though, did make much more serious threats against the Jewish community
as a result of Sanders' outspoken activism in support of civil rights. Like other
southern cities with synagogues in the 1950s, Little Rock and its synagogues
received bomb threats.

On Thursday, October 16, 1958, the FBI informed Rabbi Sanders and Rabbi
Irwin Groner of Little Rock's Orthodox Congregation Agudath Achim that
segregationists had made bomb threats against both the Reform temple and
the Orthodox synagogue. While Ira Sanders had been a very public and active
voice in support of civil rights for decades, Rabbi Groner — twenty-six years
old, in his first pulpit, and in town for only two years — had refrained from
public pronouncements (although he supported desegregation). By all reports
he and the Orthodox community were shocked that they, having kept a low

profile, had also been threatened. In Little Rock as in other southern cities, the level of actual engagement of specific rabbis or congregations in civil rights activities did not determine who was and who was not bombed or threatened with bombing. It was, instead, a nonspecific targeting of the entire Jewish community as retribution for the actions of certain members of that community; in this case, the Jews of Little Rock were being threatened in large part because of the activism of Ira Sanders.[52]

Temple president Henry Spitzberg presided over a hastily called special meeting of the boards of trustees of both the temple and the synagogue, which convened in the temple at noon on Friday, October 17, to discuss the threat. Both rabbis were present. Rabbi Groner earlier had phoned the Anti-Defamation League for further information on the threat, and the ADL told him that the threat specifically stated that the Temple, the Atlanta synagogue that had been bombed on October 12, was to be "the last to be bombed unoccupied."[53] The discussion then turned to whether the upcoming Friday evening service, only hours away, should be held or cancelled. At some point late in this meeting, Rabbi Sanders, determined that no threat would disrupt Friday evening services, reportedly stood up and said, "Gentlemen, you will have to excuse me. I will be in the pulpit this evening at 7 p.m.," and exited the meeting.[54] Whether or not Sanders actually said this — his dramatic statement does not appear in the meeting minutes — Rabbi Sanders clearly intended for services to go forward, bomb threats notwithstanding. In fact, both rabbis were in agreement on this point, and the two boards followed their lead. After moving to step up security at both facilities, the trustees voted to have Sabbath services as usual that evening and the next morning, saying, "We could not allow any group of fanatics to rout the Jewish people from their places of worship."[55] Board member Selwyn Loeb had made the motion, quickly approved, that services be held as usual. Dr. Jerome Levy then called for a second meeting to be held the next day, Saturday, October 18, to consider the question of whether to hold Sunday's religious school session as usual. The boards then discussed several matters of security, including improvements to outside lighting, hiring security guards, and establishing a committee to deal exclusively with "future problems or threats" before the meeting ended.[56]

The arrival in police hands of a second threatening letter warning of a bombing at the temple prompted the board to hold another emergency meeting that same Friday afternoon at four o'clock rather than wait until the scheduled Saturday meeting time. Sanders read the threatening letter to the trustees. The board then noted that as a result of the threats, the Little Rock police had been ordered to keep the temple under "complete surveillance" for the entire weekend. Four police cars were assigned to alternately circle the block at Fifth and Broadway, upon which sat the Temple, during that frightening weekend. Feeling they had taken all possible actions to protect the congregation, the board cancelled the planned Saturday meeting.[57]

Friday night and Saturday morning services passed without incident. Sunday religious school also went forward as usual with no disruption, though few parents braved the threat. Importantly, and perhaps surprisingly, given the gravity of the threat and the spate of synagogue bombings in other states, no one on the board ever suggested reining in Sanders; no one suggested that the rabbi lower his community profile regarding civil rights. Henry Spitzberg and the rest of the board stood firmly with their rabbi of more than thirty years throughout the period of the Central High crisis despite the bomb threats.

On Tuesday, October 21, at seven thirty in the evening, the board of Congregation B'nai Israel met for a third time to discuss further security issues. Rabbi Solomon A. Fineberg, community relations consultant of the American Jewish Committee, came to Little Rock upon being informed of the bomb threats and sat in at this meeting. The board provided for the hiring of a nightly security guard and noted that the Little Rock police continued their close, around-the-clock surveillance. The board adopted Rabbi Sanders' suggestion that "a committee of fathers [of religious school children] be constituted to guard the buildings between 9 a.m. and noon each Sunday while school was in session" and then agreed that fire drills and other evacuation contingencies be developed. The grounds committee proposed that "all shrubbery be thinned out" to deprive potential bombers of cover. The board also acted on the previous meeting's resolution to create an "emergency committee" and appointed board members Myron Lasker, Harry Pfeifer Jr., Arnold Mayersohn, M. A. Safferstone, and Jerome S. Levy to deal exclusively with security needs. Finally, Rabbi Fineberg proposed that no public mention be made of any of these contingencies for increased security: "Publicity should be minimized because the bleating of the lamb excites the tiger, and we are dealing with an element not subject to public opinion and control."[58] For these reasons, the threats and all mentions of the board's plans were kept out of the press and omitted from the temple's newsletter.

By the following month, the fear of bombings had waned, and the board rescinded some of the security measures implemented the month before, but then they imposed others. The floodlights that had been erected outside the temple each night were discontinued, but the board voted to brick up a stairwell on the Capitol Avenue side of the building. The board also agreed to provide security any time meetings were held in the temple.[59]

As with other contemporary southern rabbis, Ira Sanders' civil rights activism had frightening and potentially disastrous implications both for him and the Jewish community. Unlike the Temple in Atlanta, Little Rock's Reform temple avoided destruction, though it endured additional threats both during and after the crisis. As the Atlanta newspaper *Southern Israelite* ominously pointed out in 1959, "Jews who espouse and defend the cause of civil rights jeopardize the security" of southern Jewish communities, "threaten their social integration and economic position, and ultimately even their physical safety."[60] This had been the case in Little Rock, precisely as some of the prominent Little Rock businessman had feared. Their reticence to take a stand, in fact, was more accurately a concern over the realization of these possibilities.

In January 1960, in his annual report to the congregation, Rabbi Sanders praised the membership for its support during the Central High crisis and through the threats of bombings. He praised them for "conduct[ing] themselves with calmness, resoluteness, and courage in a most laudatory manner." He continued with pride, "Despite threats to our Temple by sinister forces from without, we conducted all of our activities with unsuspended fervor and dignity." He praised those in the congregation "who joined with the right-thinking leaders of [the] community to restore stability and normalcy" and noted that his congregation was "made of sturdier stuff than to let intimidation or fear frighten us" and had persevered by defiantly holding services and other events "several times under the threat of bombs."[61]

Sanders and his colleague Irwin Groner of Congregation Agudath Achim agreed that, even in a time of threats from extremists, the overall relationship between Little Rock Jews and non-Jews "could not conceivably be better or friendlier," a sentiment shared by many local Jewish businessmen as well and foreshadowed by earlier remarks made by J. William Fulbright, United States senator from Arkansas, who had stated in April 1955 that Arkansas was "a model for Gentile-Jew relations."[62] By 1958 Sanders had been so well established as a community leader that in some ways his Jewishness was secondary in the public mind to his civic-mindedness. For three decades he had been a well-respected and admired community leader in the same vein as high-profile Protestant or Catholic religious leaders in the city. The threats by extremists, rather than marginalizing or silencing the Jewish community, had the effect of drawing the congregation more tightly around its rabbi and making the Little Rock community at large more intolerant of anti-Semitic or racist extremism, lest their municipal image be further tarnished. Ironically, the radical anti-Semitic threats of a few lessened whatever softer anti-Semitism may have existed in the community as a whole, as Arkansas liberals and racial moderates effectively "circled the wagons" to maintain the state's relatively moderate position on civil rights. Arkansans, it seemed, did not wish to emulate the extremes seen in other southern states.

Although the Jews of Little Rock obviously never adopted any "official" Jewish position on school integration, Sanders, as "one of the leading figures in the campaign to adhere to and enforce the law of the land," stood for many as the de facto Jewish leader and spokesman on these issues.[63] The reasons for his reception were many. His position did not appreciably differ from any number of other religious liberals or moderates. His style of leadership provided an example of working for racial justice from within the system through established (or through the establishment of) civic and community organizations such as the Rotarians or the Urban League. He sought to educate from an already-established position, thirty years in the making, of moral and religious community leadership rather than one of street demonstration or controversial direct-action tactics. And finally, Little Rock—despite the momentous exception of Faubus and the reactionary response on the part of some to the desegregation of Central High—remained since World War II a more moderate environment for civil rights progress than Birmingham or Montgomery. For all of these reasons, Little Rock did not see Ira Sanders as an interloper or an "agitator" or a dangerous "other" within the larger community. Therefore, although there were threats from fringe elements, the Jewish community did not suffer appreciable consequences as a result of his public and steady brand of moral activism.

During the events of 1957 to 1959, Sanders' work on behalf of social justice was a source of pride for Reform Jews and Jewish organizations, and he received both encouragement and congratulations from colleagues around the country. Organizations such as the UAHC offered key support. Chairman Cyrus Gordon of the Commission on Social Action commended Sanders for his "strong leadership" in the community, calling it "the only bright spot in the Little Rock situation." He asked Sanders to forward his views on desegregation "for the benefit of those [southern rabbis] who will be confronting similar situations."[64] Gordon wanted to hold Sanders and his work up as an example for other Reform rabbis to emulate.

The Central Conference of American Rabbis (CCAR), the American Jewish Congress, the New York Association of Reform Rabbis, and other groups also offered support and encouragement to Sanders. "The Jewish community," wrote Richard Cohen, regional director of the American Jewish Congress, "should be proud of the public position you took in your testimony on the four bills and in the essentially moral position you took." Likewise, the New York association leadership rallied behind their former colleague, saying they were "confident that [Sanders would] bring to this problem the ethical and moral insights of Judaism and that [he would] labor zealously for its just and moral solution." Perhaps the most significant message came from Maurice Eisendrath, the president of the UAHC. Rabbi Eisendrath wired Sanders shortly after the start of the 1957 school year congratulating him on his "splendid leadership in mobilizing the religious community of Little Rock to take concerted moves towards the removal of strife." Eisendrath told Sanders that he intended to hold the Little Rock rabbi up as a role model for the entire UAHC membership in the upcoming mid-October meetings in Cincinnati in order "to urge efforts similar to [his] in communities throughout the nation, both North and South." He thanked Sanders on behalf of the UAHC member congregations—the vast majority of Reform congregations in the United States were affiliated with UAHC—for his "vivid demonstration of the need to apply today's mandates to [the] realm of social action."[65] Clearly, Sanders' work in Little Rock was having a national as well as local impact.

As the Central High crisis abated, and Arkansas moved into the 1960s, Rabbi Sanders considered his future. He celebrated his sixty-seventh birthday in 1961, by which time he had served Congregation B'nai Israel for thirty-five dynamic and active years. With the addition of the five years he served as rabbi in Allentown and another two in Manhattan, Sanders had served a total of forty-two years in the rabbinate. The *Arkansas Democrat* recognized Rabbi Sanders' contributions in April: "As the leader [of the Little Rock Jewish community, Sanders] has espoused all causes that stand for improvement of the community." Then in May 1961, the *Arkansas Gazette* again celebrated Sanders' ability to "immerse himself in the whole life of the community without thought of narrow sectarianism." Dr. Sanders' "contagious enthusiasm has diminished not one whit over the years, and his broad interpretation of the role of the spiritual leader has attracted increasingly wide admiration and respect." That deep respect also came from his peers. The director of the American Jewish Archives, reflecting on the views of Sanders' contemporaries in the rabbinate, called him "one of the most highly respected men in the Central Conference of American Rabbis." Fellow civil rights advocate and rabbi James Wax of Memphis congratulated his friend, telling Sanders, "You have personified the noblest teachings of our religion." Martha Allis, executive secretary of the Pulaski County Tuberculosis Association, an organization Sanders had served after his arrival more than three decades earlier, added, "I am always so grateful that you decided to cast your lot in Little Rock because you have made such a wonderful contribution to every phase of community life in our city. I know of no one more beloved by all denominations of the city than you."[66]

In these final years of his ministry, Rabbi Sanders seldom missed an opportunity to interject messages of racial equality and fairness in his public addresses, and he frequently made them the centerpiece of his sermons. In November 1961, for example, Sanders offered the invocation at the formal ceremonial laying of the cornerstone for the new federal building in downtown Little Rock. He prayed it would be built upon the foundations of "justice and freedom under law," saying, "May we never forget that when our human statutes fail to implement Thy divine rule of liberty and equality for all, we cannot find favor in Thy sight."[67]

The year 1961 became a year of reflection for Rabbi Sanders. His thirty-fifth anniversary with the temple moved him to consider a change. At the 1962 annual meeting of the congregation, Rabbi Sanders surprised the gathering with his request that he "be retired." He had told no one of his decision other than the congregation president, to whom he had talked "as late as five o'clock that afternoon." But this was no snap judgment; rather, it represented for Rabbi Sanders the culmination of a year's thought on the matter. Accordingly, on August 31, 1963, "the congregation officially retired [him] and elevated [him] to Rabbi Emeritus."[68] Before that retirement became effective, however, there remained one last great cause for which Rabbi Sanders would fight.

The Conference

Our words must be translated into deeds of love and justice.
—IRA SANDERS, 1963

On January 14, 1963, Protestant, Catholic, and Jewish leaders gathered in Chicago to convene the National Conference on Religion and Race. At this conclave, they expressed their common anti-segregationist convictions, stating, "Racial discrimination and prejudice are moral problems at their roots, and . . . racial segregation is one of the most crucial problems facing our religious institutions and our democracy." Inspired by this national interfaith conference, Rabbi Sanders, in the final year of his ministry, met in Little Rock on April 22 with Rev. Kenneth Teegarden, president of the Arkansas Council of Churches, and the Most Reverend Albert L. Fletcher, bishop of the Catholic Diocese of Little Rock, and together they formed the Greater Little Rock Conference on Religion and Human Relations.[69] They said of the effort, "We sincerely believe that this proposed conference can provide a unique opportunity for religiously committed people in our area to speak with one voice on racial issues. . . . It can provide leadership for interreligious projects aimed at the creation of genuine human respect, understanding, and acceptance among all our people."[70] This core of three called a meeting at which 108 representatives from twenty-three Protestant groups, both Little Rock Jewish congregations, one Greek Orthodox church, and many Roman Catholic institutions attended.[71]

On behalf of this larger group, a multiracial quartet consisting of Sanders, Fletcher, Teegarden, and Bishop John D. Bright, head of the African Methodist Episcopal (AME) churches of Arkansas and Oklahoma, together drafted "An Appeal to Conscience," a statement intended for wide distribution to congregations in Little Rock, and designed for public reading. "We believe the racial problem is the most serious domestic problem facing our nation," the statement read, "and it demands the attention of every citizen." Racial discrimination, though, cannot be solved by laws alone. "We appeal to all men of good will in the Greater Little Rock area to take an active part in solving this moral evil" through acts of mutual respect and cooperation based on moral laws of justice and equality. The statement also included proposed discussion questions the four had drafted for congregations to use in stimulating dialogue on the issue. The Conference agreed that anything members wanted added to the statement would require "the approval of these top men."[72]

The clergymen agreed to meet monthly to help define and then work to solve racial issues for Arkansas and specifically the Little Rock area. The group also sought cooperation with existing civic institutions to better facilitate racial harmony. In June, the group named Sanders to head the steering committee, which was responsible for fulfilling the mandate of identifying causes for the group to address. "Our words," Sanders wrote, "must be translated into deeds of love and justice." One of the first measures the steering committee recommended was the desegregation of worship services at congregations in the area. The Conference urged its members to take proactive steps in inviting and welcoming people of different races into their services and their congregations. They proposed such first steps as inviting choirs from predominantly black or white churches to sing at churches on the other side of the racial divide, and inviting clergy to preach at other pulpits—all in an effort to reach out in fellowship across racial lines.[73]

The Conference, though, concerned itself with more than just the desegregation of religious institutions. It also tackled the much more complex and controversial issue of housing discrimination and residential segregation. Pres. John F. Kennedy had not yet signed Executive Order 11063, which prohibited discrimination in the sale, leasing, or rental of properties owned or operated by the government or provided with federal funds after November 20, 1962. Little Rock housing projects were still rigidly segregated by race as a matter of course, openly and unapologetically.[74] Little Rock's subsidized low-rent housing followed the pattern of "Negroes to the east, whites to the west." Recent urban renewal projects, despite the presidential order, had exacerbated and continued this practice. The Conference committed itself to halting "the trend toward ghettoizing" as a positive means to "affect immediate economic ends." To accomplish this, Sanders and the steering committee drafted a position paper entitled "Confronting the Little Rock Housing Problem," outlining a plan of action to combat housing discrimination. Churches and synagogues, the paper stated, could "encourage inclusiveness" by keeping congregants aware of and sympathetic to "the housing needs of Negroes in the community," encouraging and assisting "the poorly-housed to break out of their environmental housing trap," and influencing decision makers to improve African American access to all housing. The report concluded,

> The evidence convinces us we are moving from a city of tolerable diversity in housing to the dangerous conditions prevailing in eastern and northern cities—the condition of racial ghettos and of economic ghettos. The forces pushing this trend toward residential apartheid are powerful and entrenched, appealing to basic anti-democratic human desires and prejudices. Strong affirmative resolution to change the trend will be required. This is an emergency. Unless action is taken during the *process* of change, it will be too late. What has happened to other cities need not happen in this Southern city.[75]

Ira Sanders' involvement with the Conference stretched on for many years following his 1963 retirement from the pulpit as the group pursued equal housing opportunities for several years, working to create equal access to housing for Little Rock families regardless of race. In October 1964, members voted to rename the organization the Greater Little Rock Conference on Religion and Race to more accurately reflect its aims and mission of racial equality. The following year, Rabbi Sanders became the vice chairman of the group, continuing to promote the ideals of the Conference and give it positive direction.[76] Three months later, during a meeting on March 1, 1966, member Sam Allen related his experience of selling his home in an all-white neighborhood to a black family. He reported being harassed by neighbors and realtors and "receiving threats by phone and by mail." The Conference leadership offered their support and reiterated to the members that they must "make their stand in support of integrated housing clear to their congregations." Sanders, moved by Allen's predicament, suggested that the group throw him a testimonial dinner to honor his commitment to the cause.[77]

In a special meeting held only two days later, more details came out. Allen had sold his home to Mr. and Mrs. Sam Anderson, an African American carpenter and his wife. Local contractor George Bronson, an employer of Anderson and a supporter of fair housing, told the Conference members he had been instructed to fire the carpenter as retribution for his moving into an all-white neighborhood. Bronson refused to do so and as a result was himself fired by the firm for which he worked. Moved by his actions, the Conference pledged to give Bronson the necessary financial support to reestablish himself and resume his work as a building contractor, through which Anderson could also work. Sanders and the rest of the Conference were so impressed with Mr. Bronson that they named him to the steering committee of the organization. In April 1967, the Conference membership elected Ira Sanders chairman of the organization one month before his seventy-third birthday. In accepting the responsibility, Sanders said, "serving God with a commitment to our fellow man, according to law, is my allegiance to the Committee." The group continued its efforts at community outreach and breaking down racial barriers, remaining active in the local community throughout the decade in the areas of housing and welfare.[78]

The most active phase of Ira Sanders' career was approaching its end. However, that did not mean he would withdraw from the community or from his dedication to social and racial justice. There still was work to do.

—8—

Honors, Laurels, and Plaudits

1963–1985

IRA SANDERS' 1963 RETIREMENT prompted reflection from the Little Rock community he had so diligently served for more than three decades. The *Arkansas Gazette* pondered what the new phase in the life of such a "moving force in community affairs" would be. The newspaper opined, "It is good to know that Little Rock is not going to lose the benefits of [Sanders'] keen and lively mind and his social vision."[1] He remained an active advocate for social justice for many years after his retirement, directing the Arkansas Mental Health Hygiene Association, serving on the boards of the Arkansas Association for Mental Health, the Arkansas Tuberculosis Association, the Urban League of Greater Little Rock, and the Arkansas Lighthouse for the Blind and as a trustee for the Little Rock Public Library, the first organization with which he became involved when he arrived in September 1926, and on whose board he would serve until 1978.

Sanders' retirement neither ended his civic activism nor dimmed his desire to pursue social justice. Besides his continuing efforts on behalf of equal housing as a founder and leader of the Greater Little Rock Conference on Religion and Race, in the spring of 1964, during the first year of his retirement, Sanders actively promoted the reestablishment of one of his proudest accomplishments. The Little Rock School of Social Work had been defunct since the early years of the Great Depression. But there were people in need, he told a gathering of the Arkansas chapter of the National Association of Social Workers in Little Rock. "Common decency," he said, "does not permit us to neglect them. There is an acute shortage of trained social workers, and the time is ripe for those of us who realize that social work is an art and have dedicated our lives to its enlargement should put our minds and wills together so that Arkansas may soon boast of a School of Social Work."[2] Sanders' dream came to fruition soon after, in 1969, when the Graduate Social Work Program was established at the University of Arkansas at Little Rock, offering a master's degree. In retirement Sanders remained vigilant regarding affairs related to social work in Arkansas. In 1965, when Gov. Orval Faubus vetoed salary appropriations for the Child Welfare Division of the State Welfare Department, eliminating director Ruth Johnston's position as well as ninety-one other jobs in the process, including all of the professional social workers, Sanders took action. The Arkansas Conference on Social Welfare (ACSW) expressed "deep concern," and the ACSW quickly appointed a committee headed by Sanders whose responsibility would be "to continue that surveillance that our state may be assured that the quality of child welfare services will be maintained according to long established professional standards."[3] Sanders and his committee kept a watchful eye on developments related to social welfare.

On June 6, 1965, Sanders participated in the dedication ceremony for the new Arkansas Lighthouse for the Blind facility at Sixty-Ninth and Murray Streets in Little Rock. Future governor Winthrop Rockefeller gave the main address at this groundbreaking ceremony. Sanders and Rev. Jeff Smith had cofounded the organization in 1940, which provided "employment, training, and services" to blind and visually impaired citizens, and Sanders remained on the board for more than three decades. By the 1960s, the Arkansas Lighthouse for the Blind began manufacturing materials for the United States government, including detonators later shipped to Vietnam in 1966. Department of Defense contracts remained "the backbone of its client base."[4]

Since the establishment of the State of Israel in 1948, Rabbi Sanders had dedicated himself to its support and success. One form that support came in was bond drives, nineteen of which Sanders had led since Israel's inception. In 1967, Ariel Eshel, deputy director general of the Israeli Ministry of Foreign Affairs, presented Rabbi Sanders with an award on behalf of Israel for his "contributions, influence, and leadership for 40 years in the Little Rock and Arkansas Jewish community." The awards dinner took place on June 4, 1967, at the Hotel Marion in Little Rock and was attended by more than three hundred people. The occasion also marked the nineteenth anniversary of the establishment of the State of Israel. Eshel lauded Sanders "with deep gratitude for the support of Israel and the preservation of its people," particularly in his efforts to raise funds for Jewish immigration to Israel by organizing annual bond drives since 1948, one for each year of Israel's existence. *Arkansas Gazette* publisher J. N. Heiskell, a long-time friend of Sanders and fellow member of the library board of trustees, said, "When we survey the long years of service of Rabbi Ira Sanders to his God and to his fellow man, we must wonder how one man could have been engaged in so many activities." He added, "His activities fall under the same pattern—a desire to turn men's eyes to those tall white peaks

Ariel Eshel (*left*) and Ira Sanders (*right*), 1967.
Photo courtesy of the *Arkansas Democrat-Gazette*.

which hold the greatest purpose on the earth: service to man." At this ceremony, the Urban League of Greater Little Rock also presented Sanders with
a "Certificate of Merit and Appreciation" in recognition of his thirty years of
service and his role as a founder of the organization.[5]

The dinner honoring Rabbi Sanders fell on the evening of June 4, 1967.
Eshel and Sanders held a brief press conference that morning at the Little Rock
airport when the deputy director general arrived. Eshel lamented the Egyptian
blockade of the Gulf of Aqaba: "Aggression has been committed," he said, and
then he expressed the hope that "mankind can force the aggressor to revoke this
unilateral action" and asserted that if it could not, something had to be done.
The following day, the Six-Day War began. In reaction to the deployment of
Egyptian forces along the Israeli border, Israel launched a stunningly successful
preemptive attack against the Egyptians and moved to take the Gaza Strip and

the Sinai Peninsula from Egypt, the Golan Heights from Syria, and the West Bank from Jordan. Sanders recalled going to bed late that evening, only to be awakened by a phone call and news that the fighting had begun. Sanders feared for the outcome for Israel: "Great tears streamed down [my] face as [I] felt the full impact of the event."[6]

In February 1968 the Arkansas region of the National Conference of Christians and Jews (NCCJ) announced the selection of Rabbi Sanders as the recipient of its Brotherhood and Humanitarian Award. The recipient in 1967 had been Gov. Winthrop Rockefeller. Sanders accepted the award in Little Rock at a gala on May 27 at which over one thousand people of all religious and social backgrounds gathered to recognize Sanders' tireless work in Arkansas on behalf of the cause of equality. Local businessman Frank Lyon, selected to chair the event, called Sanders "one of America's truly great men and great leaders." Governor Rockefeller, unable to attend, added his congratulations via telegram for Sanders' forty-three years of "unremitting work for social reform in Little Rock."[7]

The dinner was held at the Robinson Memorial auditorium, and singer Bob McGrath (of soon-to-be *Sesame Street* fame) provided entertainment. Lieutenant governor Maurice "Footsie" Britt, a former Detroit Lion and World War II Medal of Honor recipient, presented Sanders with a gold medallion in addition to his award, which came in the form of an engraved bronze plaque. The *Arkansas Democrat* approvingly said Sanders' talk at the dinner was, "to the surprise of no one," the "best speech of the evening." The rabbi presented "the same lesson that he [had] expressed in a thousand different ways over the years: 'We must learn to live together or we shall vanish as a passing race of fallen giants.'"[8] Sanders also said, "I have great hope for the future of the world," even in the midst of the turmoil and social upheaval of 1968. Social and racial justice remained the key. Sanders called for "brotherhood among men of all races and faiths" and said that "such brotherhood must begin on the individual level." The rabbi stated that each man must seek out the other, and once met, the two would "form the first couplet of a long and beautiful love poem, a psalm of psalms, dedicated to the brotherhood of man." For Sanders, America's future rested "not on black power or white power, but on cultural pluralism, neither of which segment can survive without the other."[9] Sanders was unhappy with the nation's priorities: "I want to see less money spent on going to the moon and on the senseless Vietnam War and more being spent for the eradication of poverty, crime, and other maladjustments of society which produce an Oswald who kills a president of the United States." He also expressed concerns about societal and campus unrest: "There is too much educating of the minds and far too little educating of the emotions being done."[10] He called for more readily available counselling and psychological assistance at the nation's universities and colleges. The Presbyterian minister who closed the gathering offered the simplest of benedictions, summing up the feelings of many as he gave "thanks to God for seeing to it that Dr. Sanders had come to Arkansas to live."[11] Soon after this event, Sanders appeared on the local NBC television affiliate KARK as a guest on the NCCJ-sponsored public service program *People and Patterns*.[12]

From Life to Life

Call me Rabbi.
—IRA SANDERS, 1985

All of the honors and plaudits conferred upon Ira Sanders both during his career and after his retirement speak to the tremendous impact he had on Little Rock over the decades since his arrival in 1926. Reflecting on his years in Arkansas in a pair of interviews conducted in 1977 and 1978, Rabbi Sanders admired the ways in which Little Rock had so greatly evolved since his arrival, having "moved from a closed to an open community, more diverse, more cosmopolitan, a place where cultural pluralism should be fulfilled, in which each group has a part to play."[13] The fierce Jim Crow restrictions he had challenged in the early twentieth century had long since given way to a more open and egalitarian society. The "wilderness," as he derisively described Little Rock upon his arrival, had grown into a progressive metropolitan area with a social service and racial justice infrastructure. And he had helped develop or broker this enduring infrastructure through the Little Rock School of Social Work, the Urban League of Greater Little Rock, the Lighthouse for the Blind, and a variety of other social welfare and community service agencies. His leadership and his drive to make a difference in ways both large and small had paid enormous dividends. The modern, diverse, cosmopolitan Little Rock he admired in 1978 was in many ways the culmination of the fruits of his own labors over the decades.[14]

In retirement, Rabbi Sanders took on a new role as rabbi emeritus at Temple B'nai Israel.[15] His successor, Elijah Ezekiel "Zeke" Palnick, at twenty-eight years of age, was forty years his junior. He recalls their first meeting: "Splendidly arrayed in a crisp and spotless white shirt, tie, and brown suit, [Sanders] waited in his office on a beautiful June afternoon in 1963 to welcome Irene and me to Little Rock and Temple B'nai Israel." Sanders tried to reassure young Palnick, "If you accept this call and succeed me as rabbi, you will never talk about me as your friends talk about my friends." By this Sanders meant that Palnick need not have any concerns about him undercutting his authority or usurping his role as rabbi; instead, he offered unconditional support and loyalty. "From that moment on," Palnick recalled, "he became my teacher and my friend, my rabbi, part of our family." Palnick served Congregation B'nai Israel for twenty-four years, and for nearly all that time, Sanders stood by his side as a mentor and guide.[16]

A civil rights activist in his own right, Palnick had played a significant role in the desegregation of the University of Alabama. He continued, and in many ways expanded on, Sanders' tradition of community activism in Little Rock, leading and participating in direct action campaigns and marches.[17] "Ira fought for the things he believed in," Palnick remembered, and he built on the tradition, using the pulpit to persuade on the issue of civil rights, "probably too much," he later recalled. Palnick loved and admired Sanders, who "had earlier been a fighter in the battle" for racial justice, and he saw himself very much in the Sanders mode, viewing his tenure in Little Rock as a continuation of Sanders' tenure. Despite their wide age differences, Palnick said, "I don't think there was an iota of difference in the way we thought about the great social issues."[18] Rabbi Palnick's rabbinate, especially in his first ten years in the Little Rock pulpit, reflected a generational shift that could be seen across the southern Jewish civil rights leadership toward more forthright activism and direct action campaigns, a shift that mirrored the overall evolution of the civil rights movement in general.

Rabbi Sanders began work on his autobiography, "The Journal of a Southern Rabbi," in 1973 and wrote on and off for the next several years, never completing it. Because of his penchant for precision of language, he wrote portions of it over and over, rewriting and fine-tuning, while other sections are little more than basic ideas and conceptions of possible topics. What survives is a combination of typewritten and handwritten manuscripts. They are written in the third person, as Sanders chose to refer to himself by his Hebrew name "Isaac"—often "Isaac, son of Aaron"—or sometimes as "he," rather than "Ira" or "I." This choice, combined with his customary formality, resulted in some awkward and stilted prose at times, as in his opening sentence, which describes his encounter with Clarence Darrow: "Isaac, son of Aaron, was in the thirty-sixth year of his life when, on November 16, 1930, a committee of three men met the train that brought the renowned Clarence Darrow to Little Rock, Arkansas for a debate with Isaac."[19] He filled out his memoir by adding some of his sermons and other public addresses to the work as well. As he began to lose his eyesight, he used dictation to continue the work.

Rabbi Sanders at his eightieth birthday celebration, 1974.
Courtesy Temple B'nai Israel, Little Rock, Arkansas.

Congregation B'nai Israel honored Rabbi Sanders' fiftieth anniversary with
the temple on September 8, 1976, by holding a celebration in the modern and
magnificent new facility in West Little Rock, which had been dedicated in 1975
and remains the congregation's home. The new temple incorporated many
cherished elements and items from the congregation's previous home. It was
designed by congregant and architect Eugene P. Levy, who decades earlier as a
young boy attended the temple's religious school. Levy reflected on his childhood under the sometimes imposing presence of his rabbi by saying that he
"did not know the difference between Rabbi Sanders and God." The old temple
at Fifth (later Capitol Avenue) and Broadway in downtown Little Rock, the
congregation's home since May 1897, had been sold and torn down to make way
for the modernization of the downtown area. At the well-attended celebration
of Dr. Sanders' half-century in Little Rock, the congregation presented their
rabbi emeritus with an official portrait and a "love gift" of fifteen thousand dollars, among other gifts.[20] The portrait was displayed in the new temple and still
hangs in the temple library.

Tragedy struck Rabbi Sanders and the congregational family when, on June 28, 1978, Dr. Sanders' wife of fifty-six years, Selma Loeb Sanders, died.[21] With a sly wit and a sparkling sense of humor, but never as comfortable in the public eye as Ira, Selma had been a quiet, reserved woman less involved than her husband with community affairs. The exception was her participation (along with hundreds of others) in the Women's Emergency Committee to Open our Schools (WEC) during the Little Rock Central High School crisis. Over the years, though, she helped the rabbi with his sermons and addresses, skillfully editing his work. Rabbi Palnick presided over the funeral service; in his eulogy, Palnick recalled, "Selma Sanders never let anyone hold her husband too cheap. Fearfully protective, genuinely funny at times, with a rapier wit to pierce pretensions, she ensured their honest name."[22]

Sanders spent his final years in ill health, wrapped in the love and support of the Little Rock community, as a figure of profound admiration. This cofounder of the Arkansas Lighthouse for the Blind began himself to lose his sight during his last decade, and he was legally blind for the final five years of his life. He underwent two separate surgeries for cataracts in both eyes in 1980, but progressive macular degeneration eventually robbed him of all but rudimentary peripheral vision. His spirits flagged, and a diagnosis of leukemia made Sanders even more pessimistic about his future. Dr. Hampton Roy, his friend and his ophthalmic surgeon, scolded Sanders over his attitude, telling the rabbi he "should be ashamed of [himself]" and reminding him of his promise to stay positive in the wake of his blindness.[23] Friends, loved ones, and the community rallied around their ailing rabbi to offer support in many different ways. A lifelong avid reader and lover of books, Sanders feared the loss of his sight would rob him of the enjoyment of books, but friends, congregants, and loved ones stepped forward and volunteered to read to him. On a regular basis, friends sat with him and served as his eyes, reading to him from his substantial library. Others ran errands, shopped, helped him write his memoirs and manage his mail, and cooked for him. Rabbi Sanders' lifetime of devotion to the Little Rock community and his congregation now came back to him a hundredfold.[24]

As Sanders' health continued to falter, Rabbi Palnick wrote to him in 1984 on the occasion of his mentor's ninetieth birthday in order to express, perhaps for the last time, what Sanders had meant to him; in doing so, he spoke for the community as a whole. "You have been an inspiration to me," he wrote. "I have found in you a model to follow and a pattern to copy." Palnick told his rabbi emeritus, "You have modeled for me courage in the face of adversity and a faith that does not shrink."[25] In 1985, nearing death, Ira Sanders spent his last days in the hospital. The infirmities of age and illness had weakened his body but not his dignity and spirit. On the last day of his life, a hospital aide came to Rabbi Sanders' room to assist him in rolling over in the bed. As she worked to move him, she prompted him, "Move over, Ira." Upon hearing those words, Sanders paused and, though weak and blind, turned his head toward her. "You don't know me well enough to call me Ira," he said. "Call me Rabbi." Despite the ravages of illness and age that afflicted his physical state, his dignity, mental acuity, and sense of propriety remained as strong as ever. "Call me Rabbi" were the last words he spoke before he died on April 8, 1985, just weeks short of his ninety-first birthday.[26]

In life, Rabbi Ira Sanders enjoyed reading poetry and himself had a felicity for writing poetry. In the many funeral services over which he presided, he often read a poem from an anonymous author he found particularly meaningful. Rabbi Palnick read this poem at Sanders' funeral:

There is no death.
What we call death is but a sudden change.
Because we know not where it leads, therefore it seemeth strange.
There is no death.
What we call death is but a restful sleep.
They wake not soon who slumber so; therefore we mourn, we weep.
There is no death.
What we call death is but surcease from strife.
They do not die whom we call dead.
They go from life to life.

After a most productive and meaningful ninety years, Rabbi Sanders was at rest, on a journey "from life to life."[27]

As a testament to Ira Sanders, the *Arkansas Democrat* honored him in 1986 as part of the Arkansas sesquicentennial celebration the newspaper termed "Project Pride," which celebrated the accomplishments of Arkansans who had made significant community, state, and national contributions over the state's 150-year history. Simply headlined "Rabbi Sanders Sought Rights for Minorities," the article was a fitting tribute for a rabbi who in 1977 had summed up his career similarly: "The part of my ministry which has appealed to me the most, of course, has been my stand on integration."[28]

There is no better summation of Ira Sanders' life, his philosophy, or his contributions to the life and history of Arkansas than the following excerpt from one of his most eloquent and heartfelt sermons. Inspired in part by his reading of the 1956 work *Justice and Judaism*, it was delivered on January 10, 1959, in the aftermath of the Little Rock Central High School affair. I offer it as a fitting conclusion to the life and work of the rabbi:

> In the Jewish tradition man is called the co-worker and partner of God in the creation of a better world. Judaism insists that we must apply constantly the sharp, ethical insights of the Prophets to the specific social problems of our generation. We do this through social action. We must battle against those conditions in inequality that deny any man his inalienable rights of free opportunity to education or economic security or civil liberties. We must fight those infringements of civil rights that deny any citizen of this land due regard for his civil liberties. We must carry on the battle for FEPC [Fair Employment Practices Commission], for fair employment practices, for the opportunity of a man to get a job without preference or discrimination shown because of race or color or creed. We must carry on the torch that has been lighted by the United States Supreme Court for desegregation. We must stand firm for legal rights and see to it that there is no second-class citizenship in the United States.
>
> Such a program translates our faith into concrete social action. . . . Such a program of social action works for the economic welfare of the entire country. Such a program seeks to avoid those tensions in areas of social distress that breed anti-Semitism. Such a program of social action upholds and defends and furthers democracy. Jewish religious bodies, and certainly members of Reform temples, have a deep responsibility to seek to strengthen democracy and the ideals of justice. We must bridge the gap between concession and commitment, between word and deed, by working for the establishment of a greater share of social justice to all.[29]

APPENDIX 1

The Rabbis of Little Rock's Congregation B'nai Israel

RABBI	TERM OF SERVICE	LENGTH OF SERVICE
Samuel Peck	1867–1868	1 year
(vacant)	*1868–1872*	
Jacob Bloch	1872–1880	8 years
N. J. Benson	1881–1884	3 years
Joseph Stolz	1884–1887	3 years
E. Eisenberg	1888	<1 year
Emmanuel Schreiber	1889–1891	2 years
Charles Rubenstein	1891–1897	6 years
Harry H. Mayer	1897–1899	2 years
Louis Wolsey	1899–1907	8 years
Louis Witt	1907–1919	12 years
James Heller	1920	1 year
Emanuel Jack	1921–1925	4 years
(vacant)	*1925–1926*	
Ira E. Sanders	1926–1963	37 years
Elijah E. Palnick	1963–1987	24 years
Eugene H. Levy	1987–2011	24 years
David Lipper	2012–2013	1 year
Barry Block	2013–	

Note: Rabbi Ira Sanders' tenure of nearly thirty-seven years was longer than the combined terms of service of the congregation's first *nine* rabbis. Together with his twenty-two years as rabbi emeritus, his rabbinate ushered in a period of increased stability and tenure lengths among the temple's subsequent rabbis.

Source: Ira Sanders and Elijah E. Palnick, eds., *One Hundred Years: Congregation B'nai Israel* (Little Rock: Congregation B'nai Israel, 1966), 83.

APPENDIX 2

Rabbi Ira Sanders' Speech before the Arkansas General Assembly,
February 18, 1957

I am Ira E. Sanders, rabbi of Congregation B'nai Israel, Little Rock. I have been its spiritual leader for almost thirty-one years. However, tonight I speak as a private citizen. I am representing no organization and no group. This I wish to be recorded most emphatically.

The state of Arkansas is very dear to me. It has provided me the opportunity to serve many causes in social welfare, touching both colored and white citizens, Jew and Christian alike. And in recognition of these efforts, the University of Arkansas in 1951 conferred upon me its highest honorary degree—Doctor of Humane Letters. I say this with the deepest humility, so that you may know why I doubly love this State and want to keep unsullied its good name. I would be unworthy of the sacred trust did I not raise my voice in protest of all four measures.

Why do I ask you, the senators of our state, to defeat these measures?

Above my love for Arkansas comes my devotion to America. This country protects your rights and mine through the finest interlocking of democratic processes in the world—its executive, its legislative, and its judicial departments. In the domain of the last of these, I regard the Supreme Court as the final democratic authority of the land, because it is the combined wisdom of all the people through the ballot box which gives to these legislators the high privilege of confirming or rejecting appointments of justices made by our chief executive, the president of the United States.

Because of the high legal talents with which they are endowed, it is their duty to interpret the Constitution as befit men of such high trust. Once they pass on the constitutionality of the law, it should become operative as the law of the land. Higher than the legal law, however, stands the moral law—those imperishable mandates which are the ethical repository of the best in our Judeo-Christian concept of life. Both Judaism and Christianity posit the dictum: "We shall have one law." And a great prophet among my people, Malachi, once said, "Have we all one Father, hath not one God made us all."

I believe that the words of Leviticus 25 are the bedrocks upon which American democracy alone can survive. That are these words inscribed on our Liberty Bell: "Ye shall proclaim liberty throughout the land unto all the inhabitants thereof." Our nation must be based on liberty and justice for all peoples, whose contributions to the cultural pluralism of our land have been great and varied. The dignity of the individual must never be destroyed by granting the state those powers which would deny anyone the liberty and the freedom guaranteed by the Constitution. These four bills on which we are speaking tonight were all concerned with the thought of circumventing the highest legal authority of the land. They will never stand the test of time, for higher than the legal law of the land stands this moral law of God. It operates slowly but surely, and in the end justice will prevail.

You have just passed a magnificent tax law to help the state financially. The increased revenue will bring untold good into the state, and industry from afar will want to come within our blessed boundaries to give to all of us increased economic, cultural and spiritual enrichment. If these measures which deny America's traditional guarantees of individual freedom and liberty are allowed to pass, the state you and I love will lose first an increased economy coming from new industries and secondly it will be held morally in just opprobrium before the country. And what you have done to bring industry into the state will be overwhelmingly nullified.

When Jesus died on the cross, He repeated those immortal words: "Father forgive them for they know not what they do." Legislators! May future generations reading the statute books of Arkansas laws not be compelled to say these words of you. For the sake of the glorious heritage Arkansas may yet give to our beloved America, defeat, I pray you, in toto, these four measures, and the God of all men will bless your handiwork.

Source: Ira E. Sanders. Papers. Box 1, file 15, Congregation B'nai Israel Archives, Little Rock, Arkansas.

APPENDIX 3

*Organizations in Which Rabbi Ira E. Sanders
Played a Significant Role*

American Council for Judaism
American Jewish Joint Distribution Committee
Arkansas Association for Mental Health
Arkansas Conference on Social Welfare
Arkansas Committee of the Displaced Persons Commission
Arkansas Eugenics Association
Arkansas Human Betterment League
Arkansas Jewish Assembly
Arkansas Lighthouse for the Blind
Arkansas Mental Health Hygiene Association
Arkansas Tuberculosis Association
Association of Southern Women for the Prevention of Lynching
Central Conference of American Rabbis
Congregation B'nai Israel
Congregation Keneseth Israel
Family Welfare Agency
Federation of Jewish Charities
Greater Little Rock Conference on Religion and Race
Greater Little Rock Ministerial Alliance
Jewish Chautauqua Society
Jewish Community Center of Allentown
Jewish Welfare Fund
Little Rock Central Council of Social Agencies
Little Rock Public Library
Little Rock Rotary Club
Little Rock School of Social Work
Ministry of Reconciliation
National Association for the Advancement of Colored People
National Association of Social Workers

National Conference of Christians and Jews
Palestine Foundation Fund
Pennsylvania Federation of Religious School Teachers
Planned Parenthood Association of Arkansas
Pulaski County Public Welfare Commission
Social Welfare Bureau (Little Rock)
Southwestern Assembly of Religious School Teachers
St. Louis–Little Rock Hospitals, Inc.
Temple Israel of the City of New York
Temple Men's Club (Little Rock)
Union of American Hebrew Congregations
University of Arkansas
Urban League of Greater Little Rock
Young Men's Hebrew Association

NOTES

Introduction

1. "Bills on Segregation Defended as Legal, Deplored as Unjust," *Arkansas Gazette*, February 19, 1957, 1; Ira Sanders oral history, 1977, transcribed interview with Charlotte Gadberry, December 5, 1977, Oral History Collection, UALR Center for Arkansas History and Culture, Arkansas Studies Institute, Little Rock, Arkansas [hereafter cited as ISOH transcript (1977)], 18. The audio of this interview is available at https://arstudies.contentdm.oclc.org/cdm/compoundobject/collection/p1532coll1/id/12585/rec/14.

2. ISOH transcript (1977), 18.

3. "Brotherhood," *Arkansas Gazette*, February 28, 1950, discusses Sanders' community work as coming without fanfare or "benefit of a publicity chairman."

4. "Bills on Segregation Defended as Legal, Deplored as Unjust," *Arkansas Gazette*, February 19, 1957, 1. The speech is fully discussed in chapter 7 and is reprinted in its entirety as appendix 2.

5. Moses, "The Law of Life is the Law of Service: Rabbi Ira Sanders and the Quest for Racial and Social Justice in Arkansas, 1926–1963," *Southern Jewish History* 10 (2007): 159–203; "The Jewish Experience in Arkansas: Rabbi Ira Sanders' Quest for Racial and Social Justice, 1926–1963," *Pulaski County Historical Review* 58 (Fall 2010): 96–116.

6. Besides the works cited and discussed in this introduction, see also Eric L. Goldstein, *The Price of Whiteness: Jews, Race, and American Identity* (Princeton: Princeton University Press, 2006); Debra Schultz, *Going South: Jewish Women in the Civil Rights Movement* (New York: New York University Press, 2001); Cheryl Greenberg, "The Southern Jewish Community and the Struggle for Civil Rights," in *African Americans and Jews in the Twentieth Century: Studies in Convergence and Conflict*, ed. V. P. Franklin et al. (Columbia: University of Missouri Press, 1999), 123–64; Seth Forman, "The Unbearable Whiteness of Being Jewish: Desegregation in the South and the Crisis of Jewish Liberalism," *American Jewish History* 85 (June 1997): 121–42; Eli N. Evans, *The Provincials: A Personal History of Jews in the South* (New York: Atheneum, 1973); Leonard Dinnerstein and Mary Dale Palsson, eds., *Jews in the South* (Baton Rouge: Louisiana State University Press, 1973); Leonard Dinnerstein, "Southern Jewry and the Desegregation Crisis, 1954–1970," *American Jewish Historical Quarterly* 62 (March 1973): 231–41.

7. Carolyn LeMaster, "Ira Eugene Sanders (1894–1985)," *The Encyclopedia of Arkansas History and Culture*, http://www.encyclopediaofarkansas.net/encyclopedia/entry-detail.aspx?entryID=1755.

8. Clive Webb, *Fight against Fear: Southern Jews and Black Civil Rights* (Athens: University of Georgia Press, 2001), 174.

9. Krause, "Rabbis and Negro Rights," 27, 29.

10. Mark Cowett, *Birmingham's Rabbi: Morris Newfield and Alabama, 1895–1940* (Tuscaloosa: University of Alabama Press, 1986), xi.

11. "Rabbi Sanders' Service," *Arkansas Gazette*, June 9, 1963.

12. "Prophetic Judaism" as a term came into general usage in the late 1950s and refers "not only to Amos and Ezekiel," writes Melissa Greene, "but—across two decades—to the humanitarianism of a small group of rabbis manning frontier outposts in hostile territory" during the civil rights movement. These rabbis made the "connection between the words of the prophets" and the African American movement "for civil equality." Melissa Fay Greene, *The Temple Bombing* (Reading, MA: Addison-Wesley, 1996), 178.

Chapter 1. Before Little Rock: 1894–1926

1. "The Journal of a Southern Rabbi" (hereafter referred to as Sanders Journal), p. 12, Temple Archives, Congregation B'nai Israel (hereafter cited as Temple Archives), box 1, Little Rock, Arkansas. This manuscript was a memoir that Sanders began in 1973 but never finished. Sanders wrote in the third person, referring to himself by his Hebrew name Isaac.

2. Flora Sanders to Carolyn LeMaster, April 29, 2004, series I, subseries III, box 9, file 7, Carolyn LeMaster Arkansas Jewish History Collection, Butler Center for Arkansas Studies, Arkansas Studies Institute, Little Rock, Arkansas (hereafter referred to as LeMaster Collection); Paula Sanders, telephone interview with the author, November 16, 2017. See also Sanders Journal, 13–16; ISOH transcript (1977), 1.

3. Sanders Journal, 13–15; Flora Sanders, telephone interview, November 6, 2017; Paula Sanders, telephone interview, November 16, 2017.

4. Sanders Journal, 17–20. Sanders later said, "I especially became interested [as a child] in the promotion of good will between peoples and felt I could serve better in that capacity as a rabbi." Ira Sanders oral history, 1978, transcribed interview with Charlotte Gadberry, January 18, 1978, Oral History Collection, UALR Center for Arkansas History and Culture, Arkansas Studies Institute, Little Rock, Arkansas [hereafter ISOH transcript (1978)], 15. The audio of this interview is available at https://arstudies.contentdm.oclc.org/cdm/compoundobject/collection/p15532coll1/id/12585/show/12584/rec/16.

5. Sanders Journal, 19.

6. Sanders Journal, 19–20.

7. Sanders Journal, 19–20.

8. Sanders Journal, 24–25. Sanders purposefully left his landlady unnamed in his memoir.

9. Sanders Journal, 25–26. Liebert went on to pulpits in San Rafael and Long Beach, California.

10. Sanders Journal, 25–27. Franklin went on to pulpits in Vicksburg, Mississippi, and succeeded Rabbi Liebert at Temple Israel in Long Beach, California.

11. Sanders Journal, 27–28; Ira E. Sanders and Elijah E. Palnick, eds., *One Hundred Years: Congregation B'nai Israel* (Little Rock, 1966), 67.

12. Sanders Journal, 32–32D.

13. Meyer Jacob to Sanders, February 11, 1919; Max Kahn to Sanders, March 8, 1919; Congregation Keneseth Israel to Sanders, March 25, 1919, box 1, Ira E. Sanders Papers, UALR Center for Arkansas History and Culture, Arkansas Studies Institute, Little Rock, Arkansas, [hereafter cited as Sanders Papers, UALR].

14. Sanders Journal, 34.

15. Sanders, "Business, Allentown, and the Jew," *The Community Voice* 1 (June 1920): 4–5, series 1, subseries III, box 8, file 8, LeMaster Collection; see also Sanders Journal, 35–36.

16. Sanders Journal, 35–36; ISOH transcript (1977), 4–5; Lynn Dumenil, *The Modern Temper: American Culture and Society in the 1920s* (New York: Hill and Wang, 1995), 167. In his journal, Sanders recalled travelling to New York once a week, but he stated in a 1977 interview that he did so twice a week.

17. Center for Jewish History, "Guide to the American Jewish Joint Committee Collection," Center for Jewish History, accessed January 25, 2016, http://findingaids .cjh.org/?pID=121489.

18. "Jacob Henry Schiff," Jewish Virtual Library, accessed May 27, 2016, http:// www.jewishvirtuallibrary.org/jsource/biography/schiff.html. Schiff died September 25, 1920.

19. Sanders Journal, 34–35.

20. Sanders Journal, 39. The Chautauqua was an educational movement prominent from the late nineteenth century, a combination of education and entertainment that featured speakers on wide varieties of topics.

21. Sanders Journal, 37; Rabbi Elijah E. "Zeke" Palnick, interview with the author, November 16, 2004, Little Rock, Arkansas. Palnick succeeded Sanders as the rabbi of Congregation B'nai Israel of Little Rock, serving from 1963 to 1986. During almost all of that time, Sanders served as rabbi emeritus and had an office alongside Palnick's. Rabbi Palnick considered Sanders a mentor and dear friend. Sanders' evolving view of Zionism is discussed in chapter 5 of this work.

22. Flora Sanders, email to Carolyn LeMaster, June 11, 2004, copy in series I, subseries III, box 9, file 7, LeMaster Collection.

23. ISOH transcript (1977), 3; Sanders Journal, 37–39. A love letter from Selma is at 37a–37b.

24. Rabbi Elijah E. Palnick, voice recording on the occasion of Rabbi Sanders' one-hundredth Birthday, May 5, 1994, cassette tape, Temple Archives.

25. Sanders to the Jewish National Workers' Alliance, Branch no. 103, July 26, 1920, series I, subseries III, box 8, file 8, LeMaster Collection.

26. "Allentown Congregation Shows Its Appreciation to Rabbi Ira E. Sanders," "Rabbi Sanders Accepts Charge in Metropolis," unknown newspaper clippings, n.d., series I, subseries II, box 8, file 8, LeMaster Collection. The Young Men's Hebrew Association, first established in New York in 1874, was the Jewish analog to the YMCA. They were later renamed Jewish Community Centers, or JCCs.

27. "Rabbi Sanders in Charge of Temple," *Allentown Morning Call* [1919?]; *Templegram* [Congregation Keneseth Israel newsletter], inaugural issue (November 1922). Both in series I, subseries III, box 8, file 8, LeMaster Collection.

28. "Memorial Service at Keneseth Israel," unknown newspaper clipping, February 11, 1924, box 1, file 4, Sanders Papers, UALR.

29. "Our History," Temple Israel of the City of New York, accessed August 24, 2015, http://www.templeisraelnyc.org/about-us/our-history.

30. Maurice Harris, telegram to Ira Sanders, May 27, 1924, with Sanders' handwritten response on back, box 1, Sanders Papers, UALR.

31. "Rabbi Ira Sanders Called to New York," *Kansas City Jewish Chronicle*, June 20, 1924, 4.

32. Sanders, "The Law of Life is the Law of Service," Temple Israel of the City of New York, September 24, 1924, reprinted in Sanders Journal, 40–40A. Temple Israel printed a synopsis of the previous Friday evening's sermons each Wednesday. (Sanders added many of his New York sermons to his journal, inserted and paginated alphabetically following page 40.)

33. "Rabbi Ira Sanders — Logic and Persuasion," *Arkansas Gazette*, February 21, 1954; Flora Sanders, interview with the author, May 22, 2007, Little Rock, Arkansas. To this author's ear, Sanders' voice sounds something like the precise diction of radio journalist H. V. Kaltenborn.

34. Sanders quoted in "Rabbi Ira Sanders — Logic and Persuasion," *Arkansas Gazette*, February 21, 1954.

35. "Haman Alive," sermon of April 2, 1925, in Sanders Journal, 40CC. Sanders' unpublished memoir itself is an example of his penchant for unduly formal language, making it often ponderous and essentially unpublishable.

36. Flora Sanders interview, May 22, 2007.

37. "After the Election," sermon of November 14, 1924, in Sanders Journal, 40H–40J.

38. ISOH transcript (1977), 5–6; Flora Sanders, telephone interview with the author, November 6, 2004; Flora Sanders interview, May 22, 2007; ISOH transcript (1978), 10.

39. ISOH transcript (1977), 5. On Lillian Wald, see Marjorie N. Feld, *Lillian Wald: A Biography* (Chapel Hill: University of North Carolina Press, 2009); see also "Women of Valor," Jewish Women's Archive, accessed May 11, 2007, http://www.jwa.org/exhibits/wov/wald/lwbio.html.

40. "NAACP: 100 Years of History," NAACP, accessed January 25, 2016, http://www.naacp.org/pages/naacp-history.

41. Flora Sanders, email message to the author, June 1, 2015; Flora Sanders interview, May 22, 2007.

Chapter 2. Rabbi Sanders Goes to Arkansas: 1926–1934

1. Eli N. Evans, *The Provincials: A Personal History of Jews in the South* (New York: Atheneum, 1973), 96–97.

2. See LeMaster, *A Corner of the Tapestry*, for an encyclopedic history of the Jewish presence in Arkansas. See esp. p. 58 on the early history of the Little Rock Jews.

3. See LeMaster, *A Corner of the Tapestry*, 190; Sanders and Palnick, *One Hundred Years*. Maurice Altheimer anglicized the pronunciation of his name: "MAU-ris," not "Mah-REES."

4. LeMaster, *A Corner of the Tapestry*, 63; Gary P. Zola and Marc Dollinger, eds., *American Jewish History: A Primary Source Reader* (Waltham, MA: Brandeis University Press, 2014), 204. See also Charles C. Alexander, *The Ku Klux Klan in the*

Southwest (Norman: University of Oklahoma Press, 1995) and Kenneth C. Barnes, *Anti-Catholicism in Arkansas: How Politicians, the Press, the Klan, and Religious Leaders Imagined an Enemy* (Fayetteville: University of Arkansas Press, 2016).

5. "When the Rabbi Came, He Came to Stay," *Arkansas Democrat*, May 11, 1974.

6. Special meeting minutes, June 8, 1926, in box "Temple Business, 1924–1937," Temple Archives. Adjusted for inflation, an annual salary of $10,000 in 1926 equates to a modern salary of about $135,000 per year. It was a generous offer designed to convince Sanders to take the job.

7. Maurice Altheimer to Ira Sanders, June 9, 1926, box 2, Ira E. Sanders Papers, Temple Archives, Congregation B'nai Israel, Little Rock, Arkansas (hereafter cited as Sanders Papers, Temple).

8. Leo Pfeifer to Ira Sanders, June 12, 1926, box 2, Sanders Papers, Temple.

9. "New Rabbi for Local Temple," *Arkansas Democrat*, June 13, 1926, clipping in box 2, file 10, Sanders Papers, UALR.

10. Preston Pfeifer, telegram to Ira Sanders, June 12, 1926, box 4, file "Correspondence," Sanders Papers, Temple.

11. Myron Lasker to Sanders, June 14, 1926, box 4, file "Correspondence," Sanders Papers, Temple.

12. "They Had to Argue to Get Rabbi Sanders to Go to Little Rock—But He Has Stayed 25 Years," *Arkansas Gazette*, June 12, 1951.

13. ISOH transcript (1977), 6. The recorded high that day in Little Rock was only ninety-four degrees, but temperatures above ninety would last an additional three weeks.

14. Maurice Altheimer to D. L. Menkus, August 28, 1926, series I, subseries III, box 9, file 3, LeMaster Collection. In 1926, Rosh Hashanah fell on September 9, only eight days after Sanders' arrival.

15. He later told his daughter Flora Sanders this, according to an email message to the author, June 1, 2015.

16. ISOH transcript (1978), 10; "Rabbi Ira E. Sanders—Logic and Persuasion," *Arkansas Gazette*, February 21, 1954; Sanders and Palnick, *One Hundred Years*, 67; *Arkansas Gazette*, June 21, 1951. Flora Sanders also commented on her father's initial belief that coming to Little Rock "was a big mistake."

17. "When the Rabbi Came, He Came to Stay," *Arkansas Democrat*, May 11, 1974.

18. Board meeting minutes, October 12, 1926, box "Temple Business, 1924–1937," Temple Archives. The weekly publication of the *Chronicle* lasted one month only, most likely due to the lack of new material to fill it every week. Beginning in November 1926, the newsletter was issued bi-weekly for a time.

19. Annual meeting minutes, January 31, 1927, box "Temple Business, 1924–1937," Temple Archives. The meeting was held as a dinner that year, again on the unanimously approved suggestion of Rabbi Sanders during the board meeting of January 4.

20. See appendix 1.

21. Annual meeting minutes, January 29, 1928; president's report, January 29, 1928; board meeting minutes, February 14, 1928; board meeting minutes, October 23, 1928. All in box "Temple Business 1924–1937," Temple Archives.

22. Sanders to Lasker Ehrman, temple board vice-president, May 7, 1928, box 4, Sanders Papers, Temple.

23. Annual meeting minutes, January 27, 1929; board meeting minutes, June 11,

1929. Both in box "Temple Business 1924–1937," Temple Archives. A salary of $12,000 in 1929 dollars equates to about $175,000 in 2018 dollars. Sanders was well paid.

24. See Fon Louise Gordon, *Caste and Class: The Black Experience in Arkansas, 1880–1920* (Athens: University of Georgia Press, 1995); see also Cherisse Jones-Branch's excellent summary "Segregation and Desegregation," in *Encyclopedia of Arkansas History and Culture*, accessed May 2, 2016, http://www.encyclopediaof arkansas.net/encyclopedia/entry-detail.aspx?entryID=3079.

25. Jones-Branch, "Segregation and Desegregation"; Ben F. Johnson, *Arkansas in Modern America, 1930–1999* (Fayetteville: University of Arkansas Press, 2000), 6; Gordon, *Caste and Class*; *The Civil Rights Cases*, 109 U.S. 3 (1883); *Plessy v. Ferguson*, 163 U.S. 537 (1896); John William Graves, "Jim Crow in Arkansas: A Reconsideration of Urban Race Relations in the Post-Reconstruction South," *Journal of Southern History* 55 (August 1989): 421–48.

26. Flora Sanders, telephone interview with the author, October 27, 2006.

27. ISOH transcript (1977), 12–13. In recounting the story in this interview later in life, Sanders could not bring himself to use the offensive racial slur spoken by the conductor and which he detested, but he made plain what was said.

28. ISOH transcript (1977), 13; *Arkansas Gazette*, May 11, 1974. Unfortunately, though fragments of the sermon appear in his journal and later interviews, the sermon itself is lost.

29. The Mosaic Templars of America is an African American fraternal organization founded in 1882 and headquartered in Little Rock. See "Mosaic Templars of America," http://www.encyclopediaofarkansas.net/encyclopedia/entry-detail.aspx?entryID =1186.

30. "With Officers Making No Attempt at Restraint, Mob Burns Negro's Body and Creates a Reign of Terror," *Arkansas Gazette*, May 5, 1927, 1; "Mob Burns Man's Body in Little Rock Street," *Washington Post*, May 5, 1927, 1; Brian Greer, "The Last Lynching: A New Look at Little Rock's Last Episode of Deadly Mob Justice," *Arkansas Times*, August 4, 2000, 12–19; ISOH transcript (1978), 11–12.

31. Webb, *Fight against Fear*, 174; Harvard Sitkoff, *A New Deal for Blacks: The Emergence of Civil Rights as a National Issue: The Depression Decade* (New York: Oxford University Press, 1978), 274–275; ISOH transcript (1978), 12. On the ASWPL, see also Henry E. Barber, "The Association of Southern Women for the Prevention of Lynching, 1930–1942," *Phylon* 34 (December 1973): 378–89.

32. I am not suggesting that Sanders' sermons on racial justice were met with universal acclaim; this seems unlikely, and I'm fairly certain some congregants would have disagreed with him, particularly on issues of race. Such discord simply does not appear in the historical record.

33. On the Leo Frank case, see Steve Oney, *And the Dead Shall Rise: The Murder of Mary Phagan and the Lynching of Leo Frank* (New York: Vintage, 2004).

34. Flora Sanders, telephone interview with the author, November 18, 2015.

35. Jerry Jacobson, interview with the author, June 2, 2015; Maxwell "Mac" Lyons II, interview with the author, June 1, 2015; James Pfeifer, interview with the author, June 1, 2015.

36. "Rabbi Ira E. Sanders—Logic and Persuasion," *Arkansas Gazette*, February 21, 1954.

37. Alan Thalheimer, interview with the author, March 29, 2016, Little Rock, Arkansas.

38. "Seventieth Anniversary Service and Dedication of the New Altar," program, March 5, 1937, series III, subseries I, box 2 file 2, LeMaster Collection. In 2003 the UAHC became the Union for Reform Judaism.

39. Flora Sanders, telephone interview with the author, November 18, 2015; interview with the author, May 22, 2007, Little Rock, Arkansas.

40. Sanders Journal, 57–58.

41. For example, as to kosher laws and other rituals, the Pittsburgh Platform states, "We hold that all such Mosaic and rabbinical laws as regulated diet, priestly purity, and dress originated in ages and under the influence of ideas entirely foreign to our present mental and spiritual state. They fail to impress the modern Jew with a spirit of priestly holiness; their observance in our days is apt rather to obstruct than to further modern spiritual elevation." Full text of the Pittsburgh Platform is available at Central Conference of American Rabbis, "1885 Pittsburgh Conference," accessed June 8, 2015, http://ccarnet.org/rabbis-speak/platforms/declaration-principles. See also Michael A. Meyer, *Response to Modernity: A History of the Reform Movement in Judaism* (Detroit: Wayne State University Press, 1995); Paul Johnson, *A History of the Jews* (New York: Harper, 1987), 370.

42. ISOH transcript (1977), 17.

43. ISOH transcript (1978), 15.

44. Sanders quoted in *Arkansas Gazette*, June 8, 1963.

45. David Marx, a rabbi in Atlanta, is a good example and provides a nice comparison. See Mark K. Bauman and Arnold Shankman, "The Rabbi as Ethnic Broker: The Case of David Marx," *Journal of American Ethnic History* 2 (Spring 1983): 51–68; George R. Wilkes, "Rabbi Dr. David Marx and the Unity Club: Organized Jewish-Christian Dialogue, Liberalism, and Religious Diversity in Early Twentieth-Century Atlanta," *Southern Jewish History* 9 (2006): 35–68.

46. ISOH transcript (1978), 7–8; Sanders Journal, 37.

47. Newspaper clipping discussing Sanders' selection as president of the Little Rock Central Council of Social Agencies, 1927, box 1, Sanders Papers, Temple. The Community Fund was established in 1923 as a means to provide "a more effective, economical, and systematic plan of caring for [Little Rock's] poor and needy." Community Fund pamphlet, 1927, series I, subseries III, box 9, file 1, LeMaster Collection; also in box 2, file 1, Sanders Papers, Temple.

48. ISOH transcript (1977), 7–8; Sanders Journal, 37.

49. Sanders Journal, 37–38.

50. "Announcement—Little Rock School of Social Work 1928–1929," series V, box 1, file 6, LeMaster Collection; see also flyer announcing the opening of the Little Rock School of Social Work, box 1, Sanders Papers, Temple; Sanders Journal, 38.

51. ISOH transcript (1977), 10; Sanders Journal, 38; "Rabbi Ira E. Sanders—Logic and Persuasion," *Arkansas Gazette*, February 21, 1954; LeMaster, *Corner of the Tapestry*, 64.

52. ISOH transcript (1977), 10; *Arkansas Democrat*, May 11, 1974.

53. Sanders, speech before the annual meeting of the Arkansas chapter of the National Association of Social Workers, March 21, 1964, Little Rock, Arkansas, in

box 2, "Sermons and Addresses," Sanders Papers, Temple; LeMaster, *Corner of the Tapestry*, 480; "Rabbi Ira E. Sanders—Logic and Persuasion," *Arkansas Gazette*, February 21, 1954.

54. Sadye Allen Thompson, interview with Carolyn LeMaster, March 15, 1982, series V, box 1, file 11, LeMaster Collection.

Chapter 3. Race and Poverty in the Great Depression: 1929–1937

1. Sanders played no significant role in immediate Mississippi River flood relief, having just arrived in Arkansas. He was focused on Little Rock's issues of poverty and need. On the flood and its effects, see "Flood of 1927," *Encyclopedia of Arkansas History and Culture*, accessed November 1, 2017, http://www.encyclopediaofarkansas .net/encyclopedia/entry-detail.aspx?entryID=2202. See also Russell E. Bearden, "Arkansas' Worst Disaster: The Great Mississippi River Flood of 1927," *Arkansas Review: A Journal of Delta Studies* 34 (August 2003): 79–97; Pete Daniel, *Deep'n as it Come: The 1927 Mississippi River Flood* (Fayetteville: University of Arkansas Press, 1996).

2. Elizabeth C. Perry and F. Hampton Roy, "The Rabbi and Clarence Darrow," *Pulaski County Historical Review* 28 (Summer 1980): 2; "Rabbi Will End 37 Years at B'nai Israel August 31," *Arkansas Gazette*, June 8, 1963, 2A; Sanders Journal, 2.

3. Sanders Journal, 1–2.

4. "Agnostic and Rabbi Debate 'Immortality,'" *Arkansas Gazette*, November 4, 1930, 18; Sanders Journal, 3–4.

5. "Agnostic and Rabbi Debate 'Immortality,'" *Arkansas Gazette*, November 4, 1930, 18; Perry and Roy, "The Rabbi and Clarence Darrow," 3.

6. Raida Pfeifer, quoted in "The Great Debate That Drew an Encore," *Focal Point*, December 1999, p. 3. *Focal Point* is the newsletter of the organization Friends of Central Arkansas Libraries. Copy in box 2, file 14, Sanders Papers, Temple.

7. Paul Quillian to Sanders, November 4, 1930, box 1, Sanders Papers, UALR; LeMaster, *A Corner of the Tapestry*, 316; "Rabbi Will End 37 Years at B'nai Israel August 31," *Arkansas Gazette*, June 8, 1963, 2A.

8. My analysis is strongly informed by John Galbraith, whose critical analyses of the causes of the Depression remain for me the most satisfying, as strikingly trenchant now as then. John Kenneth Galbraith, *The Great Crash 1929* (Boston: Houghton Mifflin, 1954; reprint ed., Mariner Books, 2009), 168–96. See also John Garraty, *The Great Depression* (New York: Harcourt, 1986), which offers a worldwide perspective.

9. Johnson, *Arkansas in Modern America*, 1–12; for more on Hoover and the drought, see David E. Hamilton, "Herbert Hoover and the Great Drought of 1930," *Journal of American History* 68 (March 1982): 850–75; Nan Woodruff, "The Failure of Relief during the Arkansas Drought, 1930–1931," *Arkansas Historical Quarterly* 39 (Winter 1980): 301–13; see also "Drought of 1930–1931," accessed July 6, 2015, *Encyclopedia of Arkansas History and Culture*, http://www.encyclopediaofarkansas. net/encyclopedia/entry-detail.aspx?entryID=4344. On Hoover's approach to relief in general, see Joan Hoff Wilson, *Herbert Hoover, Forgotten Progressive* (Boston: Little, Brown, 1975); Charles Rappleye, *Herbert Hoover in the White House: The Ordeal of the Presidency* (New York: Simon and Schuster, 2016).

10. Holly Hope, "An Ambition to Be Preferred: New Deal Recovery Efforts and Architecture in Arkansas, 1933–1943," Arkansas Historic Preservation Program, Department of Arkansas Heritage, 2006, accessed March 2, 2016, https://www .arkansaspreservation.com/LiteratureRetrieve.aspx?ID=133233; "500 Farmers Storm Arkansas Town Demanding Food for their Children," *New York Times*, January 4, 1931, 1. The England crisis was resolved after a hasty telephone call to Little Rock prompted the Red Cross to authorize its local representative to give $2.50 in food to each needy family.

11. Board meeting minutes, January 14, 1930, box "Temple Business 1924–1937," file "Temple Board Business Minutes 1930," Temple Archives.

12. LeMaster, *Corner of the Tapestry*, 310–14, 323.

13. ISOH transcript (1977), 15–16; ISOH transcript (1978), 7–8; Sanders Journal, 40.

14. See *Arkansas Gazette*, December 14, 1934.

15. Regarding the contract, see annual meeting minutes, January 27, 1929, box "Temple Business, 1924–1937," Temple Archives. Regarding the salary increase, see board meeting minutes, June 11, 1929, box "Temple Business, 1924–1937," Temple Archives.

16. Board meeting minutes, October 14, 1930, box "Temple Business, 1924–1937," Temple Archives, emphasis added.

17. John Henry, "The Depression and Arkansas: Historians Shine Light on Dark Era," *Arkansas Business*, March 30, 2009, http://www.arkansasbusiness.com/article /40159/the-depression-and-arkansas-historians-shine-light-on-dark-era?page=all, accessed May 25, 2010.

18. Ira Sanders to Maurice Altheimer, December 19, 1932, box 4, file "Correspondence," Sanders Papers, Temple.

19. Board meeting minutes, December 27, 1932, Box "Temple Business, 1924–1937," Temple Archives.

20. Special board meeting minutes, May 27, 1946, box 2, file 14, Sanders Papers, Temple; board meeting minutes, February 19, 1957, box "Temple Business, 1957–1964," Temple Archives.

21. ISOH transcript (1978), 7–8; Federal Emergency Relief Administration, "Unemployables in Arkansas," 1934, 1–2, 4, box 1, file 5, Arkansas Small Manuscript Materials, Butler Center for Arkansas Studies, Arkansas Studies Institute, Little Rock, Arkansas; Hope, "An Ambition to be Preferred," 15–16.

22. Patrick J. Maney, *The Roosevelt Presence: The Life and Legacy of FDR* (Berkeley: University of California Press, 1992), 59.

23. Harry Hopkins, press conference of March 30, 1934, in Washington, DC, in WPA Papers, National Archives and Records Administration, Washington, DC, Record Group 69, series 737, box 4, available online at "Work Relief Administration Press Conferences," *New Deal Network*, accessed February 17, 2016, http://newdeal .feri.org/workrelief/hop04.htm; Roosevelt quoted in Robert E. Sherwood, *Roosevelt and Hopkins: An Intimate History* (New York: Harper & Brothers, 1948), 53–55; Hope, "An Ambition to be Preferred," 14.

24. *Arkansas Democrat*, April 12, 1934, 6; LeMaster, *A Corner of the Tapestry*, 314; William J. Atto, "Brooks Hays and the New Deal," *Arkansas Historical Quarterly* 67 (Summer 2008): 172.

25. Unidentified newspaper clipping, "10-Cent Utility Bill Tax Voted for Relief," reporting an Associated Press story, dateline May 1, 1934, box 1, Sanders Papers, Temple; "Doing unto Others," brochure explaining the "voluntary tax," 1934, series I, subseries III, box 9, file 1, LeMaster Collection; *Arkansas Democrat*, April 12, 1934, 6.

26. Sanders to Arkansas Water Co., May 17, 1934, box 2, file 1, Sanders Papers, UALR.

27. E. N. McCall to Sanders, June 8, 1934, box 2, file 1, Sanders Papers, UALR; "Doing unto Others" brochure, 1934, series I, subseries III, box 9, file 1, LeMaster Collection.

28. ISOH transcript (1978), 9–10; Sanders to Judge Charles J. Mitchell, president of County Judges' Association of Arkansas, May 30, 1934, box 2, file 1, Sanders Papers, UALR.

29. Minutes, meeting of the Pulaski County Public Welfare Commission, June 4, 1934, Little Rock, Arkansas, box 2, file 1, Sanders Papers, UALR. Present at this meeting were Sanders, Lawrence Berger, John Pruniski, Hugo Norvell, Dr. J. O. Hall, and Ora Nix.

30. LeMaster, *A Corner of the Tapestry*, 314; Alison C. Greene, *No Depression in Heaven: The Great Depression, the New Deal, and the Transformation of Religion in the Delta* (New York: Oxford University Press, 2016), 142–43.

31. Sanders Journal, 58–59; ISOH transcript (1977), 17; "Urban League," *Encyclopedia of Arkansas History and Culture*, accessed September 14, 2015, http://www.encyclopediaofarkansas.net/encyclopedia/entry-detail.aspx?entryID=7936; M. Lafayette Harris to Sanders, June 12, 1951, box 1, file 2, Sanders Papers, UALR. On the Urban League, see also Touré Reed, *Not Aims but Opportunity: The Urban League and the Politics of Racial Uplift, 1910–1950* (Chapel Hill: University of North Carolina Press, 2008); Nancy J. Weiss, *The National Urban League, 1910–1940* (New York: Oxford University Press, 1974); Robert R. Wright, *Old Seeds in the New Land: History and Reminiscences of the Bar of Arkansas* (Fayetteville: University of Arkansas Press, 2001), 294.

32. *Urban League of Arkansas, Inc.: Golden Anniversary Celebration, 1937–1987* (Little Rock: The League, 1987), 10, 14; ISOH transcript (1977), 17

33. Sanders Journal, 49; "Rabbi Will End 37 Years at B'nai Israel August 31," *Arkansas Gazette*, June 8, 1963, 1. In 1947, ten years after the group's founding, Little Rock businessman and philanthropist Fred Darragh Jr. became the first white businessman to join the Urban League of Greater Little Rock. He later served on its board of directors. On Darragh, see Sarah Simmers, "In the South, but Not of the South: Fred K. Darragh, Jr.," *Pulaski County Historical Review* 57 (Winter 2009): 124–35.

34. Sanders Journal, 59; *Arkansas Democrat*, February 19, 1986.

35. *Arkansas Democrat*, April 28, 1939; Weiss, *National Urban League*, 303.

36. Ira Sanders, "Foreword," *A Survey of Negroes in Little Rock and North Little Rock* (Little Rock: Urban League of Greater Little Rock, 1941), accessed April 10, 2017, https://hdl.handle.net/2027/uc1.$b725353.

37. *Survey of Negroes*, 95.

38. *Survey of Negroes*, 2–19.

39. *Survey of Negroes*, 1, 2, 96, 97.

40. Gwendolyn Floyd, chair of the Urban League's emeritus committee, to Ira Sanders, October 24, 1972, box 2, file 7, Sanders Papers, UALR.

41. ISOH transcript (1977), 16–17; "Lighthouse has Grown from Broom, Mop Days; Quality Items Stressed," *Arkansas Gazette*, November 24, 1985, 7C.

42. Sanders Journal, 59.

Chapter 4. Birth Control, Eugenics, and "Human Betterment": 1931–1958

1. Quoted in Robert McElvaine, *The Great Depression: America, 1929–1941* (New York: Times Books, 1984), 179, as written.

2. Comstock Law, a.k.a. An Act for the Suppression of Trade in, and Circulation of, Obscene Literature and Articles of Immoral Use, ch. 258, § 2, 17 Stat. 599, enacted on March 3, 1873. On Margaret Sanger, see Ellen Chesler, *Woman of Valor: Margaret Sanger and the Birth Control Movement in America* (New York: Simon and Schuster, 2007); Jean H. Baker, *Margaret Sanger: A Life of Passion* (New York: Hill and Wang, 2011); Margaret Sanger, *Margaret Sanger: An Autobiography* (New York: W. W. Norton, 1938); Cathy Moran Hajo, *Birth Control on Main Street: Organizing Clinics in the United States, 1916–1939* (Urbana: University of Illinois Press, 2010); United States v. One Package of Japanese Pessaries, 86 F. 2nd 737 (1936).

3. Robert Kelso, *Poverty* (New York: Longman's, 1929), quoted in Matthew C. Price, *Justice between Generations: The Growing Power of the Elderly in America* (Santa Barbara, CA: Praeger, 1997), 11–12.

4. "Speaks in Behalf of Birth Control," *Arkansas Gazette*, January 20, 1932, 12.

5. Program, Arkansas Conference of Social Work (ACSW), October 12–15, 1932, series V, box 1, file 6, LeMaster Collection. Hilda Cornish chaired the session at which Sanders spoke, and from 1932 to 1935, Brooks Hays served as president of this organization. The ACSW was an affiliate of the National Conference of Social Work. Originally known as the National Conference of Charities and Correction, the group changed its name in 1917 and became the National Conference of Social Work. In 1956, it slightly changed its name again to become the National Conference on Social Welfare. See Virginia Commonwealth University Libraries Social Welfare History Project, "National Conference on Social Welfare," accessed April 23, 2018, https: // socialwelfare.library.vcu.edu/organizations/national-conference-on-social-welfare.

6. Marianne Leung, "'Better Babies': Birth Control in Arkansas during the 1930s," in *Hidden Histories of Women in the New South*, ed. Virginia Bernhard et al. (Columbia: University of Missouri Press, 1994), 54; "Planned Parenthood," *Encyclopedia of Arkansas History and Culture*, accessed July 11, 2016, http://www.encyclopediaof arkansas.net/encyclopedia/entry-detail.aspx?entryID=4286.

7. Marianne Leung, "Cornish, Hilda Kahlert," in *Arkansas Biography: A Collection of Notable Lives*, ed. Nancy A. Williams (Fayetteville: University of Arkansas Press, 2000), 74–75; Hajo, *Birth Control on Main Street*, 78–79.

8. ISOH transcript (1978), 1–2; "Mrs. Ed Cornish Dies; Led in Birth Control," *Arkansas Gazette*, November 20, 1965, 10B.

9. "Hilda Cornish (1878–1965)," *Encyclopedia of Arkansas History and Culture*, accessed November 8, 2006, http://www.encyclopediaofarkansas.net/encyclopedia

/entry-detail.aspx?entryID=1625. On Smith, see Gene Vinzant, "The Case of Hay Watson Smith: Evolution and Heresy in the Presbyterian Church," *Ozark Historical Review* 30 (Spring 2001): 57–70.

10. Raida Pfeifer, interview with Marianne Leung, March 16, 1990, Little Rock, Arkansas, quoted in Leung, "Better Babies," 64.

11. ISOH transcript (1978), 2; Leung, "'Better Babies,'" 53–54. Being "well-born" was a phrase already associated with eugenics. It was also the title of a noteworthy 1916 book on the topic, of which Sanders was likely aware, given his abiding interest in the sociology of birth control. Michael F. Guyer, *Being Well-Born: An Introduction to Eugenics* (Indianapolis: Bobbs-Merrill, 1916).

12. Leung, "Cornish," in Williams, *Arkansas Biography*, 75.

13. Leung, "'Better Babies,'" 52–53; Leung, "Making the Radical Respectable: Little Rock Clubwomen and the Cause of Birth Control during the 1930s," *Arkansas Historical Quarterly* 57 (Spring 1998), 17.

14. Hajo, *Birth Control on Main Street*, 103.

15. See Leung, "Making the Radical Respectable"; Leung, "'Better Babies,'" 60; Lutz Kaelber, "Eugenics: Compulsory Sterilization in 50 American States: Arkansas," accessed November 8, 2006, http://www.uvm.edu/~lkaelber/eugenics/AR/AR.html.

16. Flyer, Arkansas Eugenics Association, n.d., in Clarence James Gamble Papers, 1920–1970s, series I, box 2, file 38, Center for the History of Medicine, Francis A. Countway Library of Medicine, Harvard Medical School, Boston, Massachusetts, hereafter cited as Gamble Papers.

17. Leung, "Better Babies," 54.

18. "Mrs. Ed Cornish Dies; Led in Birth Control," *Arkansas Gazette*, November 20, 1965, 10B.

19. Report of the Little Rock Birth Control Clinic of the Arkansas Eugenics Association, February 1, 1931–January 31, 1932, box 6, file 4, Records of the Arkansas Eugenics Association, History of Public Health Collection, Historical Research Center, Library, University of Arkansas for Medical Sciences, Little Rock, Arkansas (hereafter cited as AEA Records, UAMS); Leung, "'Better Babies,'" 57.

20. "Your Community and Birth Control," Arkansas Eugenics Association pamphlet, 1937, box 6, file 4, AEA Records, UAMS; Report of the Little Rock Birth Control Clinic of the Arkansas Eugenics Association, 1931–1934, box 6, file 4, AEA Records, UAMS; Leung, "'Better Babies,'" 65, 67.

21. Reports of the Arkansas Eugenics Association for 1931–1933, box 6, file 4, AEA Records, UAMS.

22. Leung, "Making the Radical Respectable," 19, 22.

23. Thomas Fitzhugh to Hilda Cornish, September 1, 1938; Clarence Gamble to Hilda Cornish, September 6, 1938. Both in series I, box 2, file 38, Gamble Papers.

24. Leung, "Hilda Cornish (1878–1965)"; "Planned Parenthood Sets Reception," *Arkansas Gazette*, September 1, 1986, 1B; "Planned Parenthood," *Encyclopedia of Arkansas History and Culture*, accessed July 2, 2016, http://www.encyclopedia ofarkansas.net/encyclopedia/entry-detail.aspx?search=1&entryID=4286. The University of Arkansas Medical School later became the University of Arkansas for Medical Sciences.

25. Hilda Cornish to James H. McIntyre, field representative for Planned

Parenthood Federation of America, June 10, 1951, box 1, file 16, Sanders Papers, UALR.

26. Ira Sanders to Planned Parenthood Foundation of America, July 10, 1951, box 1, file 16, Sanders Papers, UALR.

27. Mrs. Ed Cornish, Dr. Ira Sanders, and Mrs. Moorhead Wright, letter to Mr. Max Howell, president of Pulaski County Juvenile Circuit Court, Little Rock, January 10, 1951, box 1, file 16, Sanders Papers, UALR.

28. Sanders and Hilda Cornish, form letter to solicit donations to the Planned Parenthood Association of Arkansas, various months and days, 1951, series V, box 1, file 10, LeMaster Collection; Sanders to Planned Parenthood Federation of America, New York, October 14, 1955, box 1, file 17, Sanders Papers, UALR.

29. Ernestine Towns to Hilda Cornish, July 16, 1951; Dorothy Vaughn to Cornish, September 11, 1952. Both in series V, box 1, file 10, LeMaster Collection. There are many such letters in this file, and many responses in which Cornish refers women to local doctors for service.

30. Hilda Cornish to Ira Sanders, December 7, 1953; Florence Griffin to Planned Parenthood Association of Arkansas, December 3, 1953. Both in box 1, file 17, Sanders Papers, UALR.

31. Jacob H. Landman, *Human Sterilization: The History of the Sexual Sterilization Movement* (New York: Macmillan, 1932), 91, 83–84; Mark A. Largent, *Breeding Contempt: The History of Coerced Sterilization in the United States* (New Brunswick, NJ: Rutgers University Press, 2008), 80; Kaelber, "Eugenics: Compulsory Sterilization in 50 American States: Mississippi," accessed January 8, 2016, http://www.uvm.edu /~lkaelber/eugenics/MS/MS.html.

32. *Buck v. Bell*, 274 U.S. 200, at 207 (1927).

33. Melanie Welch, "Politics and Poverty: Women's Reproductive Rights in Arkansas, 1942–1980," (PhD diss., Auburn University, 2009), 30–34; Lutz Kaelber, "Eugenics: Compulsory Sterilization in 50 American States: Arkansas," accessed November 8, 2006, http://www.uvm.edu/~lkaelber/eugenics/AR/AR.html.

34. ISOH transcript (1978), 3.

35. Human Betterment Foundation flyer, 1929, "Human Sterilization," DNA Learning Center, accessed April 2, 2016, https://www.dnalc.org/11673-human -sterilization-human-betterment-foundation-5-.html.

36. "Minutes of the Meeting to Organize a Human Betterment League of Arkansas," April 19, 1951, Little Rock, Arkansas, series I, box 2, file 40, Gamble Papers.

37. Besides Arkansas, Human Betterment Leagues existed in North Carolina, Georgia, Alabama, Nebraska, and Iowa, where the national organization was headquartered.

38. "Sterilization Suggested in Mental Health Plan," *Arkansas Democrat*, November 1, 1951; "Sterilization Urged to Reduce Feeblemindedness in Arkansas," *Arkansas Gazette*, November 2, 1951.

39. Gamble to Mrs. T. E. (Ida Ruth) Atkinson, AHBL secretary, August 22, 1951, series I, box 2, file 40, Gamble Papers; Gamble to the Arkansas Human Betterment League, August 22, 1951, series I, box 2, file 40, Gamble Papers; ISOH transcript (1978), 4; Adrienne Dunn, "Human Betterment League of North Carolina," North

Carolina History Project, accessed February 4, 2016, http://www.northcarolinahistory
.org/commentary/314/entry.

40. ISOH transcript (1978), 4–5. The record of Human Betterment League activity
in other states is much more ominous, notably in North Carolina. The Eugenics Board
of North Carolina approved over eight thousand sterilizations, and about seventy-six
hundred were actually carried out from 1929 to 1973 (Kaelber, "Eugenics/Sexual
Sterilizations in North Carolina," accessed February 8, 2016, http://www.uvm.edu
/~lkaelber/eugenics/NC/NC.html). African Americans accounted for 60 percent of
these procedures, though making up only 25 percent of the state's overall population.
Nothing of this nature occurred in Arkansas.

41. *Why Fear Sterilization?*, North Carolina Digital Collections, State Library of
North Carolina, accessed June 7, 2016, http://digital.ncdcr.cdm/ref/collection/p2499
01coll37/id/14955.

42. AHBL minutes, March 19, 1952; AHBL minutes, December 4, 1952. Both in
Gamble Papers, series I, box 2, file 38.

43. "Sterilization Legislation Is Explained Here," *Paragould (AR) Big Picture*, n.d.,
clipping in series I, box 2, file 41, Gamble Papers.

44. Mrs. Jamie W. Newsome to Human Betterment League of Arkansas, June 1,
1954, series I, box 2, file 43, Gamble Papers.

45. Phoebe Marousek to Jamie Newsome, June 17, 1954; Marousek to Ida Ruth
Atkinson, June 17, 1954. Both in series I, box 2, file 43, Gamble Papers.

46. Ida Ruth Atkinson to Phoebe Marousek, July 20, 1954, series I, box 2, file 43,
Gamble Papers.

47. Clarence Gamble to Winthrop Rockefeller, November 26, 1954, series I, box 2,
file 43, Gamble Papers. The new University of Arkansas Medical Center, funded in
part by a cigarette tax passed in 1951, moved to its new West Markham Street address
in 1956. See "UAMS History," University of Arkansas for Medical Sciences, accessed
June 8, 2016, http://web.uams.edu/about/uams-history/.

48. AHBL minutes, May 17, 1954, series I, box 2, file 43, Gamble Papers; House Bill
300, "An Act Authorizing Voluntary Limitation of Parenthood," series I, box 2, file
43, Gamble Papers; AHBL Minutes, January 27, 1955, series I, box 2, file 44, Gamble
Papers.

49. AHBL minutes, November 17, 1955, series I, box 2, file 44, Gamble Papers; Ida
Ruth Atkinson to Phoebe Marousek, February 20, 1957, series I, box 2, file 47, Gamble
Papers; Clarence Gamble to Marousek, April 29, 1957, and May 28, 1957, series I, box 2,
file 47, Gamble Papers; Marousek, "Report on Field Visit to Arkansas, May 1957,"
series I, box 2, file 47, Gamble Papers.

50. Marousek, "Report on Field Visit to Arkansas"; AHBL minutes, November 19,
1957. Both in series I, box 2, file 47, Gamble Papers.

Chapter 5. World War II, Zionism, Cold War: 1933–1954

1. Smith v. Allwright, 321 U.S. 649 (1944); Johnson, *Arkansas in Modern America*,
61–88.

2. See Sidney S. McMath, *Promises Kept* (Fayetteville: University of Arkansas
Press, 2003); see also Jim Lester, *A Man for Arkansas: Sid McMath and the Southern
Reform Tradition* (Little Rock: Rose Publishing, 1976).

3. ISOH transcript (1978), 17.

4. These senators who condemned Nazi Germany in March 1933 were indeed speaking out early against the abuses of Adolf Hitler. Hitler had assumed the chancellorship on January 30, 1933; on February 27, the Reichstag Fire Decree abolished many civil liberties and allowed for the imprisonment of "enemies" of the state. It was quickly followed by the passage on March 24 of the Enabling Act, which allowed Hitler to rule by decree.

5. Stephen S. Wise to Ira Sanders, June 3, 1933, box 1, file 1, Sanders Papers, Temple. For more on Wise, see A. James Rudin, *Pillar of Fire: A Biography of Stephen S. Wise* (Lubbock: Texas Tech University Press, 2015).

6. As quoted in "Senator Robinson, Mourned by Nation, was Enemy of Bigotry," *Southern Israelite*, July 23, 1937, 1; Sanders Journal, 53–54. The full text of Senator Robinson's speech is available in American Jewish Committee, *The Jews in Nazi Germany: The Factual Record of Their Persecution by the National Socialists* (New York: American Jewish Committee, 1933), 59–62, also available at http://www.ajc archives.org/AJC_DATA/Files/THR-18.PDF.

7. Sanders Journal, 51, 53; Joseph T. Robinson, letter to Benito Mussolini, May 29, 1934, box 1, Sanders Papers, Temple. The letter reads as follows:

My dear Mr. Prime Minister:
   This will introduce to your Excellency, Rabbi Ira E. Sanders of Little Rock, Arkansas, who is taking a trip to Italy, and will be in Rome for a few days beginning July of this year.
   Rabbi Sanders is an ardent student of sociological and political problems. He is an outstanding citizen of my State and enjoys the high esteem and respect of those with whom he is acquainted. He is very anxious to secure an audience with you on the occasion of his visit to Rome, an honor which will be deeply appreciated.

8. Sheldon Spear, "The United States and the Persecution of the Jews in Germany, 1933–1939," *Jewish Social Studies* 30 (October 1968): 216; Sanders Journal, 53–55.

9. They crossed the Atlantic on the passenger liner *S.S. Rex* and were in Europe from June 30 to August 18, 1934. They were in Rome from July 4 to 10. Other stops on the itinerary included Venice, Geneva, Paris, Brussels, and Amsterdam. Their tour of Europe concluded in London, and they returned on the *S.S. Laconia* on August 18. Full itinerary in series I, subseries III, box 9, file 8, LeMaster Collection.

10. See David S. Wyman, *The Abandonment of the Jews: America and the Holocaust, 1941–1945* (New York: Pantheon, 1984), esp. chapter 1; Richard Breitman and Allan J. Lichtman, *FDR and the Jews* (Cambridge: Harvard University Press, 2013), esp. chapter 4.

11. Sanders Journal, 54–55.

12. Sanders sermon, n.d., in Sanders Journal, 55–55B.

13. Sanders Journal, 54.

14. Sanders sermon, n.d., in Sanders Journal, 55B–55C.

15. Sanders, sermon of September 30, 1941, Little Rock; see also "Rabbi Blames Man for World Ills," unknown newspaper clipping, October 1, 1941, box 2, file 12, Sanders Papers, UALR.

16. Cash-and-Carry was a 1939 revision of the 1936 Neutrality Act, which allowed

the United States to sell materials to belligerent nations who paid cash up front and carried the material away on their own ships, thus insulating the United States from any risk. Since the British navy controlled the Atlantic, in essence the US sold only to the allies; additionally, the program created much-needed American jobs. The Lend-Lease Act of 1941 dropped the cash requirement and provided materials only to the allies in exchange for leases to military bases or returns of goods and services after the war. This arrangement was the single most important US contribution to the war at that time.

17. Bureau of Labor Statistics, US Department of Labor, available at stats .bls.gov.

18. *Urban League of Arkansas, Inc.: Golden Anniversary Celebration, 1937–1987*, 17.

19. Tabitha Orr, "Clifford Minton's War: The Struggle for Black Jobs in Wartime Little Rock, 1940–1946," *Arkansas Historical Quarterly* 76 (Spring 2017), 23–48; Sadye Allen Thompson, interview with LeMaster, March 15, 1982, series V, box 1, file 11, LeMaster Collection.

20. See Glenda E. Gilmore, *Defying Dixie: The Radical Roots of Civil Rights, 1919–1950* (New York: W. W. Norton, 2008), 362; Orr, "Clifford Minton's War," 23–24, 39; *Urban League of Arkansas, Inc.: Golden Anniversary Celebration, 1937–1987*, 17.

21. Orr, "Clifford Minton's War," 26, 30–31.

22. Sadye Allen Thompson, interview with LeMaster, March 15, 1982, series V, box 1, file 11, LeMaster Collection; *Urban League of Arkansas, Inc.: Golden Anniversary Celebration, 1937–1987*, 17. "The Black Cabinet" was the name given to a group of African American policy advisors to President Roosevelt, and included National Urban League executive secretary Eugene K. Jones. Robert Weaver would later become the first African American to serve as a cabinet secretary when Lyndon Johnson appointed him secretary of housing and urban development in January 1966.

23. Sadye Allen Thompson, interview with LeMaster, March 15, 1982, series V, box 1, file 11, LeMaster Collection; Carolyn Yancey Kent, "Last Hired: African American Hiring in North Pulaski County's Citadel for Defense," *Pulaski County Historical Review* 62 (Fall 2014): 77–84; Johnson, *Arkansas in Modern America*, 70–71; "World War II Ordnance Plants," *Encyclopedia of Arkansas History and Culture*, accessed February 19, 2016, http://www.encyclopediaofarkansas.net/encyclopedia/entry-detail .aspx?entryID=373

24. Sanders Journal, 10–11.

25. "The Law of Life is the Law of Service," sermon of September 19, 1924; "The Father of Reform Judaism," sermon of April 17, 1925, Temple Israel of the City of New York, in Sanders Journal, 40A–40C, 40CC–40EE.

26. Jason Lustig, "Resigning to Change: The Foundation and Transformation of the American Council for Judaism" (master's thesis, Brandeis University, 2009), v; Thomas A. Kolsky, *Jews against Zionism: The American Council for Judaism, 1942–1948* (Philadelphia: Temple University Press, 1992), 54.

27. Evans, *Provincials*, 98; Ronald Sanders, *The High Walls of Jerusalem: A History of the Balfour Declaration and the Birth of the British Mandate for Palestine* (New York: Holt, Rinehart & Winston, 1984); Meyer, *Response to Modernity*, 326.

28. Meyer, *Response to Modernity*, 331.

29. Meyer, *Response to Modernity*, 330–331.

30. "Atlantic City Statement of Principles," June 1942, in Lustig, "Resigned to Change," 212–13; Kolsky, *Jews against Zionism*, 51–52; Meyer, *Response to Modernity*, 332.

31. Lustig, "Resigned to Change," 3, 15–16, 213. Population figures in Jonathan Sarna, *American Judaism: A History* (New Haven: Yale University Press, 2004), 207, 375; "Institutional Sketch," American Council for Judaism Records, 1937–1989, accessed January 21, 2016, http://collections.americanjewisharchives.org/ms/ms0017/ms0017. html; "Atlantic City Statement of Principles," quoted in Kolsky, *Jews against Zionism*, 54.

32. *New York Times*, August 31, 1943, 4; Kolsky, *Jews against Zionism*, 203–6; Meyer, *Response to Modernity*, 333. Sanders makes no mention of his signature on this document, nor offers any later explanation of it in his journal, his correspondence, or his numerous interviews.

33. Kolsky, *Jews against Zionism*, 80; Lustig, "Resigned to Change," 82, 198, 199; Evans, *Provincials*, 102; Meyer, *Response to Modernity*, 333. Houston's Congregation Beth Israel repealed its Basic Principles in 1968.

34. LeMaster, *Corner of the Tapestry*, 64; Sanders Journal, 68; Alan Thalheimer, telephone interview with the author, March 29, 2016; Elijah E. Palnick, interview with the author, November 16, 2004, Little Rock, Arkansas.

35. Abraham Shusterman to Louis Wolsey, November 9, 1942, box 4, file 8, Louis Wolsey Papers, American Jewish Archives, Hebrew Union College—Jewish Institute of Religion, Cincinnati, Ohio (hereafter LWP).

36. Louis Witt to Elmer Berger, August 10, 1943, box 4, file 11, LWP; Lustig, "Resigned to Change," 1, 104, 107.

37. Ira Sanders to Louis Wolsey, April 17, 1944, box 4, file 6, LWP.

38. Ira Sanders to Louis Wolsey, April 17, 1944, box 4, file 6, LWP; Lustig, "Resigned to Change," 59.

39. Ira Sanders to Louis Wolsey, April 17, 1944, box 4, file 6, LWP; Wolsey to Sanders, July 21, 1944, box 4, file 6, LWP; Lustig, "Resigned to Change," 53.

40. Lustig, "Resigned to Change," 1; Wolsey, "'Support Land of Israel' is Rabbi Wolsey's Plea," *Philadelphia Jewish Exponent*, May 21, 1948; Ira Sanders to Louis Wolsey, May 26, 1948, box 4, file 6, LWP.

41. LeMaster, *A Corner of the Tapestry*, 335–36.

42. Sanders Journal, 70–71, emphasis added.

43. Sanders Journal, 67–68.

44. Sanders quoted in an unknown newspaper clipping, n.d., box 1, file 4, Sanders Papers, UALR.

45. "Records of the Displaced Persons Commission," National Archives and Records Administration, accessed September 28, 2015, http://www.archives.gov/research /guide-fed-records/groups/278.html#278.3.

46. Shira Klein, "Displaced Persons Act," in *Anti-Immigration in the United States*, vol. 1, ed. Kathleen R. Arnold (Westport, CT: Greenwood Press, 2011), 160–65. See also Haim Genezi, *America's Fair Share: The Admission and Resettlement of Displaced Persons, 1945–1952* (Detroit: Wayne State University Press, 1993).

47. "Governor Told DPs Doing Well," unknown newspaper clipping dated March 8, 1951, series III, subseries I, box 2, file 3, LeMaster Collection.

48. "Genocide Pact Approval Urged," *Arkansas Gazette*, June 7, 1950, 14.

49. "Live by Moral Law Principles for Brotherhood, Rabbi Advises," *Arkansas Gazette*, February 23, 1951, 9A.

50. Ira Sanders, baccalaureate address at the University of Arkansas, February 2, 1952, excerpted in "600 U of A Seniors Told of Red Threat," *Arkansas Gazette*, February 3, 1952, 4C.

51. "Few developments," writes historian William L. O'Neill, "were more unexpected than the surge in church membership that took place after World War II." See O'Neill, *American High: The Years of Confidence, 1945–1960* (New York: Free Press, 1986), 212–15.

52. Sanders, sermon of January 10, 1959, box 1, file 3, "Sermons and Addresses," Sanders Papers, UALR.

53. "Rabbi's Sermon Recipe Shuns Sensational Spice," *Arkansas Gazette*, June 28, 1952, 5A.

54. Citation reprinted in Sanders and Palnick, eds., *One Hundred Years*, 68.

55. M. Lafayette Harris to Sanders, June 12, 1951; Jacob Blaustein, president of the American Jewish Congress, to Sanders, March 8, 1951. Both in box 1, file 2, Sanders Papers, UALR. Harris served as president of Philander Smith College from 1936 to 1961, and Blaustein, a wealthy industrialist and philanthropist, served as president of the American Jewish Congress from 1949 to 1954 and for years in a number of diplomatic capacities promoting international human rights. On Harris, see "Dr. M. Lafayette Harris (1936–1961)," Philander Smith College, accessed February 1, 2016, http://www.philander.edu/about/dr-lafayette-harris.aspx; "Philander Smith College," *Encyclopedia of Arkansas History and Culture*, accessed February 1, 2016, http://www.encyclopediaofarkansas.net/encyclopedia/entry-detail.aspx?entryID =2165. On Blaustein, see "Jacob and Hilda Blaustein," Blaustein Philanthropic Group, Family History, http://www.blaufund.org/history/jacobandhilda.html, accessed February 1, 2016; also Marianne R. Sanua, *Let Us Prove Strong: The American Jewish Committee, 1945–2006* (Waltham, MA: Brandeis University Press, 2007).

56. Nelson Glueck to Ira Sanders, February 22, 1954, box 1, Sanders Papers, Temple.

57. Sara Alderman Murphy, *Breaking the Silence: Little Rock's Women's Emergency Committee to Open Our Schools, 1958–1963* (Fayetteville: University of Arkansas Press, 1997), 31–32, 263n5.

58. Minutes, Little Rock Public Library board of trustees, January 10, 1951, in Murphy, *Breaking the Silence*, 32.

59. *Arkansas Gazette*, November 23, 1950, 4; Georg C. Iggers was a white Jewish history professor who arrived in Little Rock in the Fall of 1950 to accept a position at historically black Philander Smith College. I agree with Rosebud Harris Tillman that Iggers' letter "should be taken as a result rather than a cause of the sentiment for integration" of the library. Tillman, "The History of Public Library Service to Negroes in Little Rock, Arkansas, 1917–1951," (MS thesis, Atlanta University, 1953), 39.

60. *Arkansas Democrat*, January 14, 1951, 11; Murphy, *Breaking the Silence*, 32; Tillman, "History of Public Library Service," 32. In 1958, Terry was be the organizing force behind the Women's Emergency Committee (WEC) during the Little Rock

Central High School crisis. For more on Adolphine Terry, see Stephanie Bayless, *Obliged to Help: Adolphine Fletcher Terry and the Progressive South* (Little Rock: Butler Center Books, 2011).

61. Ira Sanders, "Effort of Every Man Needed in TB Warfare," *Arkansas Democrat*, November 12, 1955, 9.

Chapter 6. The Southern Rabbi Meets the Civil Rights Movement: 1950–1957

1. Dorothy Woods Mitchell, interviews with the author, January 5, 2017, and March 10, 2017.

2. Clive Webb, *Fight against Fear*, 170–74; Mark K. Bauman, "Introduction," in Bauman and Kalin, *Quiet Voices*, 9. Many Reform Jews took public roles in the civil rights struggle, but, as Clive Webb also notes, "Orthodox and Conservative Jews prioritized the preservation of the faith and traditions of their own people. Although sympathetic toward the black struggle, they largely refrained from any active support." Webb, *Fight against Fear*, 170.

3. ISOH transcript (1977), 13.

4. Sanders Journal, 58.

5. Rev. Donald K. Campbell, telephone interviews with the author, October 30, 2015, and January 15, 2016. Reverend Campbell served as the pastor of Little Rock's Grace Presbyterian Church from 1961 to 1973 and as the second president (1964–1965) of the Greater Little Rock Conference on Religion and Race. It is not clear whether Sanders in fact resigned on the spot or if his resignation became effective at some future date, since the merger of the two groups did not occur officially until 1956; nevertheless, his resignation facilitated the merger.

6. Sanders quoted in Irving J. Spitzberg Jr., *Racial Politics in Little Rock, 1954–1964* (New York: Garland, 1987), 76. Ogden's forthright stand for the principles of racial justice and his later role at Little Rock Central High School in helping escort the Little Rock Nine out of harm's way cost him his congregation.

7. Dunbar H. Ogden, *My Father Said Yes: A White Pastor in Little Rock School Integration* (Nashville: Vanderbilt University Press, 2008), 140–41. Once the immediate crisis at Central High had passed, the Interracial Ministerial Alliance, through a process of gradual internal self-segregation, became "impotent and eventually died." In its place arose the Interfaith Conference, which included Christian, Jewish, and Muslim clergy.

8. "Brotherhood," *Arkansas Gazette*, February 28, 1950, clipping in box 2, Sanders Papers, UALR.

9. "Live by Moral Principles for Brotherhood, Rabbi Advises," *Arkansas Gazette*, February 23, 1951.

10. Marc Dollinger, "'Hamans' and 'Torquemadas': Southern and Northern Jewish Responses to the Civil Rights Movement, 1945–1965," in Bauman and Kalin, *Quiet Voices*, 68; Allen Krause, "Rabbis and Negro Rights in the South, 1954–1967," in *Jews in the South*, ed. Leonard Dinnerstein and Mary Dale Palsson (Baton Rouge: Louisiana State University Press, 1973), 361–62; *American Jewish Year Book* 66 (1966), 83.

11. Clive Webb, "A Tangled Web: Black-Jewish Relations in the Twentieth-Century South," in *Jewish Roots in Southern Soil: A New History*, ed. Marcie Ferris and Mark I. Greenberg (Waltham, MA: Brandeis University Press, 2006), 204.

12. "The Clergy's Opinion on Brotherhood Week," *Arkansas Gazette*, February 18, 1951.

13. Dinnerstein, "Southern Jewry and the Desegregation Crisis," 233.

14. The possibility that Jewish "otherness" might "easily become an issue" was a fear for many southern Jews, writes Mary Stanton in a discussion of Jews in Montgomery, Alabama, as one example of the phenomenon. Mary Stanton, "At One with the Majority," *Southern Jewish History* 9 (2006): 176.

15. *National Jewish Post and Opinion*, October 31, 1958, cited in Webb, *Fight against Fear*, 152.

16. Quoted in Dollinger, "'Hamans' and 'Torquemadas,'" in Bauman and Kalin, *Quiet Voices*, 70. See also Janice Rothschild Blumberg, *One Voice: Rabbi Jacob M. Rothschild and the Troubled South* (Macon, GA: Mercer University Press, 1985).

17. Dinnerstein, "Southern Jewry," 234–35.

18. Webb, *Fight against Fear*, 153. See also Neil McMillan, "The White Citizens' Council and Resistance to School Desegregation in Arkansas," *Arkansas Historical Quarterly* 66 (Summer 2007): 125–44.

19. For an excellent analysis of this phenomenon, see Jeff Woods, *Black Struggle, Red Scare: Segregation and Anti-Communism in the South, 1948-1968* (Baton Rouge: Louisiana State University Press, 2004), quote on 56. For more on Perez, see Glen Jeansonne, *Leander Perez: Boss of the Delta*, 2nd ed. (Lafayette: University of Southwestern Louisiana Press, 1995), esp. 226–28.

20. ISOH transcript (1978), 13–14.

21. Louise McLean to Ira Sanders, November 19, 1954, box 1, file 2, Sanders Papers, Temple.

22. P. Allen Krause, "The Southern Rabbi and Civil Rights," (rabbinic thesis, Hebrew Union College—Jewish Institute of Religion, 1967), 62–63.

23. "Social Action Legend Al Vorspan Reflects on 'Letter from a Birmingham Jail,'" Religious Action Center of Reform Judaism, May 21, 2013, accessed January 14, 2016, http://blogs.rj.org/rac/2013/05/21/social-action-legend-al-vorspan-reflects -on-letter-from-a-birmingham-jail.

24. Martin Luther King Jr., in a *National Jewish Post and Opinion* interview quoted in William S. Malev, "The Jew of the South in the Conflict on Segregation," *Conservative Judaism* 13 (Fall 1958): 45; see also Marc Schneier, *Shared Dreams: Martin Luther King, Jr. and the Jewish Community* (Woodstock, VT: Jewish Lights Publishing, 1999), 45.

25. Rabbi Eugene Blachschleger to Sanders, October 2, 1957, series I, subseries III, box 8, file 1, LeMaster Collection. Blachschleger, a Sanders contemporary, served Temple Beth Or as rabbi from 1933 to 1965, almost paralleling Sanders' 1926–1963 career at Congregation B'nai Israel. For more on Eugene Blachschleger, see http:// templebethor.net/aboutus/history/rabbis_blachschleger_and_baylinson, accessed June 19, 2015.

26. Quoted in Webb, *Fight against Fear*, 208. On Harry Golden, see Kimberly M. Hartnett, *Carolina Israelite: How Harry Golden Made Us Care about Jews, the South,*

and Civil Rights (Chapel Hill: University of North Carolina Press, 2015). Golden published the weekly newspaper *Carolina Israelite* from 1944 to 1968 and was the author of numerous books.

27. Alfred O. Hero Jr., "Southern Jews, Race Relations, and Foreign Policy," *Jewish Social Studies* 27 (October 1965): 216; James A. Wax, "The Attitudes of the Jews in the South toward Integration," *CCAR Journal* 26 (June 1959): 18. For more on Wax, see Patricia M. LaPointe, "The Prophetic Voice: Rabbi James A. Wax," in Bauman and Kalin, *Quiet Voices*, 152–67. "Jimmy" Wax was both a friend and admirer of Sanders, writing to him on the occasion of Sanders' thirty-fifth anniversary in the Little Rock pulpit, "You have personified the noblest teachings of our religion." Wax to Sanders, May 8, 1961, box 1, file 2, Sanders Papers, UALR.

28. Dinnerstein, "Southern Jewry," 233n10; P. Allen Krause, "Rabbis and Negro Rights in the South, 1954–1967," *American Jewish Archives* 21 (April 1969): 42–43.

29. Hinchin quoted in Dollinger, "'Hamans' and 'Torquemadas,'" in Bauman and Kalin, *Quiet Voices*, 73.

30. Albert Vorspan, "The Dilemma of the Southern Jew," *The Reconstructionist* 24 (January 9, 1959): 6–9.

31. Vorspan, 7–8. For an account of the 1958 Atlanta bombing, see Melissa Fay Greene, *The Temple Bombing* (Reading, MA: Addison-Wesley, 1996).

32. The essential work on the rabbis is Bauman and Kalin, *Quiet Voices*, which contains studies of Sanders' contemporaries, including Mantinband, Nussbaum, and Rothschild, but also Morris Newfield and Milton Grafman of Birmingham, David Jacobson of San Antonio, Sidney Wolf of Corpus Christi, and James Wax of Memphis, among others. See also Webb, *Fight against Fear*, especially chapter 8, "The Rabbis"; P. Allen Krause, *To Stand Aside or Stand Alone: Southern Reform Rabbis and the Civil Rights Movement*, ed. Mark K. Bauman with Stephen Krause (Tuscaloosa: University of Alabama Press, 2016).

33. P. Allen Krause interview with William Silverman, June 23, 1966, in Krause, *To Stand Aside or Stand Alone*, 152–53.

34. Quoted in David J. Meyer, "Fighting Segregation, Threats, and Dynamite: Rabbi William Silverman's Nashville Battle," *American Jewish Archives Journal* 60 (2008): 102.

35. Perry E. Nussbaum, Charles Mantinband, and Jacob Rothschild, "The Southern Rabbi Faces the Problem of Desegregation," *CCAR Journal* 3 (June 1956): 1; Webb, *Fight against Fear*, 185–88; Dollinger, "'Hamans' and 'Torquemadas,'" in Bauman and Kalin, *Quiet Voices*, 76; see also Gary Phillip Zola, "What Price, Amos? Perry Nussbaum's Career in Jackson, Mississippi," in Bauman and Kalin, *Quiet Voices*, 230–57. Jews made up fully two-thirds of all white Freedom Riders. As to the lack of community support in Jackson, in 1967, the year of the bombings, Nussbaum estimated that only five of Jackson's 150 Jewish families played any kind of active role in the movement, and those five were only "moderately active." See "Terror in Miss. Focuses on Jews," *New York Post*, December 6, 1967, 52; Dinnerstein, "Southern Jewry," 237.

36. Dollinger, "'Hamans' and 'Torquemadas,'" in Bauman and Kalin, *Quiet Voices*, 75–76. Grafman was one of the authors of "An Appeal for Law and Order and Common Sense," cowritten by several Birmingham clergy in 1963 as a response to the direct

action campaign by Dr. King and the SCLC then underway in Birmingham. King's response was his famed "Letter from a Birmingham Jail," April 16, 1963, available in King, *Why We Can't Wait* (New York: New American Library, 1964), 76–95.

37. Nussbaum et al, "Southern Rabbi Faces," 6.

38. Stephen Ambrose, *Eisenhower: The President* (New York: Simon and Schuster, 1984), 190; Earl Warren, *The Memoirs of Earl Warren* (Garden City, NY: Doubleday, 1977), 291.

39. Quoted in Dollinger, "'Hamans' and 'Torquemadas,'" in Bauman and Kalin, *Quiet Voices*, 72.

40. Krause, *To Stand Aside or Stand Alone*, 371–74. See also Melissa Fay Greene, *The Temple Bombing*.

41. Nussbaum et al, "Southern Rabbi Faces," 4; Webb, "Big Struggle in a Small Town: Charles Mantinband of Hattiesburg, Mississippi," in Bauman and Kalin, *Quiet Voices*, 223–24.

42. Webb, *Fight against Fear*, 199.

43. Arthur Levin, quoted in Dollinger, "'Hamans' and 'Torquemadas,'" in Bauman and Kalin, *Quiet Voices*, 72.

44. Mantinband quoted in Webb, "Big Struggle in a Small Town," in Bauman and Kalin, *Quiet Voices*, 215.

45. Webb, "Big Struggle in a Small Town," in Bauman and Kalin, *Quiet Voices*, 215; ISOH transcript (1977), 17.

46. Quoted in Webb, *Fight against Fear*, 198.

47. See John Kirk, "Integration was the Answer for Downtown Little Rock in 1963," *Arkansas Times*, September 5, 2013, accessed July 21, 2017, https://www.arktimes.com/arkansas/integration-was-the-answer-for-downtown-little-rock-in-1963/Content?oid=3031539; Kirk, "The History of the Sit-In Movement in Little Rock," *Arkansas Times*, February 1, 2012, accessed July 21, 2017, https://www.arktimes.com/arkansas/sitting-in-for-rights/Content?oid=2045790; Kirk, *Redefining the Color Line: Black Activism in Little Rock, Arkansas, 1940–1970* (Gainesville: University of Florida Press, 2002), 155–57.

48. *Southern Jewish Weekly* (Jacksonville, FL), October 10, 1958; Webb, *Fight against Fear*, 182–83.

Chapter 7. The Central High Crisis and Beyond: 1957–1963

1. S. I. Goldstein, "The Roles of an American Rabbi," *Sociology and Social Research* 38 (September—October 1953): 32.

2. *Arkansas Gazette*, February 27, 1957; Webb, *Fight against Fear*, 174; Johnson, *Arkansas in Modern America*, 136–37. The meeting would be held in the larger house chamber.

3. "State Senate Balks at Segregation Bills, Sets Public Hearing," *Arkansas Gazette*, February 16, 1957, 1.

4. "Bills on Segregation Defended as Legal, Deplored as Unjust," *Arkansas Gazette*, February 19, 1957, 1.

5. "Public Hearing on Sovereignty Bills," *Arkansas Gazette*, February 15, 1957, 4.

6. "Minister William Miller Assails Proposal to Set Up Sovereignty Board on Segregation," *Arkansas Gazette*, February 16, 1957, 2; "Bills on Segregation," *Arkansas Gazette*, February 19, 1957, 1; Daisy Bates, *The Long Shadow of Little Rock: A Memoir* (New York: David McKay, 1962; reprint ed., Fayetteville: University of Arkansas Press, 1986), 54.

7. "Bills on Segregation," *Arkansas Gazette*, February 19, 1957, 1; Bates, *Long Shadow of Little Rock*, 54–55.

8. "Bills on Segregation," *Arkansas Gazette*, February 19, 1957, 1; see also Johnny E. Williams, *African American Religion and the Civil Rights Movement in Arkansas* (Jackson: University Press of Mississippi, 2008), 108, 111–12; Ayodale Braimah, "First Missionary Baptist Church [Little Rock, Arkansas]," BlackPast .org, accessed June 29, 2015, http://www.blackpast.org/aah/first-missionary-baptist -church-little-rock-arkansas-1845.

9. ISOH transcript (1977), 18.

10. Ira Sanders, speech before the Arkansas General Assembly, February 18, 1957, Little Rock, Arkansas, in box 8, file 3, Sanders Papers, Temple. The speech is reprinted in its entirety as appendix 2.

11. Sanders, speech before the Arkansas General Assembly, February 18, 1957, Little Rock, Arkansas, in box 8, file 3, Sanders Papers, Temple; Karen Anderson, "The Little Rock School Desegregation Crisis: Moderation and Social Conflict," *Journal of Southern History* 70 (August 2004): 603.

12. Sanders, speech before the Arkansas General Assembly, February 18, 1957, Little Rock, Arkansas, in box 8, file 3, Sanders Papers, Temple; ISOH transcript (1977), 18.

13. "Arkansas Senate Approves Bills to Resist Integration," *Arkansas Gazette*, February 20, 1957.

14. *Arkansas Gazette*, February 27, 1957, 1; Bates, *Long Shadow of Little Rock*, 55.

15. Sidney S. McMath to Ira Sanders, February 19, 1957, series I, subseries III, box 8, file 1, LeMaster Collection. On McMath, see Sidney S. McMath, *Promises Kept* (Fayetteville: University of Arkansas Press, 2003); Jim Lester, *A Man for Arkansas: Sid McMath and the Southern Reform Tradition* (Little Rock: Rose Publishing, 1976).

16. Rev. Charles C. Walker to Ira Sanders, February 27, 1957, series I, subseries III, box 8, file 1, LeMaster Collection.

17. David Halberstam, *The Fifties* (New York: Villard Books, 1993), 668.

18. "Woodrow Mann Dies at 85; Sought Troops in Little Rock," *New York Times*, August 9, 2002. Mann's actions in requesting federal intervention cost him his political career.

19. Johnson, *Arkansas in Modern America*, 126.

20. "Little Rock Council on Education Report, 1952," in *A Documentary History of Arkansas*, ed. C. Fred Williams et al. (Fayetteville: University of Arkansas Press, 1984), 238–39; Johnson, *Arkansas in Modern America*, 127; "Has Arkansas Gone Liberal?" *Chicago Defender*, May 7, 1955; McMillen, "White Citizens' Council," 126; Lorraine Gates, "Power from the Pedestal: The Women's Emergency Committee and the Little Rock School Crisis," *Arkansas Historical Quarterly* 55 (Spring 1996): 26.

21. Neil R. McMillen, *The Citizens' Council: Organized Resistance to the Second*

Reconstruction, 1955–1964 (Urbana: University of Illinois Press, 1971), 95; Tony Freyer, *The Little Rock Crisis: A Constitutional Interpretation* (Westport, CT: Greenwood Press, 1984), 24.

22. On the Little Rock Central High School crisis, see Bates, *Long Shadow of Little Rock*; Freyer, *Little Rock Crisis*; Virgil Blossom, *It Has Happened Here* (New York: Harper, 1959); Karen Anderson, *Little Rock: Race and Resistance at Central High School* (Princeton, NJ: Princeton University Press, 2010); John A. Kirk, *Beyond Little Rock: The Origins and Legacies of the Central High Crisis* (Fayetteville: University of Arkansas Press, 2007); Elizabeth Jacoway and C. Fred Williams, eds., *Understanding the Little Rock Crisis: An Exercise in Remembrance and Reconciliation* (Fayetteville: University of Arkansas Press, 1999); Elizabeth Huckaby, *Crisis at Central High: Little Rock 1957–1958* (Baton Rouge: Louisiana State University Press, 1980); Juan Williams, *Eyes on the Prize: America's Civil Rights Years, 1954–1965* (New York: Viking, 1987), 91–119; Henry Hampton and Steve Fayer, eds., *Voices of Freedom: An Oral History of the Civil Rights Movement from the 1950s through the 1980s* (New York: Bantam, 1990), 35–52. For the students' perspectives, see Melba Pattillo Beals, *Warriors Don't Cry* (New York: Pocket Books, 1994); Carlotta Walls Lanier, *A Mighty Long Way: My Journey to Justice at Central High School* (New York: Random House, 2009). On Faubus, see Roy Reed, *Faubus: The Life and Times of an American Prodigal* (Fayetteville: University of Arkansas Press, 1999).

23. Faubus quoted in Harry Ashmore, *Hearts and Minds: The Anatomy of Racism from Roosevelt to Reagan* (New York: McGraw-Hill, 1982), 259; Taylor Branch, *Parting the Waters: America in the King Years, 1954–1963* (New York: Simon and Schuster, 1988), 223. On Rockefeller, see John Ward, *The Arkansas Rockefeller* (Baton Rouge: Louisiana State University Press, 1978).

24. Eisenhower's televised address, quoted in Woods, *Black Struggle, Red Scare*, 69. In this address, writes Woods, the president echoed the same concerns expressed earlier that day by secretary of state John Foster Dulles to attorney general Herbert Brownell—that is, that the Little Rock situation "was ruining [US] foreign policy."

25. Harry S. Ashmore, *Civil Rights and Wrongs: A Memoir of Race and Politics, 1944–1994* (New York: Pantheon, 1994), 131.

26. Sanders Journal, 71; Freyer, *Little Rock Crisis*, 46; LeMaster, "Arkansas Story," in *Quiet Voices*, 109.

27. LeMaster, *A Corner of the Tapestry*, 376–77; "Arkansas Story," in Bauman and Kalin, *Quiet Voices*, 109. For the work of this group, see Sara Alderman Murphy, *Breaking the Silence: Little Rock's Women's Emergency Committee to Open Our Schools, 1958–1963* (Fayetteville: University of Arkansas Press, 1997); Lorraine Gates, "Power from the Pedestal: The Women's Emergency Committee and the Little Rock School Crisis," *Arkansas Historical Quarterly* 55 (Spring 1996): 26–57.

28. Eisenhower to Robert R. Brown, quoted in Brown, *Bigger than Little Rock* (Greenwich, CT: Seabury Press, 1958), 92–93.

29. Brown, *Bigger than Little Rock*, 91, 93. Catholic bishop Albert Fletcher, Baptist minister W. O. Vaughn, and Methodist bishop Paul Martin were out of town; otherwise, they too would have attended.

30. Sanders quoted in Ernest Q. Campbell and Thomas F. Pettigrew, *Christians*

in Racial Crisis: A Study of Little Rock's Ministry (Washington, DC: Public Affairs Press, 1959), 30.

31. "Little Rock's Clergy Leads the Way," *Time*, October 14, 1957, 30.

32. Statement by Ira Sanders, October 4, 1957, in Bishop Robert R. Brown Letters, box 2, file 7, UALR Center for Arkansas History and Culture, Arkansas Studies Institute, Little Rock, Arkansas (hereafter cited as Bishop Brown Letters, UALR); Brown, *Bigger than Little Rock*, 93–94, 96–97.

33. Brown, *Bigger than Little Rock*, 95–98; Campbell and Pettigrew, *Christians in Racial Crisis*, 30.

34. Letters reprinted in Brown, *Bigger than Little Rock*, 94–95.

35. *Arkansas Democrat*, October 4, 1957; Webb, *Fight against Fear*, 176.

36. Box 2, file 9, Bishop Brown Letters, UALR; "Little Rock Asks Divine Aid on Bias," *New York Herald Tribune*, October 13, 1957; "5000 Pray Over Crisis," *Arkansas Democrat*, October 13, 1957; Brown, *Bigger than Little Rock*, 97–98.

37. "Little Rock Asks Divine Aid on Bias," *New York Herald Tribune*, October 13, 1957.

38. "Little Rock Pauses to Pray for Peace; 5,000 Persons Attend 84 Churches," *Living Church* 135 (October 27, 1957): 9. *Living Church* was published weekly by the Episcopal Church.

39. Brown, *Bigger than Little Rock*, 110.

40. Cited in Brown, *Bigger than Little Rock*, 98–99. On the Mother's League of Central High School, see Graeme Cope, "'A Thorn in the Side?' The Mother's League of Central High School and the Little Rock Desegregation Crisis of 1957," *Arkansas Historical Quarterly* 57 (Summer 1998): 160–90.

41. "Little Rock Asks Divine Aid on Bias," *New York Herald Tribune*, October 13, 1957. In 1958, Little Rock had over two hundred houses of worship and a total population of about 110,000, 25 percent of whom were African American. Sixty churches in the Little Rock area were essentially all-black, and twenty of those participated in the Ministry of Reconciliation.

42. Brown, *Bigger than Little Rock*, 122–24; Blossom, *It Has Happened Here*, 139.

43. Shimon Weber, "How Has the School Conflict Affected the Jews in Little Rock?" *Jewish Daily Forward*, October 19, 1957.

44. Ira Sanders, speech broadcast on the ABC Radio program *Message of Israel*, December 1, 1957, reprinted as Sanders, "Spiritual Maturity," *Southwest Jewish Chronicle*, n.d., series I, subseries III, box 8, file 4, LeMaster Collection. The *Southwest Jewish Chronicle*, published in Oklahoma City, covered the Jewish activities of ten states in the region.

45. Blossom, *It Has Happened Here*, 140–41.

46. LeMaster, *A Corner of the Tapestry*, 379–81, 394.

47. Spitzberg, *Racial Politics in Little Rock*, 77.

48. Sanders quoted in Spitzberg, *Racial Politics in Little Rock*, 93–94.

49. Brown, *Bigger than Little Rock*, 119, 121; flyer, Capital Citizens' Council of Little Rock, 1957, in *Race, Politics, and Memory: A Documentary History of the Little Rock School Crisis*, ed. Catherine M. Lewis and J. Richard Lewis (Fayetteville: University of Arkansas Press, 2007), 30–31; Solomon Fineberg, draft memorandum,

"Program to Deal with Organized Anti-Semitic Activity," American Jewish Committee, December 20, 1958, American Jewish Committee Digital Archives, http://ajcarchives.org/ajcarchive/DigitalArchive.aspx.

50. Webb, *Fight against Fear*, 152, 155.

51. McMillen, "White Citizens' Council," 141.

52. Little Rock is an excellent example Leonard Dinnerstein's observation ("Southern Jewry," 234) that actual Jewish involvement in civil rights activities did not necessarily correlate with bombings or bomb threats. Threatening to destroy synagogues was a way to send a message to the Jewish community as a whole or to punish that community for the actions of one of its members; in this case, Sanders. On Groner, see "A Rabbi for the Ages," *Detroit Jewish News*, January 2, 2013, accessed January 21, 2016, http://www.thejewishnews.com/2013/01/02/a-rabbi-for-the-ages/.

53. Special board meeting minutes, October 17, 1958, box "Board Meeting Minutes 1958," Temple Archives.

54. As told to Congregation B'nai Israel rabbi Barry Block in 2013 by Dr. Marvin "Sonny" Cohen, then a member of Congregation Agudath Achim. Barry Block, email to the author, October 19, 2015. This statement, however, may be apocryphal, as neither it nor any reference to it appears in the meeting minutes. In addition, according to the minutes, Dr. Cohen was not present at the meeting. Alan Thalheimer, a temple trustee in 1957 who was present at this meeting, does not recall the details of the meeting or Sanders saying this but acknowledged that such a statement "sounds like something he would say." Thalheimer, interview with the author, March 29, 2016.

55. Special board meeting minutes, October 17, 1958, box "Board Meeting Minutes 1958," Temple Archives.

56. Special board meeting minutes, October 17, 1958, box "Board Meeting Minutes 1958," Temple Archives.

57. "4 P.M. Called Meeting," October 17, 1958, box "Temple Business, 1957–1964," Temple Archives.

58. Board meeting minutes, October 21, 1958, Temple Archives.

59. Board meeting minutes, November 18, 1958, Temple Archives.

60. "Recklessness or Responsibility," *Southern Israelite*, February 27, 1959, 13.

61. Ira Sanders, "1959 Annual Report," January 25, 1960, box 2, "Services and Addresses," Sanders Papers, Temple.

62. Shimon Weber, "How Has the School Conflict Affected the Jews in Little Rock?" *Jewish Daily Forward*, October 19, 1957; Fulbright quoted in *Arkansas Gazette*, April 25, 1955, clipping in box 2, file 13, Sanders Papers, Temple. Fulbright made his remarks at a Little Rock dinner marking the three-hundredth anniversary of Jews in the New World.

63. Shimon Weber, "How Has the School Conflict Affected the Jews in Little Rock?" *Jewish Daily Forward*, October 19, 1957.

64. Cyrus Gordon to Ira Sanders, October 27, 1957, series I, subseries III, box 8, file 1, LeMaster Collection.

65. Richard Cohen to Ira Sanders, September 25, 1957; Jacob K. Shankman, president of the New York Association of Reform Rabbis, to Ira Sanders, October 11, 1957; Maurice Eisendrath, telegram to Ira Sanders, October 4, 1957. All in series I, subseries III, box 8, file 1, LeMaster Collection.

66. "Jews Contribute to Civic Righteousness," *Arkansas Democrat*, April 8, 1961; "Honoring Dr. Sanders," *Arkansas Gazette*, May 17, 1961, 4A; Jacob R. Marcus to Ira Sanders, May 11, 1961; James A. Wax to Sanders, May 8, 1961; Martha C. Allis to Sanders, April 11, 1961. All in box 1, file 2, Sanders Papers, UALR.

67. Box 1, file 3, "Sermons and Addresses," Sanders Papers, UALR.

68. ISOH transcript (1977), 18.

69. Subsequent mentions of "the Conference" refer to the Greater Little Rock Conference on Religion and Human Relations.

70. "History and Purpose," Greater Little Rock Conference on Religion and Human Relations, UALR .0214, box 1, file 2, UALR Archives and Special Collections, Arkansas Studies Institute, Little Rock, Arkansas (hereafter cited as GLRC Papers); Webb, *Fight against Fear*, 176–77; on Kenneth Teegarden, see D. Duane Cummins, *Kenneth L. Teegarden: The Man, The Church, The Time* (Fort Worth: Texas Christian University Press, 2007). Affiliated with the Christian Church (Disciples of Christ), Teegarden was a strong advocate of racial integration and social justice during the civil rights movement.

71. "Progress in Little Rock," *Christian Century*, May 8, 1963; "What Religion Says to Life in Little Rock," *Arkansas Gazette*, April 24, 1963.

72. "An Appeal to Conscience," box 1, file 4, GLRC Papers; steering committee minutes, May 21, 1963, box 1, file 5, GLRC Papers.

73. "Recommendations for Action by the Conference," box 1, file 4, GLRC Papers; Webb, *Fight against Fear*, 177.

74. Executive Order 11063, accessed May 10, 2016, US Department of Housing and Urban Development, www.hud.gov.

75. "Confronting the Little Rock Housing Problem," [1963?], box 1, file 4, GLRC Papers, emphasis in original.

76. Steering committee minutes, October 13, 1964, and December 7, 1965, box 1, file 5, GLRC Papers.

77. Steering committee minutes, March 1, 1966, box 1, file 5, GLRC Papers.

78. Steering committee minutes, April 3, 1967, box 1, file 5, GLRC Papers; "Rabbi Sanders Named to Receive NCCJ Award," *Arkansas Democrat*, February 18, 1968.

Chapter 8. Honors, Laurels, and Plaudits: 1963–1985

1. "Rabbi Sanders' Service," *Arkansas Gazette*, June 9, 1963.

2. Sanders, speech before the annual meeting of the Arkansas chapter of the National Association of Social Workers, March 21, 1964, Little Rock, Arkansas, series V, box, 1, file 8, LeMaster Collection.

3. "Child Welfare Job Cut Concerns State Group," *Arkansas Democrat*, April 8, 1965, 38.

4. "75 Years of Excellence," Arkansas Lighthouse for the Blind, http://arkansas lighthouse.org/75years.html, accessed March 8, 2016.

5. "Rabbi Sanders Due Honors from Israel," *Arkansas Democrat*, May 6, 1967, 5; "LR Rabbi Honored by Israel; Appeal Made for Support," *Arkansas Gazette*, June 5, 1967, 21A; certificate, Urban League of Greater Little Rock, box 4, Sanders Papers, Temple.

6. "Israeli Diplomat in U.S. Says at LR, if War Comes He Thinks Arabs Will Lose," *Arkansas Gazette*, June 4, 1967; Sanders Journal, 67. On the war, see Michael B. Oren, *Six Days of War: June 1967 and the Making of the Modern Middle East* (New York: Random House, 2002).

7. Winthrop Rockefeller, telegram to Ira Sanders, May 24, 1968, box 1, file 2, Sanders Papers, UALR.

8. "The Influential Rabbi," *Arkansas Democrat*, May 29, 1968, 8.

9. "Rabbi Sanders Named to Receive NCCJ Award," *Arkansas Democrat*, February 18, 1968; *Arkansas Gazette*, February 18, 1968; "1000 at Tribute to Rabbi Sanders Hear ABA Leader Condemn Violence," *Arkansas Gazette*, May 28, 1968; "Nearly 1,000 Applaud Tribute to Rabbi Ira E. Sanders," *National Conference of Christians and Jews Newsletter* (Arkansas Region), September 1968, 1, box 2, file 9, Sanders Papers, Temple.

10. *Arkansas Democrat*, May 26, 1968. In addition to his opposition to the Vietnam War, in later years Sanders would also express dismay over the Watergate affair, calling it "the saddest hour in the history of our country, without a doubt." *Arkansas Gazette*, August 10, 1974.

11. "The Influential Rabbi," *Arkansas Democrat*, May 29, 1968, 8.

12. "Nearly 1,000 Applaud Tribute to Rabbi Ira E. Sanders," *National Conference of Christians and Jews Newsletter*.

13. ISOH transcript (1978), 10–11.

14. See appendix 3 for the lengthy list of organizations and agencies founded by or impacted by Ira Sanders.

15. There are no official duties attached to the honorary title "rabbi emeritus," and the actual responsibilities, if any, vary from congregation to congregation. Generally, the rabbi emeritus should help establish the new rabbi in his or her position, may sit on the bimah, conduct services at the rabbi's invitation, and participate—again at the rabbi's invitation—in life cycle events such as bar or bat mitzvahs. The rabbi emeritus should not attend board meetings. See David R. Cohen, "Rabbis, Congregations Customize Emeritus Role," *Atlanta Jewish Times*, August 16, 2016; *Guidelines for Rabbinical-Congregational Relationships*, as adopted by the Union of Reform Judaism board of trustees and the Central Conference of American Rabbis, Fall 1984, accessed August 8, 2017, https://www.ccarnet.org/media/filer_public/2011/12/19/guidelines_rabbinicalcongregationrel.pdf

16. Elijah Palnick, recorded message on the occasion of Ira Sanders' one-hundredth birthday, May 6, 1994, cassette tape, Temple Archives. Transcript in possession of the author, 2.

17. LeMaster, "The Arkansas Story," in Bauman and Kalin, *Quiet Voices*, 112–17. On Palnick, see also Webb, *Fight against Fear*, 177–80.

18. Palnick, interview with the author, November 16, 2004, Little Rock, Arkansas; Palnick, recorded message on the occasion of Ira Sanders' one-hundredth birthday, May 6, 1994, cassette tape, Temple Archives.

19. Sanders Journal, 1.

20. "Fiftieth Anniversary Celebration," box 2, file 9, Sanders Papers, Temple; Eugene P. Levy, interview with the author, June 2, 2015; "About Us—1866–Present,"

Congregation B'nai Israel, "History," accessed August 8, 2017, http://www.bnai-israel
.us/content/about_us/history.asp.

21. *Arkansas Democrat*, June 29, 1978, 6B.

22. Palnick, recorded message on the occasion of Ira Sanders' one-hundredth birthday, May 6, 1994, cassette tape, Temple Archives.

23. Dr. F. Hampton Roy, interview with the author, September 21, 2017, Little
Rock, Arkansas. See also Elizabeth C. Perry and F. Hampton Roy, *Light in the
Shadows: Feelings about Blindness* (Little Rock: World Eye Foundation, 1982), 65–73,
which focuses on Rabbi Sanders and his coping with blindness.

24. Flora Sanders, telephone interview with the author, August 15, 2017.

25. Elijah E. Palnick to Ira Sanders, March 29, 1984, box 1, Sanders Papers,
Temple.

26. Palnick, interview with the author, November 16, 2004, Little Rock, Arkansas.

27. Palnick, interview with the author, November 16, 2004, Little Rock, Arkansas;
Palnick, recorded message on the occasion of Ira Sanders' one-hundredth birthday,
May 6, 1994, cassette tape, Temple Archives, transcription in the possession of the
author, 12. In this recording, Palnick mistakenly attributes the authorship of the poem
to Sanders.

28. *Arkansas Democrat*, February 19, 1986; ISOH transcript (1977), 17.

29. Sanders, excerpted from sermon of January 10, 1959, box 1, file 3, "Sermons and
Addresses," Sanders Papers, UALR. The sermon is partly drawn from and occasionally quotes from Albert Vorspan and Eugene J. Lipman, *Justice and Judaism: The
Work of Social Action* (New York: Union of American Hebrew Congregations, 1956),
esp. 10–11.

BIBLIOGRAPHY

Archival Collections

American Jewish Committee Digital Archives. http://ajcarchives.org/ajcarchive
/DigitalArchive.aspx.

Arkansas Eugenics Association. Records. History of Public Health Collection,
Historical Research Center, Library, University of Arkansas for Medical Sciences,
Little Rock, Arkansas.

Arkansas Small Manuscript Materials. Butler Center for Arkansas Studies, Arkansas
Studies Institute, Little Rock, Arkansas.

Brown, Bishop Robert R. Letters. UALR Center for Arkansas History and Culture,
Arkansas Studies Institute, Little Rock, Arkansas.

Darragh, Fred. Papers. Butler Center for Arkansas Studies, Arkansas Studies
Institute, Little Rock, Arkansas.

Gamble, Clarence James. Papers, 1920s–1970s. Center for the History of Medicine,
Francis A. Countway Library of Medicine, Harvard Medical School, Boston,
Massachusetts.

Greater Little Rock Conference on Religion and Human Relations. Records. UALR
Center for Arkansas History and Culture, Arkansas Studies Institute, Little Rock,
Arkansas.

LeMaster, Carolyn, Arkansas Jewish History Collection. Butler Center for Arkansas
Studies, Arkansas Studies Institute, Little Rock, Arkansas.

Palnick, Elijah E. Papers. Temple Archives, Congregation B'nai Israel, Little Rock,
Arkansas.

Sanders, Ira E. Papers. Temple Archives, Congregation B'nai Israel, Little Rock,
Arkansas.

Sanders, Ira E. Papers. UALR Center for Arkansas History and Culture, Arkansas
Studies Institute, Little Rock, Arkansas.

*Survey of Negroes in Little Rock and North Little Rock. Compiled by the Writers'
Program of the Work Projects Administration in the State of Arkansas.* Little Rock:
Urban League of Greater Little Rock, 1941. Accessed April 10, 2017. https://hdl
.handle.net/2027/uc1.$b725353.

Temple Business Records. Temple Archives, Congregation B'nai Israel, Little Rock,
Arkansas.

Urban League of Arkansas, Inc.: Golden Anniversary Celebration, 1937–1987. Little
Rock: The League, 1987. Butler Center for Arkansas Studies, Arkansas Studies
Institute, Little Rock, Arkansas.

Wolsey, Louis. Papers. American Jewish Archives, Hebrew Union College—
Jewish Institute of Religion, Cincinnati, Ohio.

Newspapers

Allentown (PA) Morning Call
Arkansas Democrat (Little Rock)
Arkansas Democrat-Gazette (Little Rock)
Arkansas Gazette (Little Rock)
Arkansas Times (Little Rock)
Atlanta Jewish Times
Chicago Defender
Jewish Daily Forward (New York City)
Jewish Exponent (Philadelphia)
Kansas City Jewish Chronicle
National Jewish Post and Opinion (Indianapolis)
New York Herald Tribune
New York Post
New York Times
Southern Israelite (Atlanta)
Southern Jewish Weekly (Jacksonville, FL)
Washington Post

Interviews and Correspondence

Campbell, Donald K. Telephone interviews, October 30, 2015 and January 15, 2016.
Jacobson, Jerry. Interview. June 2, 2015, Little Rock, Arkansas.
Jacobson, Trudy. Interview. June 2, 2015, Little Rock, Arkansas.
Levy, Gene P. Interview. June 2, 2015, Little Rock, Arkansas.
Lyons II, Maxwell. Interview. June 1, 2015, Little Rock, Arkansas.
Mitchell, Dorothy Woods. Telephone interview, May 10, 2016. Interview, March 10, 2017, Little Rock, Arkansas.
Palnick, Elijah E. Interview. November 16, 2004, Little Rock, Arkansas.
———. Voice recording on the occasion of Rabbi Sanders' one-hundredth birthday, May 5, 1994, cassette tape, Temple Archives, Congregation B'nai Israel, Little Rock, Arkansas.
Pfeifer, James. Interview. June 1, 2015, Little Rock, Arkansas.
Roy, F. Hampton. Interview. September 21, 2017, Little Rock, Arkansas.
Sanders, Flora L. Interview, May 22, 2007, Little Rock, Arkansas. Telephone interviews, November 6, 2004, October 27, 2006, November 18, 2015, and November 6, 2017. Email to author, June 1, 2015.
Sanders, Paula. Telephone interview. November 16, 2017.
Thalheimer, Alan. Telephone interview. March 29, 2016.

Encyclopedias

The Encyclopaedia Judaica. 26 Vols. New York: McMillan, 1971–1992.
Encyclopedia of Arkansas History and Culture. http://www.encyclopediaofarkansas .net.

Theses and Dissertations

Krause, P. Allen. "The Southern Rabbi and Civil Rights." Rabbinic thesis, Hebrew
Union College—Jewish Institute of Religion, 1967.
Leung, Marianne. "'Better Babies': The Arkansas Birth Control Movement during
the 1930s." PhD diss., University of Memphis, 1996.
Lustig, Jason. "Resigning to Change: The Foundation and Transformation of the
American Council for Judaism." MA thesis, Brandeis University, 2009.
Rison, David. "Arkansas during the Great Depression." PhD diss., University of
California, Los Angeles, 1974.
Tillman, Rosebud Harris. "The History of Public Library Service to Negroes in Little
Rock, Arkansas, 1917–1951." MS thesis, Atlanta University, 1953.
Welch, Melanie K. "Politics and Poverty: Women's Reproductive Rights in Arkansas,
1942–1980." PhD diss., Auburn University, 2009.

Articles

Atto, William J. "Brooks Hays and the New Deal." *Arkansas Historical Quarterly* 67
(Summer 2008): 168–86.
Barber, Henry E. "The Association of Southern Women for the Prevention of
Lynching, 1930–1942." *Phylon* 34 (December 1973): 378–89.
Barth, Jay. "Remembering the 1927 Lynching in Little Rock." *Arkansas Times*,
August 1, 2012. Accessed May 30, 2017. https://www.arktimes.com/arkansas
/remember-the-1927–lynching-in-little-rock/Content?oid=2367957.
Bauman, Mark K., and Arnold Shankman. "The Rabbi as Ethnic Broker: The Case
of David Marx." *Journal of American Ethnic History* 2 (Spring 1983): 51–68.
Bearden, Russell E. "Arkansas' Worst Disaster: The Great Mississippi River Flood
of 1927." *Arkansas Review: A Journal of Delta Studies* 34 (August 2003): 79–97.
Chappell, David L. "Diversity within a Racial Group: White People in Little Rock,
1957–1959." *Arkansas Historical Quarterly* 54 (Winter 1995): 444–56.
Cope, Graeme. "'A Thorn in the Side'? The Mother's League of Central High School
and the Little Rock Desegregation Crisis of 1957." *Arkansas Historical Quarterly* 57
(Summer 1998): 160–90.
———. "'Honest White People of the Middle and Lower Classes'? A Profile of the
Capital Citizens' Council during the Little Rock Crisis of 1957." *Arkansas Historical
Quarterly* 61 (Spring 2002): 34–58.
Dinnerstein, Leonard. "Southern Jewry and the Desegregation Crisis, 1954–1970."
American Jewish Historical Quarterly 62 (March 1973): 231–41.
Fair, Paul. "Little Rock: Then and Now." *Theory into Practice* 17 (February 1978):
39–42.
Forman, Seth. "The Unbearable Whiteness of Being Jewish: Desegregation in the
South and the Crisis of Jewish Liberalism." *American Jewish History* 85 (June 1997):
121–42.
Gates, Lorraine. "Power from the Pedestal: The Women's Emergency Committee and
the Little Rock School Crisis." *Arkansas Historical Quarterly* 55 (Spring 1996):
26–57.

Goldstein, S. I. "The Roles of an American Rabbi." *Sociology and Social Research* 38 (September–October 1953): 32–37.

Graves, John W. "Jim Crow in Arkansas: A Reconsideration of Urban Race Relations in the Post-Reconstruction South." *Journal of Southern History* 55 (August 1989): 421–48.

Greenberg, Cheryl. "The Southern Jewish Community and the Struggle for Civil Rights." In *African Americans and Jews in the Twentieth Century: Studies in Convergence and Conflict*, edited by V. P. Franklin et al., 123–64. Columbia: University of Missouri Press, 1999.

Hamilton, David E. "Herbert Hoover and the Great Drought of 1930." *Journal of American History* 68 (March 1982): 850–75.

Hero, Alfred O., Jr. "Southern Jews, Race Relations, and Foreign Policy." *Jewish Social Studies* 27 (October 1965): 213–35.

Hope, Holly. "An Ambition to Be Preferred: New Deal Recovery Efforts and Architecture in Arkansas, 1933–1943." Little Rock: Arkansas Historic Preservation Program, Department of Arkansas Heritage, 2006. Accessed March 2, 2016. https://www.arkansaspreservation.com/LiteratureRetrieve.aspx?ID=133233.

Kent, Carolyn Yancey. "Last Hired: African American Hiring in North Pulaski County's Citadel for Defense." *Pulaski County Historical Review* 62 (Fall 2014): 77–84.

Krause, P. Allen. "Rabbis and Negro Rights in the South, 1954–1967." *American Jewish Archives* 21 (April 1969): 20–47.

Leung, Marianne. "Making the Radical Respectable: Little Rock Clubwomen and the Cause of Birth Control during the 1930s." *Arkansas Historical Quarterly* 57 (Spring 1998): 17–32.

"Little Rock Pauses to Pray for Peace; 5,000 Persons Attend 84 Churches." *Living Church* 135 (October 27, 1957): 9–10.

"Little Rock's Clergy Leads the Way." *Time*, October 14, 1957, 30.

Malev, William S. "The Jew of the South in the Conflict on Segregation." *Conservative Judaism* 13 (Fall 1958): 35–47.

McMillen, Neil. "The White Citizens' Council and Organized Resistance to School Desegregation in Arkansas." *Arkansas Historical Quarterly* 30 (Summer 1971): 95–122.

Meyer, David J. "Fighting Segregation, Threats, and Dynamite: Rabbi William Silverman's Nashville Battle." *American Jewish Archives Journal* 60 (2008): 99–113.

Moses, James L. "The Jewish Experience in Arkansas: Rabbi Ira Sanders' Quest for Racial and Social Justice, 1926–1963." *Pulaski County Historical Review* 58 (Fall 2010): 96–116.

———. "'The Law of Life Is the Law of Service': Rabbi Ira Sanders and the Quest for Racial and Social Justice in Arkansas, 1926–1963." *Southern Jewish History* 10 (2007): 159–203.

Nussbaum, Perry E., Charles Mantinband, and Jacob Rothschild. "The Southern Rabbi Faces the Problem of Desegregation." *CCAR Journal* 3 (June 1956): 1–6.

Orr, Tabitha. "Clifford Minton's War: The Struggle for Black Jobs in Wartime Little Rock, 1940–1946." *Arkansas Historical Quarterly* 76 (Spring 2017): 23–48.

Simmers, Sarah. "In the South, but Not of the South: Fred K. Darragh, Jr." *Pulaski County Historical Review* 57 (Winter 2009): 124–35.

Spear, Sheldon. "The United States and the Persecution of the Jews in Germany, 1933–1939." *Jewish Social Studies* 30 (October 1968): 215–42.

Stanton, Mary. "At One with the Majority." *Southern Jewish History* 9 (2006): 141–99.

Vinzant, Gene. "The Case of Hay Watson Smith: Evolution and Heresy in the Presbyterian Church." *Ozark Historical Review* 30 (Spring 2001): 57–70.

Vorspan, Albert. "The Dilemma of the Southern Jew." *The Reconstructionist* 24 (January 9, 1959): 6–9.

Wax, James A. "The Attitudes of the Jews in the South toward Integration." *CCAR Journal* 6 (June 1959): 14–20.

Welch, Melanie K. "Not Women's Rights: Birth Control as Poverty Control in Arkansas." *Arkansas Historical Quarterly* 69 (Autumn 2010): 220–44.

Wilkes, George R. "Rabbi Dr. David Marx and the Unity Club: Organized Jewish-Christian Dialogue, Liberalism, and Religious Diversity in Early Twentieth-Century Atlanta." *Southern Jewish History* 9 (2006): 35–68.

Woodruff, Nan E. "The Failure of Relief during the Arkansas Drought of 1930–31." *Arkansas Historical Quarterly* 39 (Winter 1980): 301–13.

Books

Alexander, Charles C. *The Ku Klux Klan in the Southwest*. Norman: University of Oklahoma Press, 1995.

Ambrose, Stephen. *Eisenhower: The President*. New York: Simon and Schuster, 1984.

American Jewish Committee. *The Jews in Nazi Germany: The Factual Record of Their Persecution by the National Socialists*. New York: American Jewish Committee, 1933.

Anderson, Karen. *Little Rock: Race and Resistance at Central High School*. Princeton: Princeton University Press, 2010.

Arnold, Kathleen R., ed. *Anti-Immigration in the United States*, vol. 1. Westport, CT: Greenwood Press, 2011.

Ashmore, Harry S. *Civil Rights and Wrongs: A Memoir of Race and Politics, 1944–1994*. New York: Pantheon, 1994.

———. *Hearts and Minds: The Anatomy of Racism from Roosevelt to Reagan*. New York: McGraw-Hill, 1982.

Baker, Jean H. *Margaret Sanger: A Life of Passion*. New York: Hill and Wang, 2011.

Barnes, Kenneth C. *Anti-Catholicism in Arkansas: How Politicians, the Press, the Klan, and Religious Leaders Imagined an Enemy*. Fayetteville: University of Arkansas Press, 2016.

Bates, Daisy. *The Long Shadow of Little Rock*. New York: D. McKay, 1962; reprint ed., Fayetteville: University of Arkansas Press, 1986.

Bauman, Mark K., and Berkley Kalin, eds. *The Quiet Voices: Southern Rabbis and Black Civil Rights, 1880s to 1990s*. Tuscaloosa: University of Alabama Press, 1997.

Bayless, Stephanie. *Obliged to Help: Adolphine Fletcher Terry and the Progressive South*. Little Rock: Butler Center Books, 2011.

Beals, Melba Pattillo. *Warriors Don't Cry*. New York: Pocket Books, 1994.

Bernhard, Virginia et al, eds. *Hidden Histories of Women in the New South*. Columbia: University of Missouri Press, 1994.

Blossom, Virgil. *It Has Happened Here*. New York: Harper, 1959.

Blumberg, Janice Rothschild. *One Voice: Rabbi Jacob M. Rothschild and the Troubled South*. Macon, GA: Mercer University Press, 1985.

Branch, Taylor. *Parting the Waters: America in the King Years, 1954–1963*. New York: Simon and Schuster, 1988.

Breitman, Richard and Allan J. Lichtman. *FDR and the Jews*. Cambridge: Belknap Press of Harvard University Press, 2013.

Brown, Robert R. *Bigger than Little Rock*. Greenwich, CT: Seabury Press, 1958.

Campbell, Ernest Q., and Thomas F. Pettigrew. *Christians in Racial Crisis: A Study of Little Rock's Ministry*. Washington, DC: Public Affairs Press, 1959.

Chappell, David L. *Inside Agitators: White Southerners in the Civil Rights Movement*. Baltimore: Johns Hopkins University Press, 1994.

Chesler, Ellen. *Woman of Valor: Margaret Sanger and the Birth Control Movement in America*. New York: Simon and Schuster, 2007.

Cowett, Mark. *Birmingham's Rabbi: Morris Newfield and Alabama, 1895–1940*. Tuscaloosa: University of Alabama Press, 1986.

Cummins, D. Duane. *Kenneth L. Teegarden: The Man, The Church, The Time*. Fort Worth: Texas Christian University Press, 2007.

Daniel, Pete. *Deep'n as It Come: The 1927 Mississippi River Flood*. Fayetteville: University of Arkansas Press, 1996.

Dillard, Tom. *Statesmen, Scoundrels, and Eccentrics: A Gallery of Amazing Arkansans*. Fayetteville: University of Arkansas Press, 2010.

Dinnerstein, Leonard and Mary Dale Palsson, eds. *Jews in the South*. Baton Rouge: Louisiana State University Press, 1973.

Dumenil, Lynn. *The Modern Temper: American Culture and Society in the 1920s*. New York: Hill and Wang, 1995.

Egerton, John. *Speak Now against the Day: The Generation before the Civil Rights Movement in the South*. New York: Alfred A. Knopf, 1994.

Evans, Eli N. *The Provincials: A Personal History of the Jews of the South*. New York: Atheneum, 1973.

Feld, Marjorie N. *Lillian Wald: A Biography*. Chapel Hill: University of North Carolina Press, 2009.

Ferris, Marcie C., and Mark I. Greenberg, eds. *Jewish Roots in Southern Soil: A New History*. Waltham, MA: Brandeis University Press, 2006.

Forman, Seth. *Blacks in the Jewish Mind: A Crisis of Liberalism*. New York: New York University Press, 1998.

Freyer, Tony. *The Little Rock Crisis: A Constitutional Interpretation*. Westport, CT: Greenwood Press, 1984.

Friedland, Michael B. *Lift Up Your Voice like a Trumpet: White Clergy and the Civil Rights and Antiwar Movements, 1954–1973*. Chapel Hill: University of North Carolina Press, 1998.

Galbraith, John K. *The Great Crash, 1929*. Boston: Houghton Mifflin, 1954; reprint ed., 1988.

Genezi, Haim. *America's Fair Share: The Admission and Resettlement of Displaced Persons, 1945–1952*. Detroit: Wayne State University Press, 1993.

Gilmore, Glenda E. *Defying Dixie: The Radical Roots of Civil Rights, 1919–1950*. New York: W. W. Norton, 2008.

Goldstein, Eric L. *The Price of Whiteness: Jews, Race, and American Identity*. Princeton: Princeton University Press, 2006.

Gordon, Fon Louise. *Caste and Class: The Black Experience in Arkansas, 1880–1920*. Athens: University of Georgia Press, 1995.

Greene, Alison Collis. *No Depression in Heaven: The Great Depression, the New Deal, and the Transformation of Religion in the Delta*. New York: Oxford University Press, 2016.

Greene, Melissa Fay. *The Temple Bombing*. Reading, MA: Addison-Wesley, 1996.

Guyer, Michael F. *Being Well-Born: An Introduction to Eugenics*. Indianapolis: Bobbs-Merrill, 1916.

Hajo, Cathy M. *Birth Control on Main Street: Organizing Clinics in the United States, 1916–1939*. Urbana: University of Illinois Press, 2010.

Halberstam, David. *The Fifties*. New York: Villard Books, 1993.

Hampton, Henry and Steve Fayer, eds. *Voices of Freedom: An Oral History of the Civil Rights Movement from the 1950s through the 1980s*. New York: Bantam, 1990.

Hartnett, Kimberly M. *Carolina Israelite: How Harry Golden Made Us Care about Jews, the South, and Civil Rights*. Chapel Hill: University of North Carolina Press, 2015.

Huckaby, Elizabeth. *Crisis at Central High: Little Rock 1957–1958*. Baton Rouge: Louisiana State University Press, 1980.

Jacoway, Elizabeth and C. Fred Williams, eds. *Understanding the Little Rock Crisis: An Exercise in Remembrance and Reconciliation*. Fayetteville: University of Arkansas Press, 1999.

Jeansonne, Glen. *Leander Perez: Boss of the Delta*, 2nd ed. Lafayette: University of Southwestern Louisiana Press, 1995.

Johnson, Ben F. *Arkansas in Modern America, 1930–1999*. Fayetteville: University of Arkansas Press, 2000.

Johnson, Paul. *A History of the Jews*. New York: Harper Perennial, 1987.

King, Martin L., Jr. *Why We Can't Wait*. New York: New American Library, 1964.

Kirk, John A. *Beyond Little Rock: The Origins and Legacies of the Central High Crisis*. Fayetteville: University of Arkansas Press, 2007.

———. *Redefining the Color Line: Black Activism in Little Rock, Arkansas, 1940–1970*. Gainesville: University Press of Florida, 2002.

Kolsky, Thomas A. *Jews against Zionism: The American Council for Judaism, 1942–1948*. Philadelphia: Temple University Press, 1992.

Krause, P. Allen. *To Stand Aside or Stand Alone: Southern Reform Rabbis and the Civil Rights Movement*. Edited by Mark K. Bauman with Stephen Krause. Tuscaloosa: University of Alabama Press, 2016.

Landman, Jacob H. *Human Sterilization: The History of the Sexual Sterilization Movement*. New York: McMillan, 1932.

Lanier, Carlotta Walls. *A Mighty Long Way: My Journey to Justice at Central High School*. New York: Random House, 2009.

Largent, Mark A. *Breeding Contempt: The History of Coerced Sterilization in the United States.* New Brunswick, NJ: Rutgers University Press, 2008.

LeMaster, Carolyn. *A Corner of the Tapestry: A History of the Jewish Experience in Arkansas.* Fayetteville: University of Arkansas Press, 1994.

Lester, Jim. *A Man for Arkansas: Sid McMath and the Southern Reform Tradition.* Little Rock: Rose Publishing, 1976.

Lewis, Catherine M. and J. Richard Lewis, eds. *Race, Politics, and Memory: A Documentary History of the Little Rock School Crisis.* Fayetteville: University of Arkansas Press, 2007.

Maney, Patrick J. *The Roosevelt Presence: The Life and Legacy of FDR.* Berkeley: University of California Press, 1992.

McMath, Sidney S. *Promises Kept.* Fayetteville: University of Arkansas Press, 2003.

McMillen, Neil R. *The Citizens' Council: Organized Resistance to the Second Reconstruction, 1955–1964.* Urbana: University of Illinois Press, 1971.

Meyer, Michael A. *Response to Modernity: A History of the Reform Movement in Judaism.* Detroit: Wayne State University Press, 1995.

Murphy, Sara Alderman. *Breaking the Silence: Little Rock's Women's Emergency Committee to Open Our Schools, 1958–1963.* Fayetteville: University of Arkansas Press, 1997.

O'Neill, William L. *American High: The Years of Confidence, 1945–1960.* New York: Free Press, 1986.

Ogden, Dunbar H. *My Father Said Yes: A White Pastor in Little Rock School Integration.* Nashville: Vanderbilt University Press, 2008.

Oney, Steve. *And the Dead Shall Rise: The Murder of Mary Phagan and the Lynching of Leo Frank.* New York: Vintage, 2004.

Orem, Michael B. *Six Days of War: June 1967 and the Making of the Modern Middle East.* New York: Random House, 2002.

Perry, Elizabeth C. and F. Hampton Roy. *Light in the Shadows: Feelings about Blindness.* Little Rock: World Eye Foundation, 1982.

Price, Matthew C. *Justice between Generations: The Growing Power of the Elderly in America.* Santa Barbara, CA: Praeger, 1997.

Rappleye, Charles. *Herbert Hoover in the White House: The Ordeal of the Presidency.* New York: Simon and Schuster, 2016.

Record, Wilson and Jane Cassels Record, eds. *Little Rock U.S.A.: Materials for Analysis.* San Francisco: Chandler Publishing, 1960.

Reed, Roy. *Faubus: The Life and Times of an American Prodigal.* Fayetteville: University of Arkansas Press, 1999.

Rudin, A. James. *Pillar of Fire: A Biography of Stephen S. Wise.* Lubbock: Texas Tech University Press, 2015.

Sanders, Ira E., and Elijah E. Palnick, eds. *One Hundred Years: Congregation B'nai Israel.* Little Rock: Congregation B'nai Israel, 1966.

Sanders, Ronald. *The High Walls of Jerusalem: A History of the Balfour Declaration and the Birth of the British Mandate for Palestine.* New York: Holt, Rinehart & Winston, 1984.

Sanger, Margaret. *Margaret Sanger: An Autobiography.* New York: W. W. Norton, 1938.

Sanua, Marianne R. *Let Us Prove Strong: The American Jewish Committee, 1945–2006.* Waltham, MA: Brandeis University Press, 2007.

Sarna, Jonathan. *American Judaism: A History.* New Haven: Yale University Press, 2004.

Schneier, Marc. *Shared Dreams: Martin Luther King, Jr. and the Jewish Community.* Woodstock, VT: Jewish Lights Publishing, 1999.

Schultz, Debra. *Going South: Jewish Women in the Civil Rights Movement.* New York: New York University Press, 2001.

Sherwood, Robert E. *Roosevelt and Hopkins: An Intimate History.* New York: Harper & Brothers, 1948.

Sitkoff, Harvard. *A New Deal for Blacks: The Emergence of Civil Rights as a National Issue: The Depression Decade.* New York: Oxford University Press, 1978.

————. *The Struggle for Black Equality.* 25th Anniversary Edition. New York: Hill and Wang, 2003.

Spitzberg, Irving J., Jr. *Racial Politics in Little Rock, 1954–1964.* New York: Garland Publishing, 1987.

Verney, Kevern, and Lee Sartain, eds. *Long is the Way and Hard: One Hundred Years of the NAACP.* Fayetteville: University of Arkansas Press, 2009.

Vorspan, Albert and Eugene J. Lipman. *Justice and Judaism: The Work of Social Action.* New York: Union of American Hebrew Congregations, 1956.

Ward, John. *The Arkansas Rockefeller.* Baton Rouge: Louisiana State University Press, 1978.

Warren, Earl. *The Memoirs of Earl Warren.* Garden City, NY: Doubleday, 1977.

Webb, Clive. *Fight against Fear: Southern Jews and Black Civil Rights.* Athens: University of Georgia Press, 2001.

————, ed. *Massive Resistance: Southern Opposition to the Second Reconstruction.* New York: Oxford University Press, 2005.

Weiss, Nancy J. *The National Urban League, 1910–1940.* New York: Oxford University Press, 1974.

Weller, Cecil E. *Joe T. Robinson: Always a Loyal Democrat.* Fayetteville: University of Arkansas Press, 1998.

Williams, C. Fred, et al., eds. *A Documentary History of Arkansas.* Fayetteville: University of Arkansas Press, 1984.

Williams, Johnny E. *African American Religion and the Civil Rights Movement in Arkansas.* Jackson: University Press of Mississippi, 2008.

Williams, Juan. *Eyes on the Prize: America's Civil Rights Years, 1954–1965.* New York: Viking, 1987.

Williams, Nancy A., ed. *Arkansas Biography: A Collection of Notable Lives.* Fayetteville: University of Arkansas Press, 2000.

Wilson, Joan Hoff. *Herbert Hoover, Forgotten Progressive.* Boston: Little, Brown, 1975.

Woods, Jeff. *Black Struggle, Red Scare: Segregation and Anti-Communism in the South, 1948–1968.* Baton Rouge: Louisiana State University Press, 2004.

Wright, Robert R. *Old Seeds in the New Land: History and Reminiscences of the Bar of Arkansas.* Fayetteville: University of Arkansas Press, 2001.

Wyman, David S. *The Abandonment of the Jews: America and the Holocaust, 1941–1945.* New York: Pantheon, 1984.

Zola, Gary P. and Marc Dollinger, eds. *American Jewish History: A Primary Source Reader.* Waltham, MA: Brandeis University Press, 2014.

INDEX

A

Allen, Sam, 155–56
Allentown Morning Call, 23
Allentown, Pennsylvania: Sanders as rabbi in, 9, 18–23, 25, 38
Allis, Martha, 152
Alman, Sol, 145
Altheimer, Maurice, 29–31, 33, 35–36, 59–60
American Council for Judaism (ACJ), 95–102
American Jewish Archives (journal), 8
American Jewish Joint Distribution Committee, 19–20
Anderson, Sam, 155–56
Anti-Defamation League (ADL), 123, 148
Arkansas Association for Mental Health, 157
Arkansas Conference of Social Work, 70
Arkansas Conference on Social Welfare, 158
Arkansas Democrat (Little Rock), 31, 62, 66, 152, 160, 165
Arkansas Displaced Persons Committee, 103–104
Arkansas Eugenics Association (AEA), 10, 69–77, 79–80; principles of, 74; becomes Planned Parenthood of Arkansas, 76
Arkansas Gazette (Little Rock), 8–9, 36, 39, 40, 42, 106, 108, 114, 116–17, 129, 137, 158; segregationist boycott of, 146, 152.
Arkansas General Assembly: Sanders' 1957 speech before, 3–5, 8, 128–34, 169–70.

Arkansas Human Betterment League (AHBL), 10–11, 79–85. *See also* sterilization.
Arkansas Industrial Development Commission, 135
Arkansas Jewish Assembly, 57
Arkansas Lighthouse for the Blind, 4, 157–58, 161; Sanders as co-founder, 67.
Arkansas Mental Health Hygiene Association, 157
Arkansas National Guard, 136
Arkansas Tuberculosis Association, 4, 44, 157.
Ashmore, Harry, 134, 137
Association of Southern Women for the Prevention of Lynching, 40, 64, 109
Atkinson, Ida Ruth, 83, 85
Atlantic City Statement of Principles, 97

B

Back, Alice, 137
Bailey, Carl, 76
Balfour Declaration (1917), 96
"Basic Principles." *See* Congregation Beth Israel (Houston, TX).
Bates, Daisy, 129
Bauman, Mark K., 7, 8
Bennett, Bruce, 136
Bethune, Mary McLeod, 94
Better Understanding Week, 29. *See also* Jack, Emanuel J.
Birmingham, Alabama, 6, 122, 124, 134, 151
Birth control, 69–85
Birth Control Research Bureau (New York), 70
Blachschleger, Eugene, 118–19, 126

Blass Department Store, 29, 145–46

Blass, Gus, 145

Blaustein, Jacob, 107

blindness: Sanders copes with, 164

Blossom, Virgil, 137, 140, 142, 144–45

Boas, Franz, 19

Boaz, H. A., 46

Boggs, Marion, 113, 138

Bright, John D., 154

Britt, Maurice "Footsie", 160

Bronson, George, 155–156

Brown v. Board of Education (1954), 7, 112–13, 116–17, 119, 123–24, 128, 134, 137; Sanders' views on, 117

Brown, Robert R., 138, 140–42, 146

Buck v. Bell (1927), 79

Byrd, Harry (senator), 126

Byrd, William, 129

C

Campbell, Donald K., 113–14

Capital Citizens' Council of Little Rock (CCCLR), 117, 135, 142, 145; boycott threats of, 127, 146–47

Carter, John: lynching of, 39–40

Central Conference of American Rabbis (CCAR), 96–97, 151, 152

Central Council of Social Agencies (CCSA), 45–46

Chambers, Erle, 44, 65

Chastain, Hoyt, 129

Cherry, Francis, 133

Christophe, L. M., 65

Civil Rights Act of 1964, 126

Civil Rights Cases of 1883, 37

Civil Works Administration (CWA), 60–62

Civilian Conservation Corps (CCC), 60

Cohen, Richard, 151

Columbia University, 19, 44

communism: 11, 117, 129, 146; Sanders' views on, 104–106

Comstock Law, 69–70

Congregation Agudath Achim (Little Rock), 147, 150

Congregation B'nai Israel (Little Rock), 3, 4, 5, 7, 9, 12, 15, 26, 36, 42, 58, 91, 97, 106, 127–28, 130, 141, 152, 161–62; early history of, 28–29; Sanders elected rabbi of, 30–33; Sanders' educational reforms at, 34; bomb threats against, 11–12, 127, 147–50; relocates to West Little Rock, 163

Congregation B'nai Jehudah (Kansas City), 15

Congregation Beth Israel (Houston, TX), 98; "Basic Principles" of, 98–101

Congregation Keneseth Israel (Allentown, PA), 18, 20, 22

Congregation Rodeph Shalom (Philadelphia), 33

Cooper, W. G., 140

Corner of the Tapestry, A, 7, 101

Cornish, Hilda, 10, 70–72, 76, 79, 80, 85; and Pulaski County Public Welfare Commission, 62

County Judges' Association of Arkansas, 63

D

Dalton, Aubrey, 138

Darrow, Clarence, 10, 162; debate with Sanders, 52–54; Sanders' views on, 52–53.

Dewey, John, 19

Displaced Persons Act of 1948, 103–104

Downtown Negotiating Committee (DNC), 125

drought of 1930, 10, 27, 51, 54–55

E

Eastern Pennsylvania Joint Distribution Committee, 19

Ehrman, Lasker, 30, 36

Eisendrath, Maurice, 152

Eisenhower, Dwight D., 136, 138, 142; views on segregationists, 123

Encyclopedia of Arkansas History and Culture, 7

England, AR "food riot", 56

Eshel, Ariel, 158–59
Eugenical Sterilization Act of 1924
  (Virginia), 79
eugenics, 4, 10–11, 69–70, 72, 74–76,
  79–80, 82. *See also* Arkansas Eugenics
  Association; Arkansas Human
  Betterment League.
Evans, Eli N., 27, 96
executive order 11063 (1962), 154
executive order 8802 (1941), 94

F
Fair Employment Practices Commission
  (FEPC), 94, 166
Family Welfare Agency, 10, 57–58
Faubus, Orval, 127, 129–130, 133–37,
  140–42, 151, 158
Federal Emergency Relief
  Administration (FERA), 60, 62, 64
Fineberg, Solomon, 149
Fletcher, Albert L., 116, 153–54
Ford, Henry, 23
Frank, Emmet, 120, 126
Frank, Leo: lynching of, 41
Franklin, Harvey, 16
Free Synagogue of New York, 88
Freedom Riders, 122, 125; in Little Rock,
  125
Fulbright, J. William, 150

G
Gamble, Clarence J., 82, 84–85
German language: Sanders' proficiency
  in, 18, 22
Giddings, Frank, 19
Glueck, Nelson, 107
Golden, Harry, 119
Goldstein, S. I., 127
Goodman, Alfred L., 8
Gordon, Cyrus, 151
Grafman, Milton, 122
Great Depression: 6, 8, 10, 27, 48–49, 54,
  85; causes of, 55; Hoover administra-
  tion response to, 51, 56; Sanders' efforts
  during, 51–68. *See also* New Deal.

Greater Little Rock Conference on
  Religion and Human Relations, *aka*
  Greater Little Rock Conference on
  Religion and Race, 12, 128, 153–55,
  157
Greater Little Rock Ministerial Alliance,
  113–14; Sanders' resignation from,
  114
Groner, Irwin, 147–48, 150

H
Hall, R. C., 46, 48
Hansen, Bill, 125–26
Hardie, Richard, 140
Harris, M. Lafayette, 65, 107
Harris, Maurice, 23
Hays, Brooks, 62, 134, 136, 138
Hebrew Benevolent Congregation
  (Atlanta, GA): bombing of, 116, 148,
  150
Hebrew Union College – Jewish Institute
  of Religion (Cincinnati), 9, 43, 107;
  Sanders as student at, 15–16
Heiman, Hugo, 144
Heiskell, John N. "Ned", 108, 158
Heller, James, 28, 97
Henry Street Settlement House, 19, 26
Hess, Max, 19
Hill, Eulis, 116
Hinchin, Martin, 118, 119–20
Holocaust, 8, 11, 20, 87–92, 102
Hopkins, Harry, 61
House Bill 322, Arkansas (1957), 128–29,
  133
House Bill 323, Arkansas (1957), 128, 133
House Bill 324, Arkansas (1957), 128–29,
  133
House Bill 325, Arkansas (1957), 128, 133
House Bill 330 (Arkansas), 84
Howell, Max, 77
Human Betterment Foundation (HBF),
  80, 85
Human Betterment League of North
  Carolina, 82
Human Sterilization (pamphlet), 83

I

Iggers, George C.: and desegregation of Little Rock Public Library, 108–109
Immigration Act of 1924, 90, 97
Interracial Ministerial Alliance (IMA), 114, 138
Israel, State of, 95–96, 100–102, 158. *See also* Zionism.
Ives, Amelia B., 65

J

Jack, Emanuel J., 28–30
Jackson, Mississippi, 6, 120, 121–22, 124
Jacksonville, AR: ordnance plant in, 87, 93–94
Jacobson, Jerry, 41, 42
Jewish Chautauqua Society of Philadelphia, 20
Jewish Daily Forward, 143
Jewish National Workers' Alliance, 22
Jewish Welfare Fund, 57
Jim Crow laws, 9, 27, 37–39, 41, 48, 51, 87–88, 119, 121, 124, 161
"Jim Crow Law, The" (Sanders sermon), 39–40
Johnson, Jim, 136
Jones, Fred T., 65
"Journal of a Southern Rabbi, The" (Sanders' unfinished memoir), 162
Justice and Judaism (book), 166

K

Kahn, Sidney, 59
Kansas City, Missouri, 13; Sanders' childhood in, 14–15
kashrut (kosher laws), 42
Kelso, Robert, 70
Kempner, James, 145
Kempner's (department store), 29, 145
Kennedy, John F., 154
Keren haYesod. See Palestine Foundation Fund
King, Martin Luther, Jr., 119–20
Kirk, John, 125
Knights of the White Camellia, 29

Knowlton, Horace, 62
Kohler, Kaufmann, 16, 43
Krause, P. Allen, 7–8, 121
Kretchmar, Ruth, 137
kristallnacht, 91
Ku Klux Klan, 29

L

Landau, Moses, 122
Laney, Ben, 88, 129
Lasker, Myron, 30, 32, 149
Lasker, Rosa, 37
LeMaster, Carolyn, 7, 8, 57, 101
Lend-Lease Act of 1941, 92–93
Levin, Arthur, 123
Levy, Eugene P., 42, 163
Levy, Jerome S., 148, 149
Liebert, Julius, 16
Little Rock: Sanders' arrival in, 27, 33–34
Little Rock Birth Control Clinic, 10; founding of, 70–72, 74; service to African American women, 75; closure of, 76
Little Rock Central High School, 7, 126, 127, 146–47; desegregation crisis of 1957–58 at, 11, 119, 125, 127, 134–38, 142–44, 151–52, 164, 166
Little Rock Community Fund, 45–46
Little Rock Council on Education, 134–35
Little Rock Public Library, 4, 44, 65, 135, 157; Sanders as a trustee of, 44, 108, 157; desegregation of, 4, 108–109, 135
Little Rock Rotary Club, 105, 117–18, 151
Little Rock School of Social Work, 4, 10, 44–49, 51, 62, 93, 111, 157, 161; Sanders as founder of, 46–47; Sanders' attempt to desegregate, 47–49
Little Rock Urban Progress Association, 145
Loeb, Selwyn, 148
Lovell, J. A., 146
Lyons, Maxwell "Mac" II, 41

M

M. M. Cohn (department store), 29, 145–46
Mann, Woodrow W., 134, 136
Mantinband, Charles, 8, 119–20, 123–25
Marousek, Phoebe, 83, 85
Martin, Paul E., 140
Martineau, John, 40
Mayer, Harry, 15, 22, 28
Mayersohn, Arnold, 149
McCulloch, R. B., 129
McGrath, Bob, 160
McLean, Louise, 118
McMath, Sidney, 88, 104–105, 124, 133
Mendel, Jane, 137
Menkus, Josephine, 137
Message of Israel (ABC Radio program): Sanders as guest speaker on, 143–44
Miller, William L., 129
Minda, Albert, 22
Ministry of Reconciliation, 11, 111, 138–43; Sanders as a founder of, 138–139; opposition to, 141–142
Minton, Clifford, 93–94
Mississippi River Flood of 1927, 51, 74
Mitchell, Charles, 63
Mitchell, Dorothy Woods, 111
Montgomery, Alabama, 6, 124, 126, 134, 151
Montgomery Bus Boycott, 118–19, 125
Moore, U. E., 63
Mother's League of Central High School, 141–42
Mrs. B (boarding house landlady), 15–16
Mussolini, Benito: Sanders' attempted meeting with, 89–90

N

Nash, William, 65
Nashville, Tennessee, 6, 120; sit-ins in, 121, 125
National Association for the Advancement of Colored People (NAACP), 26, 40, 64, 109, 128–29, 135
National Association of Social Workers, 157

National Conference of Christians and Jews (NCCJ), 160
National Conference on Religion and Race, 153
National Jewish Post and Opinion, The, 116
National Recovery Administration (NRA), 62
National Urban League, 65
Navra, Morris, 28
New Deal, 58, 60–64, 94
New York Association of Reform Rabbis, 151–52
Newfield, Morris, 8
Nix, Ora, 62, 64
Nussbaum, Perry, 8, 120–25

O

O'Connell, James E., 130, 140
Ogden, Dunbar, 114, 138, 140
oratory: Sanders skills in, 24–25, 41–42
Ottenheimer, Gus, 145
Ottenheimer, Leonard, 145
Ottenheimer, Phillip, 28

P

Palestinian Foundation Fund, 20, 89, 101
Palnick, Elijah Ezekiel "Zeke", 7, 12, 161–62, 164–65
Paragould, AR, 83–84
Parchman (Mississippi State Penitentiary), 122
Peck, Sam (hotelier), 145
Peck, Samuel (rabbi), 28
Pennsylvania Federation of Religious School Teachers, 20
People and Patterns (NBC): Sanders' appearance on, 161
Perez, Leander, 117
Pfeifer, Harry, Jr., 149
Pfeifer, James, 41–42
Pfeifer, Leo, 29, 30–31
Pfeifer, Phillip, 28
Pfeifer, Preston, 32
Pfeifer, Raida, 71

Pfeifer's Department Store, 145–46
Philander Smith College, 65, 94, 107–108; sit-ins and students of, 125
Pittsburgh Platform, 43
Planned Parenthood Association of Arkansas, 4, 10, 69, 77–79, 84; financial troubles of, 77–78
Plessy v. Ferguson (1896), 37, 123
Prophetic Judaism, 9
Pruniski, John, 62
Public Works Administration (PWA), 60
Pulaski County, 51, 62–63
Pulaski County Public Welfare Commission (PWC), 10, 60, 62–64
Pulaski County Tuberculosis Association, 109, 152

Q

Quiet Voices, The: Southern Rabbis and Black Civil Rights, 7
Quillian, Rev. Paul, 52

R

"Rabbis and Negro Rights in the South, 1954–1967", 8
Refugees, 102–104
retirement: of Ira Sanders, 128, 153, 157
Rhine, Abraham, 57
Rich Hill, Missouri: Sanders birth and childhood in, 9, 13–15
Robinson, Joseph T., 43, 88–90
Rockefeller, Winthrop, 65, 84, 135, 158, 160
Rogers, Lucien, 128
Roosevelt, Franklin D., 60–62; wartime policies of, 92, 94
Rosen, Louis, 144
Rothschild, Jacob, 116, 120, 122–24
Roy, F. Hampton, 164

S

Safferstone, M. A., 149
salary: Sanders' voluntary cut in, 58–60
Samuel, Irene, 137
Samuel, John, 137
Sanders, Daniel (father), 13

Sanders, Flora Louise (daughter), 22, 24, 26, 31, 33, 42
Sanders, Gus (brother), 13–14, 22
Sanders, Ira E. *See separate entries for the individuals, organizations, institutions, or agencies associated with Ira Sanders.*
Sanders, Jessie (sister), 13
Sanders, Morris (brother), 13
Sanders, Paulina Ackerman (mother), 13–15
Sanders, Ralph (brother), 13
Sanders, Selma Loeb, 20–22, 26, 31, 33, 41, 42, 89, 137; marriage to Ira, 22; death of, 164
Sanger, Margaret, 10, 70; friendship with Hilda Cornish, 71.
Schiff, Jacob, 19
Schwartzman, Allan, 122
Scopes "Monkey Trial", 52
Separate Coach Law of 1891 (Arkansas), 37
Shusterman, Abraham, 99
Silverman, William, 120–21, 124
Sit-Ins: in Nashville, 121, 125; in Little Rock, 125–26.
Six-Day War, 159–60
Smith, Alfred: Sanders' support of in the 1928 presidential election, 43
Smith, Hay Watson, 70–72
Smith, Jeff, 67, 158
Smith, Odell, 129
Smith, Roland S., 129–30
Smith v. Allwright (1944), 87
Southern Christian Leadership Conference (SCLC), 118–19, 122
"Southern Rabbi and Civil Rights, The", 7
Southern Israelite (Newspaper), 150
Speaking of Sterilization (pamphlet), 82, 83
speeches. *See* oratory.
Spitzberg, Henry E., 137, 144–45, 148–49
sterilization, 11, 72, 75, 79–84. *See also* Arkansas Human Betterment League.
Storthz, Samuel, 57

Streetcar Segregation Act of 1903
    (Arkansas), 37; Sanders' 1926 defiance
    of, 37–39
Student Nonviolent Coordinating
    Committee (SNCC), 125
*Survey of Negroes in Little Rock and
    North Little Rock, A,* 66–67

T

Teegarden, Kenneth, 153–54
Temple Beth Israel (Jackson, MS), 122
Temple Beth Or (Montgomery, AL),
    118
Temple B'nai Israel (Little Rock). *See*
    Congregation B'nai Israel (Little
    Rock).
Temple Chronicle, 34, 43
Temple Israel of the City of New York, 4,
    9, 23, 29, 32, 36, 95; Sanders as associ-
    ate rabbi of, 24–26, 29–30
Temple Men's Club, 54, 70; founding
    of, 52
Tenenbaum, Carolyn, 137
Tenenbaum, Julius, 145
Terry, Adolphine, 108
Thalheimer, Alan, 42, 99
Thomas, Jessie O., 65
Thompson, Sadye Allen, 48–49, 93–95
Trinity Episcopal Church (Little Rock),
    140
Triplett, Hayes, 84

U

Union of American Hebrew
    Congregations (UAHC), 42, 118, 120,
    151–52
United Nations Genocide Convention,
    104–105
United States v. One Package (1936), 70
University of Arkansas, 46, 48, 88, 95;
    Sanders delivers baccalaureate address
    at, 105; Sanders receives honorary
    doctorate from, 106, 169; desegrega-
    tion of, 134
University of Arkansas, Little Rock
    (UALR), 157

University of Arkansas Law School, 65;
    desegregation of, 88
University of Arkansas Medical School,
    76, 79, 84, 88; desegregation of, 133
Urban League of Greater Little Rock, 4,
    10–11, 64, 66, 87, 92–95, 107, 109, 151,
    157, 159, 161; Sanders as a founder of,
    65; Sanders honored by, 67.

V

Vietnam War, 160
Vinsonhaler, Frank, 46
Vorspan, Albert, 118, 120

W

Wald, Lillian, 26
Walker, Charles C., 133–34
Warren, Earl, 123
Wax, James, 119
Weaver, Robert C., 94
Webb, Clive, 7, 8, 112
Why Fear Sterilization? (pamphlet), 82
Wickard, Charles, 45
Wilson, Woodrow, 23
Wise, Isaac Meyer, 95–96
Wise, Stephen S., 88–89
Witt, Louis, 28, 99
Wolsey, Louis, 28, 33, 38; and the
    American Council for Judaism, 96,
    100–101.
Women's Emergency Committee to
    Open Our Schools (WEC), 37, 164
Works Progress Administration (WPA),
    61–62, 64
World War II, 4, 6, 8, 9, 11, 20, 38, 85,
    87–88, 91–93, 102, 119, 121, 132, 134,
    151, 160
Wright, V. O., 130

Y

Young Men's Hebrew Association
    (YMHA), 22

Z

Zionism, 11, 20, 42–43, 87, 89; Sanders'
    evolution toward, 95–102

JAMES L. MOSES is professor of history
at Arkansas Tech University.